Women and Genocide

Women and Genocide

Gendered Experiences of Violence, Survival, and Resistance

Edited by JoAnn DiGeorgio-Lutz and Donna Gosbee

Women's Press
Toronto

Women and Genocide: Gendered Experiences of Violence, Survival, and Resistance
Edited by JoAnn DiGeorgio-Lutz and Donna Gosbee

First published in 2016 by
Women's Press, an imprint of Canadian Scholars' Press Inc.
425 Adelaide Street West, Suite 200
Toronto, Ontario
M5V 3C1

www.womenspress.ca

Canadian Scholars' Press Inc. gratefully acknowledges financial support for our publishing activities from the Government of Canada through the Canada Book Fund (CBF).

Library and Archives Canada Cataloguing in Publication

Women and genocide : gendered experiences of violence, survival, and resistance / edited by JoAnn DiGeorgio-Lutz and Donna Gosbee.

Includes bibliographical references and index. Issued in print and electronic formats.
ISBN 978-0-88961-582-3 (paperback).—ISBN 978-0-88961-583-0 (pdf).—ISBN 978-0-88961-584-7 (epub)

   1. Genocide—History—20th century.   2. Genocide—History—21st century.
3. Women—Crimes against—History—20th century.   4. Women—Crimes against—History—21st century. I. DiGeorgio-Lutz, JoAnn, editor II. Gosbee, Donna, 1955-, editor

HV6322.7.W64 2016   364.15,1082   C2016-900129-6
C2016-900130-X

Text design by Integra
Cover design by Em Dash Design
Cover image: "Traces," copyright 2013 by Julie Douglas

Printed and bound in Canada by Webcom

Canadä

MIX
Paper from
responsible sources
FSC **FSC® C004071**
www.fsc.org

Dedication

This book is dedicated to all women who have endured loss or violence at the hands of perpetrators of genocide: those who made it through to tell us their story, those who have suffered in silence, and those who did not survive to tell of their experiences.

For Michael and Gerry—the men in my life who made this project possible.
—JoAnn DiGeorgio-Lutz

To my son, David, my rock, my unpaid editor, and my sounding board on this project; and to JoAnn, for your belief in me.
—Donna Gosbee

Contents

JoAnn DiGeorgio-Lutz and Donna Gosbee

Samuel Totten observed that "the plight and fate" of women in genocidal circumstances is both comparable to and at the same time profoundly different from the experiences of men.[1] Can we make a similar observation when examining the lives of women in different genocidal contexts? This book explores the experiences of women and genocide utilizing narratives, memoirs, testimonies, and literature to investigate the ways in which their experiences as women are comparable and yet profoundly different. The inspiration for this book grew out of a graduate seminar on women and genocide and the lack of a general reader that could unite women's genocidal experiences under a common theoretical framework. Totten's edited bibliographic review, "Plight and Fate of Women During and Following Genocide," provides a foundation across a number of genocides that could enrich our understanding of women's experiences.[2] However, it does not unify women's individual accounts into a wider comparative framework to permit generalizations and generate reflection for future research. Helen Fein was an early pioneer of enlarging the scope of genocide studies to bring awareness of gender, dating from antiquity to the present. Her research set the stage for the comparative study of gender and genocide in which she contemplated two questions: what were the determinants of women's life chances during genocide and what was the role of sexual violence in genocide?[3] Although germane to the Holocaust, Nechama Tec cogently observes that if we neglect to consider the gendered differences of men and women relative to their coping strategies and distinct experiences, we lose opportunities to expand our knowledge.[4] The same observation can be made of women's experiences across diverse cases of genocide. Our intent in this book is to unify women's genocidal experiences under a central theme and harness the power of collective voice in the hopes of raising awareness of the intricacy of women and genocide.

There are many themes and conceptual approaches to understanding women's genocidal experiences. We began this project by asking ourselves, in what ways could any of these themes be universal among women and comparable across cases of genocide? Women's distinct genocidal experiences are now part of the growing scholarship on women and genocide. However, from a comparative perspective, women's voices remain largely unheard. What women anticipate, what resources they may utilize to survive, and how they rebuild their lives in a post-genocidal society should not be examined in isolated cases of genocide. This research seeks to bridge the gaps between isolated cases of genocide and underscores the importance of comparatively studying women's lives as well as their deaths as an important component to understanding their genocidal experiences.

The academic study of genocide is often challenged by the varied definitions of what constitutes genocide. In defining genocide, words and labels do matter. Within the scholarly community the mere invocation of the "G-word" to describe an event invites wide-ranging debate over the conceptual boundaries of genocide. These can include differences over genocidal intent and the parameters of who constitutes the victim groups. Adam Jones identified 16 different scholarly definitions across a range of diverse academic disciplines. Additionally, as Jones notes, this conceptual diversity is notably a product of the ambiguities of the 1948 United Nations Convention on the Prevention and Punishment of the Crime of Genocide.[5] Although it is often the starting point for the study of and definition of genocide, William A. Schabas reminds us that the 1948 Convention is above all a legal concept whose meaning will vary, and that, even within the limits of law, "it is imprecise to speak of a single, universally recognized meaning of genocide."[6] Despite its academic shortcomings and legal ambiguities, the 1948 Convention provides the baseline definition of genocide for all the cases in this book, regardless of their politically accepted status as recognized genocides or not. The crime of genocide is defined in international law in Article II of the Convention on the Prevention and Punishment of the Crime of Genocide as

> any of the following acts committed with intent to destroy, in whole or in part, a national, ethnical, racial or religious group, as such:
>
> (a) Killing members of the group;
> (b) Causing serious bodily or mental harm to members of the group;
> (c) Deliberately inflicting on the group conditions of life calculated to bring about its physical destruction in whole or in part;
> (d) Imposing measures intended to prevent births within the group;
> (e) Forcibly transferring children of the group to another group.[7]

Academically, the starting point for the formal study of women and genocide begins with the Holocaust. Our discussion of the literature flows from this premise. As a separate academic endeavour, the study of women and the Holocaust in the early 1980s begins with the work of pioneering scholars such as Katz and Ringelheim; Laska; and Bridenthal, Grossman, and Kaplan, who framed our view of the Holocaust from a feminist perspective.[8] While it could be argued that Katz and Ringelheim broadened our understanding of women and the Holocaust in a way that allowed for a more complete view, feminist/gendered perspectives still struggled for acceptance, even within the scholarly analysis of the Holocaust. Goldenberg's observation that feminist perspectives are often maligned because a gendered lens detracts from the larger impact of antisemitism and the destruction of all Jews regardless of gender is germane across all cases of genocide.[9] Moreover, one apparent consequence of the exclusive focus on women is that the subject matter of women in the Holocaust draws heavily on narrative and memoir—which has not always been valued for its scholarly contribution—as a framework of analysis. Ofer and Weitzman's edited volume speaks to this predicament.[10] On the one hand, they recognize that looking at the unique experiences of women has been a "missing element" in what they consider to be an "incomplete picture of Jewish life during the Holocaust."[11] On the other, although Ofer and

Weitzman's work contains chapters that provide scholarly analysis, their work still draws on the personal experiences of female survivors, which complicates the acceptance of their work alongside the larger body of Holocaust scholarship beyond the context of gender. Criticism aside, we contend that the voices of female survivors through the use of narratives, testimonies, memoirs, and literature can enhance our understanding of women's particular genocidal experiences.

Rittner and Roth's edited work, *Different Voices: Women and the Holocaust*, is the product of Rittner's query about the absence of women to Roth following the publication of his 1989 edited work with Berenbaum, which was primarily dominated by male voices.[12] Rittner and Roth's multidisciplinary work provides the much-needed academic space to previously neglected women's experiences throughout the Holocaust, in diverse contexts that range from survival in Auschwitz to women in the resistance to Nazi wives. As they note, what happened to men and women was "devastatingly alike" but "devastatingly different too."[13] In a general context, the Nazi intent was to eradicate the Jewish people. In this context Jewish women were not discriminated against compared to Jewish men. However, as Rittner and Roth remind us, our remembrance of the Holocaust will not be complete if women's voices are omitted and if the Holocaust is dominated only by the voices of men. They contextualize the gender specifics of the Holocaust with a simple yet powerful observation that "what men and women remember is not identical."[14]

In 2003, Baer and Goldenberg added a new dimension to the study of gender within the Holocaust when they included works in their edited volume *Experience and Expression: Women, the Nazis, and the Holocaust*, that brought to light the experiences of non-Jewish women.[15] Previous works had focused solely on the experiences of Jewish women during the Holocaust. Baer and Goldenberg also acknowledge the criticisms and the inherent difficulties with employing such resources as memoirs, diaries, and oral histories within the scope of Holocaust studies when they write that these sources are "constructions and reconstructions of experiences and memories. Such texts can never offer us unmediated access to the reality, the 'truth' of the Holocaust."[16]

Ten years later, Goldenberg and Shapiro expanded the premise of looking at the Holocaust through a more gendered lens with their edited volume *Different Horrors, Same Hell: Gender and the Holocaust*.[17] The editors continue the process started earlier, looking at the Holocaust from a gendered perspective, but delve further into the differences between men and women in terms of who had the power or agency and who did not. They inform us that gender theory brings about a "deepening and expansion of our knowledge of historical events, including the Holocaust, because it focuses on the relationships between humans, specifically in terms of power and control."[18]

We see this theme repeat itself through each of the genocidal events included in our volume. From the Armenian genocide to the Holocaust and subsequent genocides, power, control, and the women's loss of agency is a common thread that links these events across the divide of time.

Helene Sinnreich observes that in the area of gender and Holocaust studies more research is needed on women's experiences in different countries, the inclusion of non-Jewish women's voices, and exploration of the topic of sexual violence against women.[19] Hedgepeth and Saidel's edited volume is a comprehensive view of sexual violence against Jewish women during the Holocaust.[20] We would add that in addition to more in-depth analysis of women's experiences within the Holocaust, women's studies and genocide scholarship in general would greatly benefit from comparisons of women's experiences across cases of genocide. Comparative cases of gendered genocidal violence have benefited from the scholarship of von Joeden-Forgey and her attention to the destruction of the family as an assault on the larger group and the specific experiences of women in a wider gendered framework.[21] Von Joeden-Forgey's research, however, omits the gendered experience of women in different genocidal contexts, such as Armenia, Cambodia, and Bangladesh. Comparisons need a starting point, and given that the experiences of women and the Holocaust are at the forefront of scholarly analysis, for us, the Holocaust serves as the academic foundation for our understanding of genocide and the particular experiences of women. Our intent is not to enter the debate on gender and the Holocaust; nor is it to offer an exclusively "gendered analysis" of women's experiences.[22]

Adam Jones provides us with a cautionary tale regarding the dangers inherent in the process of "gendering" genocide. In his essay "Gender and Ethnic Conflict," Jones refers to the differing experiences for men and women during and after the Serbian "ethnic cleansing" of Bosnia-Herzegovina when he contends that "many of women's gender-specific experiences—as victims of rape, expulsion, and sometimes murder—exist against a backdrop of, and in many instances are predicated on, other kinds of victimization that disproportionately target males."[23] His point is that the women could easily be terrorized because the men, who would normally fight to protect their families, were already either murdered or incarcerated by the Serbs—targeted because they were male, and therefore perceived as potential combatants. As von Joeden-Forgey explains, early research on the Holocaust considered women's experiences as "derivative" and secondary to men's, and therefore of no significance to the history of this event. As a result, male voices composed the "literary and historical canon of the Holocaust."[24] However, as von Joeden-Forgey notes, when women finally began to be included in Holocaust research, the "cultural feminist" framework of the day emphasized the "special sphere" of women in isolation from their male counterparts. Consequently, von Joeden-Forgey contends that the inclusion of gender should examine how it inter-sects "with race, nationality, class to form identity and experience."[25] Our approach does not accentuate gender differences nor does it detract from the experiences of men during these genocidal events, but rather assures that the voices of women are heard and do form part and parcel of the historical and literary canon of their respective genocides.

Additionally, it is not our intent to detract from the Jewish woman's experience throughout the Holocaust. Rather, our intent is to examine the ways in which women's genocidal experiences contrast and compare, by examining genocides across the 20th century through women's narratives, memoirs, testimonies, and literature framed against the scholarly backdrop of the women in the Holocaust. As social scientists, we endeavoured to undertake this task by laying a conceptual foundation that allows for meaningful comparisons and the potential to posit generalizations of women's genocidal experiences as women. To that end, we draw upon Ofer and Weitzman's framework in which they identify and examine four structural sources of gender differences during the Holocaust. These are (1) the impact of "cultur-ally defined gender roles of Jewish men and women," which presupposed that men and women possess different "skills, knowledge and expertise";

(2) the Jews' "anticipatory reactions" to what they believed the Nazis would do to Jewish men alone; (3) differences in the nature and degree of conditions such as harassment, rules and regulations, arrests, and so on that the Nazis imposed on Jewish women and men; and (4) the different reactions on the part of Jewish men and women in their "everyday lives" as they attempt to cope with life in the ghettos, camps, and forests.[26]

We asked each contributor to reflect on this framework and to examine women's lives within this context. This volume's nine chapters are written by scholars and researchers from a variety of disciplines including history, gender studies, Holocaust studies, and linguistics. Their experience and research into aspects of specific genocidal events allows them to create essays that present the reader with a much more gendered view of particular genocidal actions. They are providing us with a perspective of genocide research that has previously been obscured by a more universalized approach. Goldenberg and Shapiro inform us that one of the most significant contributions made by feminist theory is "to emphasize attention and focus on individual lives and experiences. Researchers often universalize experience and understanding at the expense of theories and perspectives, and it is often easier to draw broad conclusions than to attend to the singularity of experiences."[27]

Through the use of memoirs, testimonies, personal interviews, and literature, the contributors to this volume give us a look at how individual women experienced the violence and psychological trauma of these horrific historical events. Being able to view the situation from the perspective of the women who were witnessing or experiencing these horrors gives us another framework with which to view genocide. In any given genocide we can identify multiple positions that involved women, including bystanders, victims, survivors, and perpetrators. Our intent in this collection is to give voice to women solely as victims and survivors.

Chapter Overviews

In her chapter, "Women of the Armenian Genocide: From Eyewitness Accounts to Literary Echoes," Sona Haroutyunian takes the reader into the first genocide of the 20th century—the Armenian Genocide perpetrated by the Young Turks. Given that this genocide occurred in 1915,

Haroutyunian relied on testimonies, memoirs, and literature to bring us the voices of women during the Armenian genocide. Through the voices of the women Haroutyunian has uncovered in her research, the reader is able to better understand the different stages of the genocide, and how each of those stages impacted Armenian women.

Michelle Kelso's chapter, "Romani Women and the Holocaust: Testimonies of Sexual Violence in Romanian-Controlled Transnistria," examines the understudied genocide of the Roma. Specifically, she focuses on Roma women in the Romanian landscape of the Holocaust using oral histories and archival documents. Kelso argues that women's particular experiences of the Holocaust have been marginal in dominant accounts of history and that this marginalization is both protective and problematic. She examines how Romani women processed their sufferings through the prism of Romani culture and the gendered parameters of women's roles.

In her chapter, "The Gender Dimension of the Holocaust in France," Carol Mann documents the struggles and coping mechanisms of Jewish women in France during World War II. She considers the strategies of survival put in place by women, often intuitively, to save and maintain their families despite impossible odds. Mann relies on personal interviews and the enormous archives of correspondences either written by or written to Jewish women living in France during the Nazi occupation. Additionally, she examines the roles of Jewish women and their efforts to save their husbands and children, as well as their struggle to live life in the present to fend off impending horror.

Farah Ishtiyaque's chapter on Bangladesh, "Silencing the Women: Violence through Rape in the 1971 War of Liberation," discusses the female gendercide and how the national history of Bangladesh obliterated women's experiences of partition. Ishtiyaque's essay explores literary texts and testimonials to understand how women understood the genocide of 1971 relative to their roles as wives, mothers, daughters, and sisters, among others. She is interested in relocating the lost voices of Urdu-speaking Bihari Muslim women, uncovering their experiences of wartime crimes and violence and the loss of humanity. Ishtiyaque also defines what it means to be raped and how women understand rape; and in particular, how Bihari Muslim women negotiated gendered violence in relation to the struggle for the birth of the new nation of Bangladesh.

In her chapter on Cambodia, "What Is Remembered? Gendered Silence, Sexual Violence, and the Khmer Rouge Atrocity," Theresa de Langis critiques the Extraordinary Chambers in the Courts of Cambodia (ECCC), which is adjudicating the myriad crimes against humanity allegedly committed by the most senior Khmer Rouge leaders still living and fit to stand trial. Her chapter critiques the tribunal's narrow and reluctant approach to taking up the specific crimes committed against women—namely forced marriage and sexual violence committed by Khmer Rouge state agents—offering an alternative narrative based on the testimonies of female survivors and witnesses as recorded in the Cambodian Women's Oral History Project (2013–2014). She reassesses the meaning and impact of Code 6—a Khmer Rouge policy erroneously assumed by the ECCC to be an anti-rape policy. In doing so, she discusses the nuances of how Khmer Rouge policies impacted women in particular (separation of families; starvation, forced labour, and forced transfers; and forced marriage and consequent forced pregnancies), as well as bringing to light the experiences of unique crimes specifically aimed at women (mass rape, gang rape, sexual slavery, and sexual mutilation, among others). Her chapter also discusses the responses and means of resistance utilized by women to navigate the atrocity and how these both called forth and transformed established gender roles during and after the Khmer Rouge period.

Martha C. Galvan-Mandujano's chapter, "Genocide in Central America: Testimonies of Survivors in Guatemala," examines how genocidal acts during the period known as *La Violencia* affected Mayan women in Guatemala. She shares testimonies of women from personal interviews she conducted in 2000 and 2002 during fieldwork in one of the Communities of Populations in Resistance (CPRs) in Nebaj, in the highlands of the Quiché region; testimonies from female Mayan survivors from Guatemala City; and other testimonies from different media sources. Galvan-Mandujano explores how the genocidal period affected Mayan women culturally and within the overall civil war. She examines the reactions and processes of the Mayan women to the physical and emotional circumstances they experienced during the genocide, as well as how survivors have fared physically and emotionally since *La Violencia*, as they attempt to rebuild lives that had been torn apart by violence.

In "Survival and Rescue: Women During the Rwandan Genocide," Sara E. Brown analyzes the role of women who exercised agency as rescuers during the Rwandan genocide. Women who chose to rescue during the genocide did so at great risk and in instances of limited options available to them. Brown argues that the actions and participation of women during the genocide continue to affect Rwandans today; many of the female rescuers are still rejected by their neighbours, and suffer economic hardships. Moreover, she examines how female actors within the genocide in Rwanda are often neglected by a gendered representation of the Rwandan genocide that emphasizes female passivity and victimhood.

Shirley Cloyes DioGuardi's chapter, "Breaking the Protracted Silence about Genocidal Rape in Kosova," takes a unique direction with her focus on domestic violence, patriarchy, and lack of agency for women even before the onset of the genocide. After the genocide the Kosovar women, for the most part, were encouraged to stay silent about what had happened to them. Their husbands and families did not want the shame and loss of honour that they believed rape placed on the family unit, in some cases indicating it was better if the woman died fighting rather than returning home as a victim of rape. Not only did their husbands or families want them to remain silent about their experiences during the genocide, but even the NATO allies negotiating the end of the fighting did not want women talking about it. Where do you turn when everyone is trying to silence you?

Dolores Chew examines the Gujarat genocide in her chapter, "'We Want Justice!' Women and the Gujarat Genocide." This is an interesting, and perhaps controversial, addition to our book, since many sources do not identify the violence in Gujarat in 2002 as a genocide, but rather a "communal riot." We believe the addition of this chapter helps us understand the fluidity of mass murder or genocide. Despite the best intentions of the 1948 United Nations Convention on the Prevention and Punishment of the Crime of Genocide, because genocide often occurs under the cover of war or conflict, arriving at a determination of genocide can be a convoluted and politically charged affair. Like the Armenian genocide, which is still not officially recognized as a genocidal event by some states, we see similar treatment of the Gujarat genocide, which occurred in 2002 and was directed by Hindu nationalists against Muslims in the Indian state of Gujarat. Chew exposes how Muslim women in particular were targeted by the killers. They were brutally tortured and killed to emasculate their men and to tarnish the community and its *izzat* (honour). She identifies how, even in their violation, the Muslim women of Gujarat were marginalized, demonstrating that gender reaffirms the patriarchal norm of women as property of men—reflectors of male honour. Chew uses testimonies of female survivors to inform us how women process and deal with the trauma they suffered during the violence. In most cases, the women continue to be denied a voice or any justice for the violence and loss they experienced, because of the systemic and gendered nature of not only the state, but also the cultural and social limitations placed on them within the patriarchal parameters of their community.

Notes

1. Samuel Totten, ed., *Plight and Fate of Women During and Following Genocide* (New Brunswick: Transaction Publishers, 2012), 1.
2. Ibid.
3. Helen Fein, "Genocide and Gender: The Uses of Women and Group Destiny," *Journal of Genocide Research* 1, no. 1 (1999): 43–63.
4. Nechama Tec, *Resilience and Courage: Women, Men, and the Holocaust* (New Haven: Yale University Press, 2003), 17.
5. Adam Jones, *Genocide: A Comprehensive Introduction* (New York: Routledge, 2006), 12–18.
6. William A. Schabas, "The Law and Genocide," in *The Oxford Handbook of Genocide Studies*, ed. Donald Bloxham and A. Dirk Moses (Oxford: Oxford University Press, 2010), 124–141.
7. UN General Assembly, "Convention on the Prevention and Punishment of the Crime of Genocide," December 9, 1948, United Nations, Treaty Series 78, no. 1021 (1951): 277–322, treaties.un.org/doc/Publication/UNTS/Volume%2078/volume-78-I-1021-English.pdf.
8. Esther Katz and Joan Miriam Ringelheim, eds., *Women Surviving the Holocaust* (New York: Institute for Research in History, 1983); Vera Laska, ed., *Women in the Resistance and in the Holocaust: The Voices of Eyewitnesses.* (Westport: Greenwood Press, 1983); Renate Bridenthal, Atina Grossman, and Marion Kaplan, *When Biology Became Destiny: Women in Weimar and Nazi Germany* (New York: Monthly Review Press, 1984).

9. Myrna Goldenberg, "Different Horrors, Same Hell: Women Remembering the Holocaust," in *Thinking the Unthinkable: Meanings of the Holocaust,* ed. Roger S. Gottlieb (New York: Paulist Press, 1990), 150–166.

10. Dalia Ofer and Lenore J. Weitzman, eds., *Women in the Holocaust* (New Haven: Yale University Press, 1998).

11. Ibid., 1.

12. Carol Rittner and John K. Roth, eds., *Different Voices: Women and the Holocaust* (St. Paul: Paragon House, 1993).

13. Ibid., 3.

14. Ibid., 10.

15. Elizabeth R. Baer and Myrna Goldenberg, eds., *Experience and Expression: Women, the Nazis, and the Holocaust* (Detroit: Wayne State University Press, 2003).

16. Ibid., 27.

17. Myrna Goldenberg and Amy H. Shapiro, eds., *Different Horrors, Same Hell: Gender and the Holocaust* (Seattle: University of Washington Press, 2013).

18. Ibid., 4.

19. Helene J. Sinnreich, "Women and the Holocaust," in *Plight and Fate of Women During and Following Genocide,* ed. Samuel Totten (New Brunswick: Transaction Publishers, 2012).

20. Sonja M. Hedgepeth and Rochelle G. Saidel, *Sexual Violence Against Jewish Women During the Holocaust* (Waltham: Brandeis University Press, 2010).

21. Elisa von Joeden-Forgey, "The Devil in the Details: 'Life Force Atrocities' and the Assault on the Family in Times of Conflict," *Genocide Studies and Prevention* 5, no. 1 (2010): 1–19; and also von Joeden-Forgey, "Gender and the Future of Genocide Studies Prevention," *Genocide Studies and Prevention* 7, no. 1 (2012): 89–107.

22. See correspondence between Gabriel Schoenfeld and Sara R. Horowitz, "Controversy: Feminist Approaches to the Holocaust," *Prooftexts* 21, no. 2 (2001): 279–283.

23. Adam Jones, *Gender Inclusive: Essays on Violence, Men and Feminist International Relations* (New York: Routledge, 2009), 64.

24. Elisa von Joeden-Forgey, "Gender and Genocide," in *The Oxford Handbook of Genocide Studies,* ed. Donald Bloxham and A. Dirk Moses (Oxford: Oxford University Press, 2010), 61–80.

25. Ibid.

26. Ofer and Weitzman, *Women in the Holocaust,* 1.

27. Goldenberg and Shapiro, *Different Horrors, Same Hell,* 11.

CHAPTER 1

Women of the Armenian Genocide:
From Eyewitness Accounts to Literary Echoes

Sona Haroutyunian

Armenian Genocide: An Historical Overview

Combining *geno*, from the Greek γένος for family, race or tribe, with *cide* from the Latin word for killing, Polish-Jewish lawyer Raphael Lemkin, whose family members were victims of the Jewish Holocaust, created the word *genocide* in 1944, when writing a pioneering book about Nazi Germany. By creating and defining this term, Lemkin sought to describe and categorize Nazi policies of systematic persecution and murder of the Jews under the Third Reich. While the term was created amid World War II and initially applied to the Holocaust, it was a term intended to help the world understand mass atrocity crimes throughout history and provide a legal framework to prevent genocide from occurring in the future. As a university student, Lemkin had read with considerable concern about the Young Turk deportations and mass killing of Armenians in the Ottoman Empire, and later applied the concept of genocide to the Armenian case. He was quite clear that while the term was new in World War II, the deed was not, and in fact had occurred throughout history, with the Armenian case a leading example at the beginning of the 20th century.[1]

The atrocities committed against the Armenian people of the Ottoman Empire during World War I are defined as the Armenian genocide. The Young Turk party—officially known as the Committee of Union and Progress (CUP), or *İttihat ve Terakki Cemiyeti*—which was in power at the time and dominated by Mehmed Talaat, Ismail Enver, and Ahmed Djemal, perpetrated deportations and massacres across much of the Ottoman Empire. When World War I broke out, the Young Turk government, hoping to save the core of a shrinking and greatly weakened Ottoman Empire, adopted a policy of Pan-Turkism: the establishment of a mega Turkish empire comprising all Turkic-speaking peoples of the Caucasus and Central Asia, extending to China. The intent was to either "Turkify" or eliminate all ethnic minorities within the Empire. The Armenian population became a major obstacle to the realization of this policy. Although the Young Turks made the decision in late 1911 to deport all Armenians from Western Armenia (Eastern Ottoman Empire/Turkey), they used the cover provided by World War I as a suitable opportunity for implementation of their plan.

On February 12, 1915, a key opening phase of the genocide occurred when Armenian conscripts in the Ottoman army were forcibly disarmed by their fellow Ottoman military colleagues on the order of Enver, the Minister of War. The Armenian conscripts were then either killed outright or worked/starved to death in labour and cargo transportation battalions. As a result of the conscription, and later murder, of military-age men, Armenian families and communities became increasingly vulnerable.

The second phase of the Armenian genocide began on April 24, 1915, with the mass arrest and subsequent murder of several hundred Armenian leaders in Constantinople (present-day Istanbul). Those murdered included clergy, educators, authors, professionals, and political figures—the Armenian intelligentsia. The Armenian people were now without most of their key leadership figures. The date became symbolic, as Armenians worldwide observe April 24 as a day to memorialize all victims of the Armenian genocide.

The third phase of the genocide comprised deportations and death marches of women, children, and the elderly into the Syrian desert. During these marches hundreds of thousands of Armenian victims were massacred by Ottoman soldiers, gendarmes, special killing units (Special Organization), and Kurdish irregulars. A multitude of others died because of famine, dehydration, exposure to the elements, and disease. Countless numbers of women and children were raped. Tens of thousands of Armenian Christians were forced to convert to Islam.

In the fourth phase of the genocide, vast numbers died in concentration camps in the Syrian Desert, or perished later as emaciated and malnourished survivors in refugee camps in the Near East and the Caucasus.

The fifth and final phase of the Armenian genocide emerged with the total and utter denial by the Ottoman and Turkish governments of the mass killings and elimination of the Armenian nation from its homeland. Despite the ongoing international recognition of the Armenian genocide, Turkey has consistently fought against the labelling of what happened to the Armenians as genocide.

The Armenian genocide is referred to as the first genocide of the 20th century. As such, it holds crucial historical significance. It is frequently considered the template for subsequent genocides. When Adolf Hitler sent to death men, women, and children of Polish derivation and language, with the justification of gaining the living space (*Lebensraum*) that Germany needed, he claimed, "*Wer redet heute noch von der Vernichtung der Armenier?*" ("Who still talks nowadays of the extermination of the Armenians?")[2] There were an estimated two million Armenians living in the Ottoman Empire on the eve of World War I. Approximately one and a half million Armenians perished between 1915 and 1923. About half a million Armenians, with substantial assistance from foreign aid organizations (e.g., Near East Relief), found shelter abroad, and their descendants now constitute much of the Armenian diaspora.[3]

Armenian Genocide Scholarship

The early scholarship in relation to the Armenian genocide was primarily descriptive in nature. After 1965 a body of English-language scholarly material, initially primarily by scholars of Armenian ethnicity, began to grow. Some of these works were influenced by the also-nascent field of Holocaust scholarship. In the 1970s and early 1980s a number of Holocaust scholars began to expand this approach, by taking the Holocaust experience into a comparative dimension. Robert Melson, Israel Charny, Helen Fein, Leo Kuper, and Frank Chalk—all involved in Holocaust studies—began to look at the commonalities of the Armenian and Jewish experiences. As Richard Hovannisian attested, "The challenge is for us to work together because the problem is not an Armenian problem or a Jewish problem or a Cambodian problem. It's a human problem."[4] At the same time a few Armenian scholars, primarily the leading sociologist and political historian Vahakn Dadrian—recognized as one of the "key thinkers" on the Holocaust and genocide—explored the phenomenon and made it their field of expertise.[5] Dadrian's work on modelling and conceptualizing helped establish the study of the Armenian genocide as a scholarly discipline. Also of fundamental importance were the efforts of Richard Hovannisian in creating the field of modern Armenian historical studies; training scholars who would go on to do important work on the genocide; and organizing conferences and publications.

Until the 1970s, Armenian genocide scholarship was dominated by historians, and their attention was firmly—and almost exclusively—fixed on documents, statistics, and data. Scant, if any, attention went to oral history and literary responses. Two main factors account for this state of affairs. The first is an ideological one, given that scholars were faced with the denial of the basic facts, and laboured to document and validate the factuality of the Armenian genocide. Moreover, in the name of academic objectivity, some historians were downplaying the importance of Armenian sources in the reconstruction of the history of the Armenian genocide. Still others were arguing that because those sources were testimonies from the victim group, they could not constitute valuable or reliable historical documentation, since they lacked objectivity. Following this line of reasoning, some Armenian historians, to avoid being labelled biased by international historians or Turkish scholars, have systematically avoided the use of Armenian sources in their scholarship. The second factor is eminently practical: there was no systematic initiative for collecting oral histories or considering narrative works until the 1970s. With the passage of time, scholarship on the Armenian genocide changed character from descriptive to analytical, and broadened its historical approach to encompass cultural, artistic, visual, and literary aspects, thus emphasizing the importance of eyewitness accounts, memoirs, and artistic literature, which provide a broader understanding of the Armenian genocide.[6]

In their book *Women in the Holocaust*, Dalia Ofer and Lenore J. Weitzman tell us that "questions about gender lead us to a richer and more finely nuanced understanding" of trauma.[7] Through the prism of testimonies from survivors, memoirs, and literary echoes, this chapter focuses on gendered aspects of the Armenian genocide in the experiences of its female victims. Gendered experiences were historically downplayed in scholarly works, and have only recently begun to be investigated.[8] The examination of these gender-specific aspects within the Armenian genocide can not only inform us about this particular genocide, but also contribute to comparative work with other genocides. In looking at gendered experiences within the Armenian genocide, this chapter will explore the impact of culturally defined roles of Armenian women in the late 19th and early 20th centuries; the women's awareness of events and anticipatory reactions as the genocidal process unfolded; the extent to which women were treated differently than men; and these women's reactions and processes as women to the physical and emotional circumstances of experiencing genocide.

Culturally Defined Roles of Armenian Women

Armenian culture has always assigned a strong emphasis to the family as the centre of society, with the image of "sacred mother" at its core.[9] The history of the Armenian nation has systematically acknowledged the active role women played in the public and patriotic realms, even though, traditionally, Armenian men have been responsible for the economic support of the family, and women the household.[10] Yet in the period before the genocide, women took on a two-fold role: in addition to being caring mothers and obedient wives, some also assumed public roles, led national charitable organizations, and undertook political activities by becoming party members and participating in the nascent nationalist and reformist movements.[11]

Women also acted in the field of education. In 1866, among 46 Armenian schools, 14 were for girls, with enrolment of 1,472. Girls' schools opened both in Eastern and Western Armenia, but women took on particularly active roles in Western Armenia—especially in Constantinople. After finishing school, many of these girls had the opportunity to continue their education at some of the best universities in Europe. On January 14, 1895, *The New York Times* reported, "The Armenians are as highly educated as Americans. They speak English fluently. It is taught in all the colleges."[12]

According to author Arpena Mesrobian, "the role of the Armenian woman in public and private life, although clearly differentiated from that of men, was nonetheless considered to be complementary, not inferior to the male role."[13] This, of course, does not mean that it was easy for a woman to have a place in society at the end of the 19th century. In her autobiographical narrative, *The Gardens of Silihdar*, Armenian writer Zapel Esayan recalls a visit she paid to the feminist writer Srbuhi Dussap in 1895:

> Mrs. Dussap, when she heard that I contemplated a literary career, warned me against it. For a woman, she said, there were in that career more snares than laurels. In the Armenian reality as it was, people were not ready yet to accept that a woman makes a name and a place for herself.[14]

Yet in the early 20th century—before the eruption of the genocide—Esayan not only became famous but, along with other female writers and activists such as Zabel Asadour (better known as Sibyl) and the very same Srbuhi Dussap, found her literary voice in the public sphere and advocated, supported, and struggled for women's rights. Moreover, Sibyl and Dussap designed the project The Declaration on Women's Role with articles relating to equal rights for men and women[15]; the right to choose one's profession; elimination of double moral standards that benefit men in conjugal life; the right to higher education as a means of improving child-rearing; women's equal participation in community activities; elimination of the dowry custom; acceptance of the role of women in the preservation of the nation; and the transfer of culture.

These female authors supported women's emancipation, believing that if women were able to exercise their talents through education and employment, social conditions for all Armenians could be improved.[16] Female writers also used models from Armenian history to encourage their female readers, as well as to uplift the national spirit of the women. After the Adana massacres of 1909, Armenian writer/activist Sibyl evoked the women of the Battle of Avarayr in the 5th century as an inspiration for Armenians, underlining the importance of women in educating the orphans: "Centuries ago, in the time of Vartan's troubles, the wives of martyred princes didn't lounge about on cushions, crying, in their fine palaces. In spite of all of their troubles and sorrows, they lavished great care [on children] and the children weren't allowed to remain uneducated."[17] Along with active participation in Armenia's social life, women continued to shoulder their traditional tasks of housekeeping and caring for their families. The following passage from a survivor's testimony offers a glimpse into Armenian life, customs, and rituals prior to 1915:

> We used to bake *lavash* every day.... Seven women lived peacefully in the house, daughters-in-law and sisters-in-law; the eldest woman was the manager. Elderly women, young women and girls used to wear their nice clothes and went to church ... there was church service every day.... The clothes of our country were nice.... During the feast days we made *bishi*. There was a school in our village. There was a teacher in our village. There were books. The people of our village read the Bible; they read Armenian books.[18]

Anticipatory Reactions of Armenian Women to the Genocide

The anticipatory reactions of Armenian women to what they perceived might happen to them were based primarily on the awareness of past massacres that their co-nationals had experienced more than two decades before the Armenian genocide. On July 26, 1890, *The New York Times* reported, "On June 20 the soldiery were ordered to disperse Armenians who were holding a meeting in a churchyard. The soldiers began a massacre of the Armenians, and the Turkish populace joined in the attack."[19]

There followed the Hamidian massacres of 1894 to 1896, with estimates of the dead ranging from 80,000 to 300,000, resulting in at least 50,000 orphaned children. A *New York Times* article from November 16, 1894, entitled "Massacre of Armenians: Equals the Bulgarian Butcheries Which Led to War. Over Six Thousand Murdered," reported details of a letter sent from Bitlis on October 9 from the chairman of the Armenian Patriotic Association in London to Lord Kimberley, Foreign Secretary. The letter described the horrors of the massacre in Sassoun, south of Moosh, where 27 villages were annihilated:

> On the admissions of the Turkish soldiers ... no compassion was shown to age or sex. In one place 300 or 400 women, after hav-ing been forced repeatedly to submit to the soldiery were hacked to pieces with swords and bayonets. In another place 200 weeping women begged at the commander's feet for mercy. The commander, after ordering that they be outraged, had them all dispatched with the sword. In another case 60 young brides and maidens were driven into a church and were violated and butchered until their blood flowed from the doors.[20]

The initial slaughters had not impacted the Armenians of Central and Western Anatolia. But their turn came when, in 1908, the Young Turk party came to power after the fall of Abdul Hamid II. Local massacres of Armenians began during the Holy Week of 1909 in Adana and its environs, and neither women nor children were spared.[21] As a result of these and other massacres prior to the Armenian genocide, thousands of Armenian women and their families left their hometowns in an attempt to escape the persecutions of the Ottoman Empire. This post-trauma expatriation turned out to be an anticipatory reaction that allowed some to escape the upcoming genocide.[22]

Yet many Armenian women stayed in the regions alongside their fami-lies and, besides fulfilling their traditional roles, took on added responsi-bilities in the midst of the violence and repression. As Payaslian explains, "In areas where Armenians formed armed resistance such as Van, Shabin-Karahisar and Musa Dagh ... young girls served as runners, reporting movement of Turkish soldiers and police in and about the Armenian quarter of the town.... The women were also required to serve in armed combat, although the resistance leaders were exclusively men."[23]

Women may have been more vulnerable, but the lessons of past experiences in some ways helped them in their anticipatory reactions when the actual genocide, with its deportations and massacres, began in 1915. Eyewitness testimonies and memoirs attest to how Armenian women recognized the ominous fate that awaited their people. There was an attempt by many women to join forces among friends and relatives in an effort to make sense of what was happening, and perhaps even prevent the unknown—in effect to try to save the savable. While Armenian women may not have known the degree of danger looming ahead of them prior to the genocidal events that began in 1915, there was a recognition that violence was a possibility. As Antonia Arslan's autobiographical narrative of her family's history in the book *Skylark Farm* attests, "what Armenian youth doesn't know about massacres and threats?"[24]

Difference in Treatment of Women and Men

When discussing the gendered aspects of the Holocaust, Ofer and Weitzman assert, "it is not possible to assume that women's experiences were totally different from those of men. That would be as false and misleading as to argue that their experiences were identical to men's."[25] This is also true in the case of early Armenian massacres when Turkish policy targeted all Armenians as Armenians, and the main importance was their "race," not their gender. Payaslian writes that though Armenians were targeted simply because they were Armenian, and were equally defenceless to the slaughters of the pre-genocide era whether they were men or women, they "experienced crisis of a different nature," based on gender.[26] The experiences of Armenians during the genocide that began in 1915, however, had a much more gendered aspect to it. The first act of the race annihilation program focused on men, who were murdered at the outset. Thus rendered vulnerable, it was easier to deal with the unprotected women, children, and elderly. Smbyul Berberian, a survivor from the town of Afion-Garahissar, attests to the practice by the Turks of eliminating any male resistance:

The Turks had killed my father and had tortured and slaughtered my mother's brother. They drafted my elder brother into the Turkish army. Later they drafted also my younger brother. We heard afterwards that, together with seventeen other Armenian young men, they had massacred them by night and had thrown them under the bridge. Thus, when we were deported, there were no males left in our family. They took away my five aunts in Der-Zor, later they cut off their heads, impaled the heads with their bayonets to show them to us and then they threw their corpses into the Euphrates. We found only half of the body of my mother's aunt. My mother buried her in the earth. They massacred everybody.[27]

The male survivors, mainly young boys who escaped the initial round-ups, were massacred during the deportation. Survivor Souren Sargsian recounts:

The next day the Kurds came, bringing with them the notorious Zeynal Bey and his brothers, the wicked executioners. They collected among the caravan all the little boys, bound their arms and took them farther on the mountain top, where the bonfires were burning. There they cut their heads with axes and threw them into the valley. They had done the same to the children of the previous caravans.[28]

Women, despite their own struggle to stay alive and out of danger, also tried to find ways to save the young boys who were targeted during the deportation process; realizing that without young Armenian male survivors, they—the Armenians—as a group could not survive. The efforts by the women are seen in the actions of one woman whose heroic stance was recounted by survivor Shogher Abraham Tonoyan:

There was a very old woman among us.... When smoke began to enter the stable, she gathered the children and made them lie on their faces, their nose and mouth on the ground, then she made their mothers lay on them. She made my brother also lie on the ground. She took off her apron, covered him with it and pushed me to lie down on my brother and not let him get up, even if he cried. May God bless her soul! That woman said: "*Lao*, what's the use of crying, we must act so that from each house one boy remains alive and comes out of the fire, so that their hearth is not extinguished, so that they may tell the world the acts of these godless and ruthless Turks."[29]

There are reported cases of young mothers themselves, seeing no other way out, killing their own infant male children in order to "save them" from the horrors awaiting at the hands of the Turks; but infants were also sometimes sacrificed by the mother so that older children might be saved instead. A passage from Alice Tachdjian's memoir, *Stones on the Heart*, illustrates this phenomenon:

Our two-months old baby was crying because he was hungry, there was not milk in Hripsimé's breasts, the grass that she ate on the streets caused terrible stomachache for the child. However, the poor creature was destined to die of hunger, diarrhea, or by the sword. To avoid being discovered by his cries, our mother and sister suffocated the baby in the middle of their backs, one against the other, without looking at him. He extinguished like a candle.[30]

After fulfilling the initial act of the race annihilation program by eliminating the Armenian men, it became easier for the Turks to deal with the now unprotected women, children, and elderly. Despite the fact that Interior Minister Talaat's telegrams called for Turkish troops to "exterminate entirely all the Armenians living in Turkey ... without regard for women, children, and the infirm," the path the women were forced to traverse was paved with different processes.[31]

One of those processes was to "Turkify" some Armenian women and incorporate them into the perpetrators' society through forced assimilation, which meant compulsory conversion to Islam: "Several attractive women were told they might live if they would recant their faith. They replied: 'Why should we deny Christ? We have no more reason to do so than had these,' pointing to the mangled bodies of their husbands and brothers, 'kill us, too.' This was done.... [B]etween 6,000 and 10,000 were killed. Babes were impaled on the same weapon with their mothers."[32]

According to Turkish traditional ideas, men were the bearers of ethnicity, while women and children were susceptible to assimilation.[33] A female survivor from Yozhat recounts how some high-ranking Turkish officers approached their group, and began trying to convince them to become Turks:

> "We ask you to think well. Are you willing to become Turks or not? You have seen the slaughtered people. Would you like to be similarly treated? Isn't it better for you to become Turks, otherwise you shall also be butchered...." There was an Armenian girl: her name was Arshalouys. She had long plaited hair. She was very pretty. They took her also and cut off her head. The gendarme came with her hair wrapped round his hand, brought Arshalouys' head, threw it before us, and said, "Either you become Turks, or you shall become like this."[34]

Aram Kyosseyan, from Harpoot, who survived the death marches the Armenian women and children were forced to endure, recalled,

> We had walked so much that we were exhausted. At last they ordered us to come to a halt. We stopped in a valley. They began to ask the adults: "Are you Turkish or Armenian?" Those who replied, "I am an Armenian," were set apart and those who said, "I am a Turk," were put on another side. The ones that did not deny their Armenian origin were taken to a remote place and slaughtered. The others who agreed to become Turks were saved.[35]

Another tool used by the Turks was the systematic nature of mass rapes of Armenian women and young girls. The German Consul to Trabzon, Heinrich Bergfeld, reported that "[t]he numerous rapes of women and girls, was part of a plan for the virtually complete extermination of the Armenians."[36] These rapes often took place in the presence of the women's own family members as the following witness statement attests: "Early in

July [1915] ... the leading Armenians of the town [Sassun] and the headmen of the villages were subjected to revolting tortures.... The female relatives of the victims who came to the rescue were outraged in public before the very eyes of their mutilated husbands and brothers."[37]

As Smith informs us regarding rape in times of genocidal violence, "rape signifies the masculinity and the victory of the perpetrators and the weakness and impotence of the defeated males.... The point is to humiliate the men along with the women and to signify to the men their utter powerlessness.... The functions of rape and other forms of sexual violence against males and females overlap, but diverge in certain respects."[38] We see this divergence in the difference in consequences: for example, women must address issues such as pregnancy, or the choice to keep or abandon the child in the fields after birth, as "the child is the reminder of what happened."[39]

Pregnant women were often specific targets of violence, since they were viewed as the embodiment of biological continuity.[40] One survivor of the genocide from Igdir testified, "The Turks were approaching. They cut open the bellies of pregnant Armenian women with their knives, took the babies out and impaled their heads on stakes."[41] Another survivor, Loris Papikian, confirmed this behaviour by the Turks when she recounted,

> Four officers, the dregs of humanity, who had acquired the fierceness of wild hyenas and had lost their human form, were seated at a table, had gathered near them, standing, a group of pregnant women who would probably give birth in a few days, and they were betting whether the child in the woman's womb was a male or female, and then they ordered the soldiers to open the woman's womb with a dagger and bring the child out.[42]

During the Armenian genocide the Turks not only separated men from women and children, but in some cases separated children from their mothers. Trvanda Mouradian, a survivor from Harpoot, recalled atrocities perpetrated by gendarmes on the roads of exile:

> They took us out of our village, they confined all the young people in a cave-like place, poured kerosene from an opening in the

roof and set fire to them. Then [Turkish gendarmes] gathered all the women and smashed their heads with stones. They killed my mother and grandmother with stones, too. They separated the children like lambs from their mother-sheep. I had a three-year-old sister; they took her also, together with the other children near the Balou Mourat (Euphrates) River bridge, cut their throats and threw them into the river.... Two gendarmes drove 500 people to exile."[43]

Another tragic occurrence during the Armenian genocide was that some Armenian mothers were forced to leave their children with Arabs, in an attempt to save the lives of their children. Many Armenian women realized that their child stood a better chance of survival if handed over to strangers for conversion and possible life, versus almost certain death if the child stayed with the mother.

Reactions of Women to Their Experiences in the Armenian Genocide

Many who survived the unimaginable deprivations, hardships, and torture of the deportations refused to share their trauma for decades, and in some cases forever.[44] In their minds they "translated" the history into memory, which stayed blocked within psychological borders. My great-grandparents on my mother's side, Mkrtich Atashian and Karmilè Paronikian, were from Van. During the genocide, Mkrtich was eight and Karmilè was four years old. They met in the orphanage in Yerevan, and married when Karmilè was 15 years old. They never told their family or anyone else the story of their survival—not a single word was uttered about the massacres. To any questions, they would simply answer, "We left Van a year before those events." The only thing that Mkrtich would repeat was, "We buried a pot of gold under the pear tree. If you go there, you can take it. It is certainly still there." And also, "When my father learned that the Turks entered his garden to steal apples, he went into a fury, took the axe, and began cutting the branches, shouting: 'I'd rather cut them than leave the Turks to get the fruit.'" The Turks fled the yard, saying the man was an *atesh*, (meaning fire in Persian). From here comes his last name—Atashian. Karmilè recalled her home in the district of Aygestan, where the rich people of Van lived and who were all called *barons* (from which derived their family name, Paronikian). The house was surrounded with such a big garden that her father, Stepan *agha* [lord/master in Turkish], travelled through it by mule. Instead of hedges there were quince trees dividing their garden from that of the neighbours.[45] This was the extent of what my great-grandparents were willing to discuss of their prior lives. Family members dared not ask my great-grandparents how they ended up in an orphanage, where their parents were, and so on. Relatives did not want to cause them additional trauma by asking difficult questions (though I wish they had found a way to talk to them). Yet this was also the period of the Soviet regime, when people were afraid of speaking about anything. As with my great-grandparents, so too we see that many other survivors of the Armenian genocide did not want to speak of their experiences, affirming that their "heart would not bear the tragic experience anew."[46]

Smith asserts that "the perpetrators attempt to extend their power through linking memory with pain, with the woman recalling for the rest of her life her violation and humiliation and, by extension, the shame brought upon her group."[47] And yet the traumatic effect of the national calamity was perceived by every woman or girl in her own manner. Fortunately for us, many Armenian women managed to overcome the psychological blockages to reveal the story of their survival through their testimonies or memoirs.

Nichanian writes that the "catastrophe ... transformed the memory into an archive," and that those who testified were "no more than secretaries of the archive."[48] Nichanian further describes the difficulties writer Zapel Esayan struggled with in documenting the "unnamable," the "catastrophe":

For two years, between 1916 and 1918, Esayan lived a unique obsession: to testify.... During these same years, she wrote stories where she displayed an unprecedented sense for female psychology.... She had to deal with survivors, victims, orphans ... but she no longer had a grasp of the immeasurable event. Moreover in her obsession to gather testimonies, to give them a form and translate them into French, she was the first among Armenians to record and shape the originary cantings of testimony into a discourse of evidence.[49]

During the Armenian genocide women stayed alive only after facing what scholar Lawrence Langer identified as "choiceless choices."[50] Though Langer used the term in relation to Jewish victims of the Holocaust, it is certainly applicable to the "choices" forced on Armenian women during their genocidal experiences. Some women underwent assimilation, yet others passed through indescribable tortures and physical violence. These women bravely made sacrifices to protect their children. "They are not animals scrapping for the last mouthful of bread, but women, still with one final source of strength: the thought of saving the children," writes Arslan.[51]

Armenian women sought not only to protect their families, but also to preserve the customs, traditions, and memories of their land, as well as books, photographs, and other objects. Considering the photographic metaphor of memory, Daniel Sherman observes, "Sight is the only sense powerful enough to bridge the gap between those who hold a memory rooted in bodily experience and those who, lacking such experience, nonetheless seek to share the memory."[52]

The lives of female Armenian survivors were shaken by almost immeasurable trauma. They experienced major burdens from the events and consequences of the genocide, such as lost family members and a lost homeland. Facing these challenges meant that they had to begin living life again, but in unfamiliar locations due to the forced Armenian diaspora, often without family members nearby. An excerpt from *Skylark Farm* is illustrative of the complex phenomenon of the diaspora that was created by the Armenian genocide: "My aunt always used to say: 'When I've finally had it with you, when you get too mean, I'm leaving. I'll go stay with Arussiag in Beirut, with Uncle Zareh in Aleppo, with Philip and Mildred in Boston, with my sister Nevart in Fresno, with Ani in New York, or even with cousin Michel in Copacabana.'"[53]

Conclusion

Despite the threat of annihilation of the Armenian population, and the violence they were subjected to by the Turks, some Armenian women were able to survive. These survivors spread Armenian culture and seeds across the world through the diaspora. In so doing, the Armenian identity evolved and became more diverse and complex, and contributed to an emerging multiculturalism in the 20th and 21st centuries. These women also gave us, in many cases, a record of their experiences during the genocide—whether through testimonies, interviews, memoirs, or even passed on orally to their children and their children's children. Given that the Armenian genocide occurred a century ago, and the survivors and witnesses are no longer with us, their testimonies, interviews, and memoirs are now the only record we have of their experiences. Much like the women who subsequently experienced other genocidal events in the 20th and 21st centuries, Armenian women can take their place among the comparisons across a gendered divide and enrich our understanding of the gendered experiences of genocide.

Questions

1. What are some of the reasons that women's voices regarding the Armenian genocide have been silenced?
2. How does nationalism, both Turkish and Armenian, play into the silencing of women?
3. What threats to both Armenian and Turkish masculinity and nationalism does the unsilencing of women's narratives pose?
4. How do the concepts of sexuality and genocide coincide? Why might sexuality be a concept that threatens discourses of "tradition"? How does this relate to the silencing of women in genocide narratives?

Notes

1. For stages of genocide, consider, among others, Gregory Stanton, "The Eight Stages of Genocide," in *The Genocide Studies Reader,* ed. Samuel Totten and Paul Bartrop (New York: Routledge, 2009).
2. Louis P. Lochner, *What About Germany?* (New York: Dodd, Mead & Company, 1942), 1–4. Hitler quotation is from the English version of the German document handed to Louis P. Lochner in Berlin. It first appeared in Lochner, *What About Germany?* The Nuremberg Tribunal later identified the document as L-3 or Exhibit USA-28. Two other versions of the same

document appear in Appendices II and III. For the German original compare *Akten zur Deutschen Auswartigen Politik 1918–1945.*

3. My special thanks to Alan Whitehorn, emeritus professor of political science, Royal Military College of Canada, for assisting me in bibliographic research, for putting me in contact with some of the authors cited, and for guidance on political issues of the Armenian genocide.

4. Richard Hovannisian, "So, Where Do We Go from Here?" (lecture, The State of the Art of Armenian Genocide Research: Historiography, Sources, and Future Directions workshop, Clark University, Worcester, MA, April 9–10, 2010.)

5. See Paul Robert Bartrop and Steven L. Jacobs, *Fifty Key Thinkers on the Holocaust and Genocide* (New York: Taylor & Francis, 2010), 79; or Vahakn Dadrian, "The Secret Young-Turk Ittihadist Conference and the Decision for the World War I Genocide of the Armenians," *Holocaust and Genocide Studies* 7, no. 2 (1993): 173–201; or Vahakn Dadrian, *The History of the Armenian Genocide: Ethnic Conflict from the Balkans to Anatolia to the Caucasus* (Providence: Berghahn Books, 1995); or Vahakn Dadrian, *Warrant for Genocide: Key Elements of Turko-Armenian Conflict* (New Brunswick: Transaction Publishers, 1999).

6. For a broader understanding of the genocide, see the following works. Verjine Svazlian, *The Armenian Genocide: Testimonies of the Eyewitness Survivors* (Yerevan: Gitutiun, 2011). Michael Hagopian, an educational filmmaker, gathered 400 interviews of survivors or witnesses. The University of Southern California-Shoah Foundation has preserved Hagopian's interviews. In the early 1970s Richard Hovannisian undertook the largest oral history project in the Armenian community, recording survivor stories. All 800 interviews were digitized in 2005. Richard G. Hovannisian, *The Armenian Genocide in Perspective* (New Brunswick: Transaction Books, 1986); Richard G. Hovannisian, *The Armenian Genocide: History, Politics, Ethics* (New York: St. Martin's Press, 1992); Richard G. Hovannisian and David N. Myers, eds., *Enlightenment and Diaspora: The Armenian and Jewish Cases* (Atlanta: Scholars Press, 1999). In 1983, the Zoryan Institute undertook an oral history program aimed at documenting survivor experiences on videotape. These and other oral history projects were of critical importance, since researchers began their work while there were a handful of survivors still alive. Without their work, the memories and experiences of these survivors or witnesses would have been lost to history. Rubina Peroomian (1993, 2008, 2012) took up the mantle of Armenian genocide literary scholarship

in the 1990s. With the publication of several books, she furnished a database of relevant literary responses and analyses of a number of texts.

7. Dalia Ofer and Lenore J. Weitzman, eds., *Women in the Holocaust* (New Haven: Yale University Press, 1998).

8. On gender issues during the Armenian Genocide, consider, among others, Roger W. Smith, "Genocide and the Politics of Rape," in *Genocide Matters: Ongoing Issues and Emerging Perspectives*, ed. Joyce Apsel and Ernesto Verdeja (New York: Routledge, 2013); Igor Kuznetsova and Rita Kuznetsova, "(Gendered) Unwritten Culture: Turkish Armenians, Ahishka Turks, Abkhaz," (lecture, Gender, Ethnicity and the National State: Anatolia and Its Neighbouring Regions, Hrant Dink Memorial Workshop 2009 Proceedings, Sabanci University, Istanbul), accessed September 1, 2014, www.hrant-dink.org/picture_library/HDMW-Proceedings%202009.pdf; Ayse Gül Altinay, "Gendered Silences, Gendered Memories," (Hrant Dink Memorial Workshop 2009 Proceedings, Sabanci University, Istanbul); Claudia Card, "Genocide and Social Death," in *Genocide's Aftermath: Responsibility and Repair*, ed. Claudia Card and Armen T. Marsoobian (Hoboken: Wiley-Blackwell, 2007), 10–11; Katharine Derderian, "Common Fate, Different Experience: Gender-Specific Aspects of the Armenian Genocide, 1915–1917," *Holocaust and Genocide Studies* 19, no. 1 (2005); Rubina Peroomian, "When Death Is a Blessing and Life a Prolonged Agony: Women Victims of Genocide," in *Genocide, Perspectives II: Essays on Holocaust and Genocide*, eds. Colin Tatz, Pater Arnold, and Sandra Tatz (Sydney: Brandl & Schlesinger with the Australian Institute for Holocaust and Genocide Studies, 2003), 314–332; Matthias Bjørnlund, "'A Fate Worse Than Dying:' Sexual Violence During the Armenian Genocide," in *Brutality and Desire: War and Sexuality in Europe's Twentieth Century*, ed. Dagmar Herzog (London: Palgrave Macmillan, 2011), 16–59; Roger W. Smith, "Women and Genocide: Notes on an Unwritten History," *Holocaust and Genocide Studies*, VIII, no. 3 (Winter 1994): 315–334; Donald E. Miller and Lorna Touryan Miller, *Survivors: An Oral History of the Armenian Genocide* (Berkely: University of California Press, 1993); Eliz Sanasarian "Gender Distinction in the Genocidal Process: A Preliminary Study of the Armenian Case," *Holocaust and Genocide Studies*, IV, no. 4 (1989): 449–461.

9. Sona Zeitlian, *The Role of Armenian Women During the Revolutionary Movement* (Hraztan: Sarkis Zeitlian Publications, 1992); Sona Zeitlian "Nationalism and the Development of Armenian Women's Rights Movement," in *Armenian Women in a Changing World*, ed. Barbara

Merguerian and Doris Jafferian (Belmont: Armenian International Women's Association Press, 1995), 84; Anny Bakalian, *Armenian-Americans: From Being to Feeling Armenian* (New Brunswick: Transaction Publishers, 1993), 14; Anna Ohanyan, "State-Society Nexus and Gender: Armenian Women in Post-Communist Context," in *Women and Politics Around the World: A Comparative History and Survey*, ed. Joyce Gelb and Marian Lief Palley, vol. 2 (Santa Barbara: ABC-CLIO, 2009).

10. In ancient times the Armenian women were treated as equal members of society in certain spheres, as evidenced in the code of Shahapivan (443 BCE): "... women [have] a right to possess a family property in case the husband deserted his wife without any reason," as well as indicating that a wife had the right "to bring a new husband home." Fifth-century Armenian historian Eghishe documented the revolt of the Armenians against the Sassanid Persians and dedicated a number of pages to praising the merits of Armenian women. See Robert Thomson, trans., *Elishe, History of Vardan and the Armenian War* (Cambridge: Harvard University Press, 1982, 9). Many writers saw parallels in the story of Armenians struggling against the Persian Empire in 451 CE and their own situation as a conquered people living in the Ottoman Empire. See Victoria Rowe, *A History of Armenian Women's Writing, 1880–1922* (Cambridge: Cambridge Scholars Press, 2003), 34–35.

11. Zabel Asaour (literary pseudonym Sybil) was one of the founders of the Society of Nation-Dedicated Armenian Women, an organization that supported the construction, maintenance, and operation of Armenian girl schools throughout the Armenian-populated districts of the Ottoman Empire (http://armenianhouse.org/sipil/sipil-en.html, accessed September 15, 2015); consider also Agop J. Hacikyan, Gabriel Basmajian, and Edward S. Franchuk, *The Heritage of Armenian Literature: From the Eighteenth Century to Modern Times* (Detroit: Wayne State University Press, 2005), 541–542. Among other societies and organizations in which women took part were National Society (*Hamazgayin*) from Murad-Raphaelyan College, Siunyats Society (*Siunyats*) in Izmir, The Devoted Society (*Andznver*) in Constantinople, Senekerimian Society (*Senekerimyan*) in Sebastia, The Society of Education Advocates (*Usumnasirats*) in Brusa, The Society of Smbatian and Devout (*Smbatyan* and *Hogeser*) in Kharberd city, The Devoted Society (*Andznver*) in Huseynik, The Society of Education Advocates and Patriots (*Usumnasiracts* and *Azgasirats*) in Mezreh, Vardan Society (*Vardanyan*), Ararat Educational Society (*Araratyan krtakan*) and Eastern

School Society (*Dprotsasirats Arevelyan*) in Chmshkatsag, Artzn Society (*Artznyan*), Education Advocates (*Usumnasirats*), Society of Reading Lovers (*Yntercasirats*), and Sisakan (*Sisakan*) in Erzurum, www.genocide-museum. am/eng/online_exhibition_13.php.

12. Vosgan Mekhitarian and Vahan Ohanian, eds., *Armenians at the Twilight of the Ottoman Era: News Reports from the International Press*, vol. 1, *The New York Times 1890–1914* (Yerevan: Genocide Documentation and Research Center, 2011), 133.

13. Arpena Mesrobian, *To Preserve the Armenian People: The Armenian Relief Society, 1910–1970* (Boston: Armenian Relief Society, 1972).

14. Marc Nichanian, *Writers of Disaster: Armenian Literature in the Twentieth Century* (London: Taderon Press, 2002), 191.

15. For more information on the role of Armenian women prior to 1915, see Zabel Esayian, "La Role de la Femme Arménienne pendant la Guerre," *Revue des Études Arméniennes* (1922) 12: 1–138. See also Victoria Rowe (2000), *The "New Armenian Women": Armenian Women's Writing in the Ottoman Empire, 1880–1915* (Ph.D. Thesis, Graduate Department of Near and Middle Eastern Civilization, University of Toronto). https://tspace. library.utoronto.ca/bitstream/1807/13580/1/NQ53820.pdf, accessed September 15, 2015. For information on The Declaration of Women's Role, see http://hetq.am/arm/news/33007/hay-kiny-patmutyan-khorqeric.html/ accessed September 15, 2015.

16. Rowe, *A History of Armenian Women's Writing*, 17.

17. Sibyl, "Aganver Hayuhik" in *Yerker* (Yerevan: 1965). See also Rowe, *A History of Armenian Women's Writing*, 35. Consider also Zapel Esayan's accounts of the Armenian massacres of 1909 in Peroomian, *When Death Is a Blessing and Life a Prolonged Agony*, 322.

18. Testimony of Shoger Abraham Tonoyan (b. 1901, Moosh Verdenis village). Verjine Svazlian, *The Armenian Genocide: Testimonies of the Eyewitness Survivors* (Yerevan: Gitutian Publishing, 2011), 97.

19. Mekhitarian and Ohanian, *Armenians at the Twilight*, 1.

20. Ibid., 40.

21. Derderian, "Common Fate," 2.

22. The main wave of emigration was to the United States, where a number of women's committees had already formed in New York, Philadelphia, Boston, and Providence to help the immigrants in facing their new reality. New York was also where the Armenian Relief Society was founded in 1910, becoming the second Armenian women's philanthropic organization, after the

Armenian Red Cross. For more information, see Arra Avakian, *Armenia: A Journey Through History* (Fresno: The Electric Press of America, 2009), 81. Also see Hagop Ohanessian, "The Armenian Relief Society (ARS): A Case Study of Armenian-American Women in the Twentieth Century" (master's thesis, California State University, 2014).

23. Simon Payaslian, "Genocide and Women," in *The Oxford Encyclopedia of Women in World History*, vol. 2 (Oxford: Oxford University Press, 2008), 364.

24. Antonia Arslan, *Skylark Farm*, trans. G. Brock (New York: Alfred A. Knopf, 2006), 107.

25. Ofer and Weitzman, *Women in the Holocaust*, 2.

26. Payaslian, "Genocide and Women," 364.

27. Svazlian, *The Armenian Genocide*, 384.

28. Ibid., 315.

29. Ibid., 97.

30. Alice Tachdjian, *Pietre sul cuore* (Milan: Sperling & Kupfer Editori S.p.A., 2003), 94.

31. Tessa Hofmann, ed. *Der Völkermord an den Armeniern vo Gerich: Der Prozess Talaat Pascha* (Göttingen: Die Gesellschaft, 1980), 133–136; also see Derderian, "Common Fate," 1–25.

32. Mekhitarian and Ohanian, *Armenians at the Twilight*, 40.

33. Derderian, "Common Fate," 4.

34. Svazlian, *The Armenian Genocide*, 351–352.

35. Ibid., 273.

36. Vahakn Dadrian, "The Armenian Genocide: An Interpretation," in *America and the Armenian Genocide of 1915*, ed. Jay Winter (Cambridge: Cambridge University Press, 2008), 83.

37. James Bryce, ed., *The Treatment of the Armenians in the Ottoman Empire, 1915–1916* (London: G. P. Putnam's Sons, 1916), 85.

38. Roger W. Smith, "Genocide and the Politics of Rape," in *Genocide Matters: Ongoing Issues and Emerging Perspectives*, ed. Joyce Apsel and Ernesto Verdeja (New York: Routledge, 2013), 90.

39. Helsinki Watch, *War Crimes in Bosnia-Hercegovina*, vol. II (New York: Human Rights Watch, 1993), 219.

40. Derderian, "Common Fate," 9.

41. Svazlian, *The Armenian Genocide*, 176.

42. Ibid., 214.

43. Ibid., 313.

44. Ibid., 352.

45. Dr. Sedmar Atashian, daughter of Armenian genocide survivors Mkrtich and Karmilè.

46. Svazlian, *The Armenian Genocide*, 351.

47. Smith, "Genocide and the Politics of Rape," 92.

48. Nichanian, *Writers of Disaster*, 233.

49. Ibid., 196.

50. Lawrence Langer, *Versions of Survival, The Holocaust and the Human Spirit* (Albany: State University of New York Press, 1982).

51. Arslan, *Skylark Farm*, 5.

52. Daniel J. Sherman, *The Construction of Memory in Interwar France* (Chicago: University of Chicago Press, 1999), 14.

53. Arslan, *Skylark Farm*, 5.

CHAPTER 2

Romani Women and the Holocaust:
Testimonies of Sexual Violence in Romanian-Controlled Transnistria

Michelle Kelso

Introduction

On a muggy July day under the shade of a willow tree, I sat on a rickety plastic chair crowded near my research assistants, both women, attentively listening to and recording the words of Silvia S., a 79-year-old Romani woman.[1] Silvia's long grey hair was plaited into two braids interwoven with orange ribbon, and hanging in front of her ears, her head covered by a floral print scarf. The hairstyle, coupled with her ankle-length pleated skirts, signalled her traditional Romani heritage. The bright yellows, oranges, and reds of Silvia's clothing competed with the faded and chipped pastel painted murals on the exterior of her house that depicted mythical mermaids and sea creatures, alongside forest fauna and flora. Silvia, sitting across from us in front of her dilapidated house, asked us, "Hitler, what did he have against Gypsies and Jews?"[2] Although several Roma spoke with us that day, Silvia's narrative stayed with me, a story that revealed the horror of sexual violence amid the multilayered persecutions that Romani women and their families suffered during the Holocaust.

Silvia, from a nomadic coppersmith family, survived genocide against Roma enacted by Nazis and their complicit partners during World War II. The Nazis deemed Roma to be racially inferior and labelled them as asocials and criminals, killing, alongside their accomplices, some 500,000 Roma during the Holocaust. The Romanian regime, allied with Germany, deported more than 25,000 Roma to camps in occupied Ukraine, where many died from wretchedness and brutalities. The Romanian space has only taken on significance in Holocaust studies since 1989, as post-communist investigations into archives grew dramatically during the transition period.[3] As Roland Clark noted, this brought to light Romania's independent killing and infliction of suffering on Jews and Roma as the second-largest perpetrator of Holocaust crimes, after Nazi Germany.[4]

Twenty years ago, I began researching the Roma Holocaust after meeting Romani women who shared their life histories, including their memories of their deportation to and internment in Romanian-run camps. Whereas I knew Roma had been victims of Nazism, I was unaware of the Romanian state's role in the Holocaust. The women's narratives were startling and emotive, revealing hidden sorrows. I searched for corroborative sources, finding few.[5] I soon discovered an erasure of Romani sufferings in Holocaust historiography, or what anthropologist Michel-Rolph Trouillot elucidated as a silencing of the past of the powerless.[6] As Europe's largest transnational minority, Roma were historically, and are presently, often impoverished, marginalized, and discriminated against.[7] Scholars paid scant attention to the genocide of Roma, which was and continues to be infrequently taught in school curricula.[8] Romanian academics I met either denied that the Holocaust took place, or said they knew nothing of it.[9] Archivists in state institutions obstructed my research, selectively providing files or even outright denying access to relevant documents.[10]

I began doing ethnography in mainly *căldărari* communities made up of survivors and their families to discover how and when Roma remembered the Holocaust, while doggedly also visiting archives.[11] Based in Bucharest, my field sites dotted the map primarily of southern Romania, where over nine years I engaged in what Peter Wogan has termed "deep hanging out" in Romani enclaves.[12] I interspersed fieldwork with civil society endeavours, my work evolving into a participatory-action lens as I worked on Holocaust compensation and education programs.[13] More than 200 Roma graciously allowed me to interview them, telling me of their lives before, during, and after their persecutions. They spoke and sometimes sang in Romani of camps in *ando Bugo* (Bug River), and other sites of Romani destruction and death, remembered privately in the sanctity of their homes. As persons who rarely visited the inside of classrooms and were infrequent consumers of materials on the subject, Romani survivors' accounts powerfully reflected their collective tragedy. In gathering Silvia's and others' accounts of genocide, I was entering into what historian Annette Wieviorka called a "compassion pact" with my respondents, who entrusted me with their testimonies.[14] In return, I promised to share their experiences with others.

Over the years I wrote academic pieces, directed a documentary film, and produced teaching materials to help rectify the lacunae regarding the Romani genocide.[15] The paucity of resources available meant that I felt a pressure to present an overview of the genocide, incorporating both Romani women's and men's narratives, but not focusing separately on gender. Only recently, while teaching courses on genocide, have I returned to the role of gender in atrocities. As historian Sybil Milton recognized, among the few works focusing on Romani peoples, studies on Romani women were "scattered and isolated," and at best "fragmentary."[16] Little has changed since Milton's pioneering work on Romani women in the Nazi camps appeared, and it yet looms large, beckoning others like myself to follow in her formidable footsteps.

In this chapter, I will revisit the paradigm put forth by Dalia Ofer and Lenore J. Weitzman regarding the role of gender during the Holocaust, amending it to allow for the experiences of Romani women deported from Romania to Transnistria.[17] In concentrating on their questions of how women experienced the Holocaust differently than men and how women physically and emotionally processed genocide, I will focus on the intersectionality of gender and ethnicity by looking specifically at sexual violence directed at Romani women in Romanian camps. By nesting sexual violence within larger narrative accounts, I aim to understand foremost how Romani women reacted to and resisted genocidal policies, including how they dealt with sexual aggressions. I employ *sexual violence* as an all-encompassing term, using it to describe unwanted sexualized acts forced upon victims that include, but are not limited to, rape.

The purpose of this writing is to fill a void in the literature about Romani experiences as well as to assess the double plight of Romani women as genocide victims. Romani narratives, fieldwork in communities, archival sources, and other primary and secondary literature aid me in addressing these questions. Among the myriad survivor narratives I collected, two were selected as case studies to provide portraits of individual women whose overall experiences reflect the collective, and, as well, because both women were victims of sexual violence. To shed light on the experiences of Romani women in Transnistria, I must turn mainly to testimonies, as historical documents do not reveal sexual violence against Roma. Indeed, scholars of sexual violence against Jewish women have discovered testimony as the main source of knowledge revealing the brutality unleashed on victims.[18]

Testimony about sexual violence was difficult not only for respondents to give, but also for me as a researcher to record. Romani women often would not speak about it if any other relatives were present, due to cultural prohibitions. Rarely did survivors use the Romanian word for rape (*viol*); rather, they used euphemisms like *și-au bătut joc de femei*, which can mean "they made fun of women," or "they took advantage of women" or more seriously, "they raped women." While sexual violence is widely recognized as a difficult subject to discuss among many cultures, Romani culture included, it was not the only impediment to discussing gender-based violence. My own status as a young foreign scholar also initially created a barrier to broaching the topic. In 1995 when I began interviewing women, I hesitated to directly question elderly women who were my grandmother's age about sexual violence because it seemed disrespectful to the respondents and was uncomfortable for me as researcher. I naively rationalized that if women had been sexually assaulted, they would include that as part of their narratives. Sometimes survivors did tell me about rapes, but my then-budding Romanian language skills did not equip me with the adequate vocabulary to grasp what they were trying to convey. Other times women told of other women being raped, but not of their own experiences. Over time, I learned both the subtleties of Romanian, and also to set aside my own discomfort in probing such difficult topics, asking with care about sexual violence. I also learned to clear the interview area of other listeners so that women could share their experiences, if they so chose, in a culturally sensitive way. Before delving into the two case studies as an assessment of localized Romani women's experiences, I will offer a brief reconceptualization of the Ofer and Weitzman model, followed by an historical synopsis of the Romani genocide.

Adjusting the Ofer and Weitzman Lens

In their seminal volume, Ofer and Weitzman employed a gender lens for a more nuanced understanding of the Holocaust. While there is much to praise in their model—which called for a paradigmatic shift in Holocaust studies to include gendered experiences, notably an expansion of concepts of resistance to include women's experiences—there is much that remains unresolved as well. Their framework, spanning from the role of culture to women's reactions and processes during the Holocaust, is predicated upon Jewish women's experiences in certain Nazi-controlled spaces. I find this problematic for two reasons. First, in ethnicizing the gender lens of the Holocaust to include only Jewish women, the framework fails to account for a broader perspective of female victims' experiences under Nazism. Romani women were also persecuted, first for their ethnicity and then for their gender.[19] I argue that the inclusion of Romani women in a gender analysis of the Holocaust will offer a more holistic approach to Holocaust studies. I thus follow the proposal of Judith Gerson and Diane Wolfe, who, among others, argue that more inclusive scholarship that adds Roma into the paradigm of the Holocaust will "yield more sophisticated and nuanced knowledge" of the phenomenon.[20] Stated differently, I am revamping Ofer and Weitzman's initial pitch for gender inclusion in increasing understanding of the Holocaust by making the same pitch for ethnic inclusion. In doing so, I add my voice to scholars such as Raul Hilberg, Henry Friedlander, Sybil Milton, Radu Ioanid, Jean Ancel, Viorel Achim, and Michael Stewart, who have articulated that Nazi bio-racial policies toward Jews and Roma must be studied in tandem.[21]

Second, Ofer and Weitzman's framework offers a limited perspective of Holocaust spaces by concentrating on certain geographical areas under

Nazi control, which often creates a seeming uniformity of Holocaust experiences when, in fact, there was not. A focus on German-run death and concentration camps can lead to a generalization of prisoner experiences that can be misleading. For example, one often reads that during the Holocaust, women were traumatized by hair removal, public nudity, and camp uniforms.[22] These experiences were not shared by all female Holocaust victims, and must be geographically contextualized. This seeming uniformity of perspective on Jewish women's suffering most likely stems from Cold War–era access to archival records and testimonies, which meant atrocities committed in occupied Soviet territories were often omitted from scholarship. In communist bloc countries, gaining access to Holocaust-related archives was difficult and a fuller accounting of the Holocaust in those spaces was not possible prior to 1989–1991. A Soviet-inspired narrative of Nazism was constructed and predominated, obscuring local perpetrator involvement and ethnicities of victims, presenting a censored historical record.[23]

After the collapse of communism in the East, Holocaust scholarship moved beyond Iron Curtain perimeters to include, in particular, former Soviet-influenced spaces, where, beginning in 1941, the Nazis and their accomplices honed their killing techniques, murdering millions.[24] Inquiries into Romanian, Hungarian, Slovakian, Yugoslavian, Ukrainian, and Bulgarian spaces, for example, widen the scope of perpetrators, victims, and bystanders, reshaping our knowledge of the Holocaust. Therefore, an analysis of Romanian space may shift the script of defeminization of women in the ways that have previously been described. Historian Dan Stone suggests that researchers must look to a more complex understanding of mass killing of Jews, de-centring antisemitism as the explanation and looking instead at interlocking and inseparable projects of genocide.[25] I thus propose that widening the Ofer and Weitzman model to include these configurations beyond a German-Jewish paradigm will lend greater understanding of perpetrations and victimizations during the Holocaust.

Since both the Romanian Holocaust and the plight of the Roma in Romanian territories are yet little known, I provide below a summation of the state's genocidal policies against its Romani citizens to contextualize the narratives of Romani women's responses to genocide in the following section.

The Holocaust in Romania: The Fate of the Roma

The rumblings of Romania's entry into the escalating war in Europe permeated national discussions after Germany invaded Poland in 1939. King Carol II found himself isolated and under pressure from an increasingly popular, pro-fascist Iron Guard party after Romania lost territories to Hungary, Bulgaria, and the USSR in 1940.[26] In a tense political climate, Carol abdicated his throne to his son Mihai, but gave much of the monarchy's power to the appointed prime minister, General Ion Antonescu. A career military man, Antonescu entered into a coalition with the Iron Guard (which failed in 1941) and, with the backing of Germany, he became dictator of Romania. Romania entered the war on the side of the Axis in the June 1941 invasion of the Soviet Union. As Romanian troops advanced toward the front lines, Antonescu and his cabinet simultaneously ordered attacks on Jews in the Bessarabia and Bukovina regions in a "cleansing the land" campaign enacted during summer 1941.[27] Romanian troops initially murdered between 45,000 and 60,000 Jews before pushing the survivors into Axis-controlled Ukraine.[28]

Hitler offered—and Antonescu accepted—governance over part of southeast Ukrainian territory near the Black Sea, including Odessa as well as part of a newly created territory named Transnistria.[29] Romanian control stretched from the Dniester River to the Bug River, while the Germans administered from the Bug to the Dnieper.[30] Transnistria became the destination for Antonescu's deportations, and the site of massive Jewish and Romani suffering, or what one author called the Holocaust's forgotten cemetery.[31] Romani survivors would later refer to their genocide as *ando Bugo*, or in the Romani language "at the Bug River." The Bug marked the periphery of the Romanian regime's control over their lives, and they conflated all their horrors into the symbol of the river, along whose banks their dead would remain.

The destruction of Romanian Jews and Roma was part of Antonescu's larger bio-political plan to bring the country back to an ethnic Romanian base, which meant a massive restructuring of the population.[32] Dubbed "Romanianization," the policies were similar to those of Nazi Aryanization, and began before Antonescu came to power. The laws passed to isolate and rob Jews of their wealth, and later policies to deport and murder them, were employed in similar ways against the Roma after 1942.[33] More than 150,000 Jews were deported to ghettos and camps in Transnistria, and preyed upon by Romanian, German, and local death squads.[34] The area was already home to a substantial Ukrainian Jewish population that would also be subjected to deportations, incarceration, and killings. Daily life for Jews was precarious, and most deportees died from typhus, starvation, exposure, or exhaustion from hard labour detail, or were killed in mass shootings.[35]

Once the genocide of Jews was underway, Antonescu targeted the Romani minority, which a century before had been enslaved in the Romanian territories. By 1942, the Romani population numbered 208,700, the majority of whom were rural inhabitants.[36] Post-slavery, in the absence of integration policies, the Roma remained a splintered and impoverished group that few, other than staunch eugenicists, viewed as a threat to an ethnic Romanian state.[37] In the early 1940s, most Roma lived in grinding poverty, segregated in disenfranchised rural enclaves. Their socio-economic status was the lowest in the country, and this arguably greatly facilitated their persecution. Roma had little pan-ethnic consciousness and self-identified mainly based on men's professions. For example, coppersmiths (*căldărari*), blacksmiths (*fierari*), comb-makers (*pieptănari*), and silversmiths (*argintari*) were a few of the Romani subgroups, each declaring itself ethnically distinct from the others.[38] Roma also worked as field hands and domestics. Romani craftsmen, aided by their female relatives, were often tied to rural areas where their skills were essential to agriculture. Some lived nomadically, travelling to sell and barter their goods, while others were settled in villages, towns, and cities. Most Roma lived in rural areas.

During the interwar period, Roma, like their compatriots, had migrated increasingly to cities for work. Romani groups were in various states of integration after emancipation, ranging from the least integrated—or those who spoke the Romani language and kept Romani traditions, as the nomads did—to the most integrated, who had completely assimilated into Romanian society, often passing as non-Roma. Nomadic Roma were highly visible, as their colourful caravans and dress acted as cultural markers, making them easily identifiable to Romanian authorities, and thus, easily deportable. Men often had long moustaches and beards, and both men and women wore their hair long. Women's clothing also set them apart as nomads. Women wore ankle-length, brightly coloured skirts and headscarves. Women also frequently wore part if not all of their families' wealth—gold and silver coins—either woven into their braids or as jewellery.

Culturally Defined Roles of Romani Women

Roma, like their Romanian neighbours, lived a patriarchal lifestyle indifferent to their group affiliation. Like women elsewhere, Romani women were responsible for raising children and keeping the household. However, Roma subgroups had differing social norms regarding gender. Families that kept *tradiţii romane*, or Romani language and cultural laws, had strict gender norms. Above all else, women were expected to be pure, and their purity greatly affected families' social standing and community relations. There was an expectation of virginity for girls before marriage; and after marriage, women were to remain faithful to their husbands. Deviance from the norm was harshly punished. Roma women from many traditional groups could not work outside their homes, a norm put in place to minimize their contact with non-Romani men. Not all Roma kept traditions, however, as some had assimilated into Romanian society. In those groups, Romani women worked as domestic servants and street vendors, but still lived under a patriarchal system.

Anticipatory Reactions of Romani Women to the Genocide

Once Jewish deportations and exterminations were underway in Transnistria in 1941, the then-experienced regime began deporting Roma in summer 1942. Even though Roma were persecuted throughout Nazi-controlled Europe, Antonescu's actions reflected the particulars of his regime.[39]

Disturbed by what he called marauding Gypsy gangs, Antonescu justified his deportation of Roma under the guise of keeping public order.[40] Authorities established two categories of *ţigani* (Gypsies) to deport to Transnistria: nomads and settled *ţigani*, who were "a burden and a danger to public order."[41] Missives also labelled Roma as "heterogeneous elements" and "parasites."[42] Unlike the Jews, who previous Romanian governments had targeted, first through restrictive legislation and later through heinous attacks, Roma had experienced little change in their status as citizens prior to expulsion.[43]

Over a four-month period from June through September 1942, Romanian gendarmes deported more than 25,000 Roma to Transnistria.[44] Deportation lists reveal that the majority of deportees were children, followed by women, and then men. By the end of August 1942, officials estimated that 11,441 nomads had arrived in Transnistria, deported in their own wagons under armed police escorts.[45] Slightly more nomadic women than men were deported, 2,375 versus 2,352, respectively.[46] Weeks later in mid-September, some 13,176 settled *ţigani* were deported by cargo trains.[47] Primarily men fit the deportation criteria of "criminals and delinquents," but women were also deported for their supposed delinquency. The families of so-called socially deviant Roma were swept up as well. Significantly more settled women than men were deported, 3,780 versus 3,187, respectively.[48] The greater number of women most likely reflected the precariousness of their social situations. The majority of women were deported because of their relationships to men in their households (mothers, sisters, girlfriends, wives, etc.). According to historian Radu Ioanid, the deportations were improvised, arbitrary, and corrupt.[49]

There was virtually no warning that the Antonescu regime would persecute Roma, thus Roma had few, if any, anticipatory reactions. This differed from the persecution of the Jews, which was somewhat foreshadowed by legislative initiatives, in-country work details and antisemitic public discourses. The deportations caught Romani victims and their compatriots alike by surprise. The expulsion of the nomads was noticed, but not regarded necessarily as nefarious by the majority, since authorities often moved nomads from village to village.[50] Only when deportations began among settled Roma did the regime's actions trouble some prominent local figures. Politician Constantin Bratianu, the Queen Mother Elena of Romania, and renowned musician George Enescu all privately intervened on behalf of Roma.[51] Some local officials and landed gentry also failed to comply with the deportation orders, protecting Roma in their districts. However, there was no public outcry against Antonescu's deportations of Roma and no major interventions on their behalf.

The Killing Fields of Transnistria

Once in Transnistria, Romanian gendarmes transferred Roma to makeshift camps primarily along the Bug River, where they were to labour in return for food and housing. Roma stayed in family groups, dumped in ghettos in towns and villages, or on Soviet-style farms. For Roma placed in evacuated Ukrainian homes, housing was miserably overcrowded, with multiple families occupying single-family dwellings lacking sanitary facilities, wood for cooking or heating, and basic amenities. Nomads recounted being left in open fields, or crammed into barns, pigpens, and dug-out earthen shelters (*bordei*) on farms. Occasionally Roma and Jews were in the same camps, often with separate housing and work details. Conditions in camps vastly differed, and much depended on local Romanian administrators. Camps had at least two Romanian gendarmes, who relied upon locals to perform tasks such as guard duties. The fate of the Roma was dependent on the mercy of the Romanian commanders. Food allocation, work details, and camp organization all factored into the likelihood of survival among deportees.

Authorities relied upon Romani leaders—all men—to organize the deportees in labour details and for food distribution.[52] Men and women did forced labour, primarily in agriculture, but also in forests, on roadways, and for other war-related tasks. When allocated, food rations were based on workload. Gendarme reports and survivor testimonies reveal that men and women faced similar pressures, predominantly because they lived in family groups. While all survivors spoke of the unrelenting hunger plaguing them, primarily women were tasked with finding food. Food rations were distributed to workers, discriminating along age and not gender, as the elderly and the very young were exempted from work and received little to no allocations. Roma used all available resources to keep from starving. Romani women and men bartered with locals: clothes for food. In the Romanian-run camps, deportees were not given uniforms and kept their own clothing. Locals appreciated the embroidered blouses that traditional Romani women and men wore.[53] A young mother recalled trading with local women who asked the price for her clothes: "I told them whatever ... they gave me a bucket of corn meal and I gave the dress and blouse off my body."[54] Another woman recalled foraging for grasses and roots to eat,[55] because her father had already sold all their intact clothing for food, and they were left in rags. Roma also began stealing and begging from locals. If caught outside camp, they risked beatings and shootings. One man—a boy at the time—recalled watching a guard shoot his father, who died holding two small potatoes that he had taken from a nearby field.[56] Parents often sent their children to steal or beg, rationalizing that guards would show mercy if children were caught. One child-survivor said that the only Russian words she remembered were "Lady, give me a piece of bread please."[57]

Difference in Treatment of Women and Men

Romani women in camps had some differing realities from men. For instance, women were not in positions of organizational power in camps, as were men. After exhausting days labouring, women were expected to cook meals, care-take, and complete other family responsibilities that were culturally designated as "women's work," just as they had prior to internment. Survivors told of the stress on mothers caused by trying to feed their children. One mother cried to a neighbour, distraught because she did not have bread to give her children.[58] Her daughter remembered this mother's sacrifice, as she gave her portion of food to the children. Weakened, the mother died of typhus a few months after arriving in Transnistria. The plight of single women, especially those with children, was even harder, as they shouldered all the familial responsibilities. One woman whose husband was a soldier on the front spoke of caring for their five children, who would cry for food, stating that it "was harder for women than for men."[59] Women's homemaking skills were vital to a family's survival. One man recalled that after his wife died from disease his father forced him to immediately remarry, Romani style, stating that without a woman to make food for them, they would die too.[60] Additionally, women bore the responsibility for pregnancies and infant children, which were additional stresses on their wasted bodies. Sexual violence was also a constant threat for women, although as testimonies will reveal in the following section, attacks had physical and emotional consequences for men as well.

During the nearly two years of internment, Romanian policies caused misery and death. Romanian authorities maintained a starvation policy with infrequent or no delivery of food. Diseases such as typhus and dysentery preyed on the weakened Roma living in filthy, cramped dwellings. In the Oceacov district, gendarmes reported to Bucharest that *ţigani* were reduced to "mere shadows" and were "almost wild."[61] They noted in particular the shocking nakedness of women, who they described as having their genitalia exposed. Another camp reported the haunting sight of the Gypsies who "die worse than animals" and "are buried without a priest."[62] Survivors reported that corpses were thrown in large pits, buried shallowly in makeshift graves, or even left in fields where animals devoured the dead.[63] Mortality rates rose with the onslaught of disease. Typhus destroyed thousands as it spread quickly among Romani prisoners. The former prefect of Oceacov wrote that a typhus epidemic ravaged the *ţigani*, killing between 3,000 and 4,000 in his district alone.[64]

Despite the overwhelming deprivation, archival sources and testimony reveal that Roma refused to wait for death. Many resisted Romanian policies through work evasion, theft of food and provisions, and escape.[65] They flummoxed and frustrated camp guards, who reported that Roma were constantly bucking the rules to survive.[66] It is difficult to use gender as a defining variable in the kinds of resistance that occurred, as archival and oral history evidence suggest that women and men participated in the same types of resistance. As these records are sporadic, estimating in what proportion women and men resisted genocide is also problematic. For example, escape was a means of thwarting the power of the state over their bodies. Gendarmes reported that miserable living situations prompted Roma to escape, as they were "naked, without good housing and fuel for winter."[67] In one month alone, some 1,000 Roma escaped from Berezovka and Oceacov regions, only to be caught and sent again to camps.[68] Despite increasing guard details, by the end of 1943 nearly 800 Roma managed to clandestinely re-enter Romania from Transnistria.[69]

In spring of 1944, the Soviet army recaptured its occupied territories, and Axis troops retreated across Transnistria. Liberation of Jews and Roma effectively occurred through abandonment by their guards, who left them to the perils of an oncoming front line. On August 23, 1944, King Mihai dissolved the Antonescu government, proclaiming an armistice with the Allied powers. Antonescu was arrested, and two days later Romania declared war on Germany. An estimated 11,000 Roma had died in Transnistria.[70] In 1946, Antonescu and his three top henchmen were executed, in part for crimes against humanity for the persecution of Jews and Roma in Transnistria.

Reactions of Romani Women to Their Experiences During the Genocide

Once the genocide was under way, Romani women and men responded to the persecution, from outside and inside the camp system. Due to space limitations, I will focus on the latter, turning to testimonies in this section to illustrate the kinds of reactions that women and their families had to the destructive policies of the state.

The Fortune Teller

The first time I met Melentina C. in 1998, she pulled a deck of tattered cards out of her apron pocket with a gnarled, nut-brown hand. "What do you say, miss? Tell your fortune?" From another pocket came a crumpled packet of unfiltered Carpaţi cigarettes, from which a lifelong brand loyalty had left Melentina with a deeply gravelled voice. A former Romani neighbour (and relative of Melentina by marriage) drove with me to Melentina's village an hour outside of Bucharest. Typically, non-Romani women showed up at the 70-year-old's door for card readings, not for Holocaust discussions. Melentina lit up her smoke, offering me a deal. She would talk to me about *ando Bugo*, but only after I bought a card reading. I agreed. Over the years of researching in Romani communities, numerous traditional Romani women who had survived Transnistrian camps and earned their living telling fortunes to non-Roma had read my cards.

Women told me that fortune-telling, or *drabarel* in the Romani language, was a skill handed down from their mothers and grandmothers, who learned it from their mothers and grandmothers. Generations of Romani women supplemented their husbands' earnings by counselling, mainly through cards, other women (and sometimes men) about their love woes, domestic strife, and other quotidian minutiae. Fortune tellers (*romni kai drabarel*), I surmised after observing tens of Romani women interacting with their Romanian clients, were rather like therapists for poor people. Clients, some of whom had decades-long relationships with fortune tellers, brought their troubles to these women and in exchange for beans, rice, cigarettes, or much-preferred cash, receiving a willing listener and sometimes partner in helping them ameliorate their futures. Melentina's acumen, enhanced by age and quirkiness, was reputed beyond her village. While Melentina's forte remained cards, she also read tea leaves and coffee grounds. "These cards are how I survived Transnistria," she told me.[71]

In following Henry Greenspan's suggestion to take testimony repeatedly from the same person to really understand the "context of recounting," I interviewed Melentina several times—sometimes alone and sometimes with my assistants—about her life before, during, and after *ando Bugo*.[72] Melentina was just 13 when she "married," in Romani fashion, her 17-year-old husband. Her parents were traditional Roma, which meant for a teenage Melentina that a marriage would be arranged for her. Most traditional Roma married young, too young for their unions to be legalized, and families held their own ceremonies to unite young couples. Melentina was unusual in that she circumvented tradition by choosing her own husband, with whom she eloped to the displeasure of both their parents. "The first time I met him, I was carrying a bucket of water from the [village] fountain. But it was heavy for me and he took it just like that and helped me. He could carry two, running." Thereafter the young couple met up at a pub that held dances in the evenings. It was when they were dancing traditional folk dances like the hora that Melentina really appreciated her new beau. "I found him so attractive," she said. "He was so handsome; he wasn't dark in the face. He sang, whistled, danced." Lightness of complexion, among the mainly dark-skinned and dark-eyed Roma, was coveted.

At a young age, Melentina picked up fortune-telling from her mother, which put money in her pocket. Though her husband had a seventh-grade education and a cobbler's apprenticeship, Melentina had never set foot in a school and declared that she could not even scribble her name. The couple survived economically, initially through her husband's work as a cobbler while in the village; and later, after moving to Bucharest, through his job as a construction worker for the national railway—which, ironically, would be used later by the Antonescu regime to deport Roma. Melentina recalled that while his income bought only their groceries, they still managed to have fun on Sundays going to community dances. Once settled in Bucharest, she said, "We had a good time then. We would gather on a paved field, lighting it up with a *hora*. We'd go to a film."

The good times were short-lived. Her husband entered the army for his required three-year military service, was released home, and a year later was drafted when the war broke out. During his times in service, Melentina returned to her parents' home. In 1942, police classified Melentina's family as nomads, deporting her extended family to Transnistria. Relatives of service men were to have been excluded from the deportation, but police widely ignored the exemption. Melentina was interned in various camps scattered along the Bug River.

Rations were scarce. Melentina recounted that just two cups of cornmeal were given per day per person. The harshness of the physical labour along with the worsening living conditions that began killing Roma prompted her to strategize measures to save her life. "After a while, I didn't want to work anymore. So I just pretended that I was completely crazy. I walked around naked, screaming. I didn't want to go dig with a hoe. That earth was as hard as cement." She thus evaded work detail, which left her free to formulate ways to survive.

Melentina learned Russian. "My luck was that I told fortunes. I earned a living from it. I would read the fortunes of local women. They used to pay me in milk and cheese, in bread or flour. God helped me earn a living." Fortune-telling, however, was not enough to keep her family fed. The miserable living conditions broke her, and she fell ill with typhus. Melentina openly talked of turning to theft from nearby storage units and houses to keep her family alive. "We Gypsy women went to steal together. Whoever didn't steal didn't have food. There were some who didn't steal, they ate what they received—onions, corn, cornmeal. But they didn't get hardly any food. So they died." Melentina explained that the local men were mostly away fighting at the front and few were left behind to guard them. The Romanian police were in the village, but not on the farm. While most Roma worked in the fields during the day, Melentina scrounged for food. Once caught stealing a chicken, locals beat Melentina so badly they broke her arm. "It took me a month to heal ... I had to set my arm with an impro-vised splint because there wasn't a doctor to put it in a cast." Beatings did not scare her, she declared. Death—the alternative to stealing—did.

German soldiers also terrified her. One afternoon Melentina and some other women, including her niece, went to get water from a nearby well to wash themselves and their clothes. They saw German troops parked in a nearby field. Melentina said, "They wanted to take my niece to rape her (să-și bată joc de ea) because she was really beautiful. We got between her [and the soldiers] and ran home. They came after us. There they beat us really badly," she said, gesturing, hitting her open palm with the side of her other hand. "We were being brutalized." The women tried to hide under the bed, but the soldiers went after them, "beating us until we were nearly senseless." Melentina's brother was there, and tried to stop the Germans. "When my brother jumped up to protect me, to save me from their hands, he died. Bang! Shot twice," she said, her hand mimicking the motion of a gun discharging and a body falling. "My heart broke seeing my brother shot before me by the Germans. My elderly father, the same. [The Germans] had their way with us, as they had wanted to."

Melentina watched her parents, three of her brothers, one sister, and other relatives die before her husband, a soldier, discovered and brought the remaining members of his family home in 1944, shortly before the war ended. After returning home Melentina continued drabarel to sustain her family. Well into her seventies, Melentina could often be found wan-dering one of the main markets in Bucharest, telling fortunes to Turkish vendors. An enthusiast for my research, Melentina acted as one of my guides, or what social scientists call "key informers." She eagerly took me to her sister, one of her ex-husbands (she married four times), and several of her neighbours who had also been deported.

The Coppersmith's Wife

Across the eastern and southern provinces of Romania, Romani survivors and their families live in villages, towns, and cities. While less than 15 percent of Roma in the pre-war years were nomadic, by the 1960s communist authorities had forcibly settled all Roma. After 1989, some Roma with permanent residencies began nomadizing with caravans in warmer months to sell goods, primarily in rural areas, before the government clamped down on travelling with horse carts as the country moved closer to European Union accession in 2007. Some formerly nomadic groups, like Silvia S. and her family, maintain much of the nomadic culture, as dress, language, and Romani laws still dominate in her extended *căldărari* kin group.

A mutual acquaintance introduced me to Silvia, who invited my team to interview her. After we settled into Silvia's courtyard, rigging up the camera and audio equipment, she began by telling us that she was born in a caravan, as her parents were nomads who travelled with their tents and wagons. As she was slightly hard of hearing, we had to raise our voices for Silvia to hear our questions, which she sometimes clarified in Romani before answering in Romanian. "My father was a coppersmith, making pots, buckets and stills," she told us.[73] Shortly before their deportation, she married her husband, Istrate, also a coppersmith. Their entire clan was rounded up in 1942, and Silvia remembered local police crying after them; she believed, in retrospect, that it was because they knew the Roma were going to their deaths.

"They put us in a camp with Jews, there in Transnistria. The Jews were on one side, and we Gypsies were on the other." Thrown into a large barn, the two ethnicities were housed together but on separate sides of the facility. Silvia said that guards hauled Jews and Gypsies out to work at six in the morning, returning with them at six in the evening. "We worked in cornfields. We worked in the forests." Her co-workers in the wheat fields were young, beautiful Jewish women. Silvia witnessed a massacre of Jews. "A large pit was made and the Jews were lined up and they shot them."

Germans shot with automatic rifles so that the Jews would fall in the pre-dug pits, she recalled. "When we saw this, we cried. [We thought] this will happen to us, too."

Silvia recounted the precariousness of life in the Transnistrian camp, from the most brutal shootings and beatings, to the daily struggle to find food. Like most survivors, Silvia commented on pitiful daily rations, just 200 grams (a cup and a half) of cornmeal with which to make polenta. "I learned Russian and got along well with the Russian women," she chuckled, telling us some Russian words for foods. Their household goods, like rugs, towels, and pots, and even their clothing, were traded for food. "We gave our things to the Russian [local] women, and they gave us flour, beans, potatoes. And they asked for our beads, and we gave them." Some 65 years later, during our interview, Silvia wore around her neck two strands of amber beads, which Roma women believe bring prosperity, much like the ones she traded for food in camps. Women also made use of the gold and silver coins woven into their hair, a cultural marker of traditional *căldărari* Romani women. "We had coins in our braids," she said, gesturing to her grey strands "and we gave them, we gave them so that we could live." To trade, Silvia had to leave the camp, which was risky. When caught by guards, Silvia said, they were brutally beaten.

They survived Transnistrian camps, she explained, because, when crossing into Transnistria, her family had hidden their gold—which they doled out to buy food. She surmised that "Those who had money, survived. Those who didn't died." When the front fell in 1944, a Romanian guard told them to leave. Her father, husband, and brother stole some horses and wagons from the Soviet farm, and they left the camp "naked, undressed," she stressed. Eventually they made their way to Tighina, a crossing point to Romania. En route, Silvia, then 16, gave birth to twins—a boy and a girl. "I threw the girl away," she said. "I gave birth, afraid the Germans were coming. My sister told me 'Leave her.' I put her down. Maybe we weren't going to come back either." Although Silvia and her family survived a typhus epidemic, starvation, and random brutality in the camps, it was, ironically, on the road home where most of Silvia's family would perish, including her infant daughter whom she set out to die. Her story poured out faster and faster, paradoxically detailed and ambiguous, without having a clear direction. She talked of relatives dying and of altercations with German soldiers.

Lawrence Langer wrote that Holocaust narratives were "not a series of links in a chain whose pattern of connections can be easily traced, but a cycle of sparks erupting unpredictably from a dark landscape" that does not always offer "the steady ray of stable insight."[74] Silvia's jumbled recounting of an encounter with German soldiers is evidence of memory sparks, and we—the intruders on her process—waited as her thoughts surfaced. She told us that near Tighina, they ran into German soldiers who were on the road. The Germans were on foot, their trucks left behind on the muddied road. They demanded the horses, and her husband refused. The Germans, she says, then threw Istrate into an open fire. "His arms were burnt where the Germans threw him into the fire," she said, repeating, gesturing to her husband. Later Silvia had him show us his scarred forearms, badges of resistance to the Germans' terror. She explained that the soldiers made them get down from their wagons, and the path was muddy. "We ran away from the Germans. The Germans beat us, they beat us, and the Germans wanted to take the women. And we ran away." This was her first reference to the possibility of rape. She backtracked:

> They grabbed my father. They beat him so that we would get down from the wagons. We got away then. I had children in my arms.... I didn't want to get down, because I had this boy in my arms. A German was pulling on me. "Get down. Get down." "I won't get down. I won't get down. I won't get down." They didn't have guns anymore. When they had guns, they would shoot. When someone defied them, they would shoot. A German came and took this old man [referring to her husband] who was young then, took him and threw him in the fire. They took our horses.

In the fracas, Silvia said, German soldiers shot Romani women. Cosmina, a Romanian doctoral student assisting me, questioned her again about the death of her siblings, their fate unclear. "They died of cold. Germans shot them," Silvia answered. I asked for clarification, confused by the chronology. Silvia disclosed that her 14-year-old sister Gurita died. "A German shot her. He wanted to take her and she didn't go, and he shot her."

Even though she implied it, Silvia avoided using the word *rape*. She repeated that Germans tried to take away her sister. My Romani assistant, Marioara, and I understood immediately Silvia's difficulty in saying what had happened. Romani women are not supposed to talk about rape due to Romani cultural restrictions. Marioara, also from a traditional *căldărari* family, learned to let go of this cultural prohibition to ask respondents about sexual assaults against them because, as she told me often, people need to know what happened to Romani women in camps.

Marioara pressed Silvia to be more specific, first in Romani, then in Romanian. She understood that although the two women had been only briefly acquainted, perhaps their shared culture might ease Silvia's reservations. Silvia repeated, "He wanted to take her. She was grown up and he wanted to take her to someplace else." Marioara voiced the words that Silvia could not: "To rape her (*să-şi bată joc de ea*)?" Silvia answered yes, and the two women switched into the Romani language. During their exchange, Marioara tried to assuage Silvia's fears. "I am shamed to say," Silvia told us, switching back to Romanian. We knew speaking of rape was difficult for Silvia, as it was for all the women we interviewed. We tried assuring her the shame was all on the part of the German. She continued, revealing that three of her sisters were shot by Germans who were trying "to take" the women away or, in effect, attempting to rape them.

I asked again for clarification: Three sisters shot in the same place? Silvia paused. A young woman standing nearby us began to tell us how they died. Silvia cut her off, saying, "We stayed buried alive underground." We were stunned at the seeming non sequitur. Our transcript reads as follows:

INTERVIEWER: What did the German want to do?

SILVIA: He took me from the wagon. I had the boy in my arms. He threw the boy down, and he grabbed me. My husband jumped in so the German wouldn't take me. He beat him and threw him in the fire. He tried [to save me], my father tried, many others tried and got me out of the German's hands. They took me from the German's hands ... he wanted to ... I am too ashamed to say.

Overcome, Silvia could not get the words out. Cosmina urged her to continue. "So that he could take me, so that he could rape me. Yes. I am so ashamed. I cannot say any more."

Once again we told her that the shame was not hers. "He took me when ..." she began. "I was near the horse wagon, then I went away. He took my sister and raped her [și-a bătut joc de dânsa]. She died, she died. He raped her.... Yes.... Many started in ... Germans. I am ashamed to say.... They were beautiful [my sisters], they had beautiful breasts." Silvia repeats that her sister Agripina, 20, was also raped and died. It was as if once the word *rape* was out, Silvia could not stop saying it. "I am very ashamed." It is uncertain whether Silvia's shame was in speaking of the gang rapes, or if it was survivor's guilt for living when her sisters had died. We interviewers remained silent, our inquisitiveness stymied. The brutality unleashed on two young women I had never met overwhelmed me, as did the lasting trauma of their deaths on the frail, green-eyed woman seated before me who still grieved.

Silvia returned to being buried alive, which happened after the other rapes had occurred. Silvia recounted that at night the German soldiers came, putting their hands on the chests of those sleeping to identify women. To avoid further rapes, which led to death, her male relatives devised a drastic plan, a testament of their resistance to German perpetration. Silvia's father, brother, and brother-in-law dug a large hole in the ground and made the women get inside. "They put a pipe in [for air], and then put earth on top of us," she said. She and her mother, as well as her sisters-in-law, were in the pit. Their menfolk slept on top of the hole during the night. Incredulous, we asked how they breathed. "We couldn't. We almost died in the hole. They left just a little bit [for air].... We were crying in there." Her sister-in-law, who Silvia described as fat and strong, suffocated in the hole. Silvia blamed her death on the Germans as well.

Silvia told us that, in a separate incident, her mother was also later raped and shot by Germans. When they took her mother away, the rest of women hid, and later their men searched for her. "[They] found her dead. Father, crying, screaming, crying, screaming. We left her on the road. There was nothing else we could do. We ran so that we could escape." It was a bitter twist of fate that the family could not dig even the shallowest of graves for

Silvia's mother, who days before had been buried alive in a pit. In total, four women in Silvia's family were killed as a result of either a sexual assault or the act of avoiding one.

Silvia explained that one evening before we came, she and Istrate cried together, remembering their tragedies. "Only God knows what we suffered," she said. "We left here a wealthy people with gold, with money and there they took it. And we came and died, the dead, who died on the road." She emphasized that no one should suffer as they did at the hands of the Germans. Almost an afterthought, Silvia mentioned that, years later, they met up with Jewish friends who were in the camps, crying together for their collective sufferings. "They brought us Gypsies and Jews, they brought us [to Transnistria] and killed us. They raped the Jewish girls and women, too," she revealed. Silvia's thoughts came full circle, asking once again *why* they were persecuted: "What did Germans have with us Gypsies and Jews? What did Hitler have against us Gypsies and Jews?"

Women as Unruly Historical Actors

Canonic texts of the Holocaust rarely mention Romani suffering, but when they do, it is often added in—an afterthought to discussions of the Holocaust.[75] Testimonies offer a perspective on how social actors like Melentina and Silvia, disenfranchised and marginalized from power structures and their institutions, make sense of their life experiences given the national and international context of collective memory of the Holocaust. Men and women often recounted similar experiences and reactions during the genocide, although some aspects were more pronounced for women, such as child-caring. Since Roma remained in family groups, gendered experiences and responses are not as distinct as Ofer and Weitzman's model suggests, even when turning to sexual violence. These women are "unruly actors," as conceptualized by Daina Eglitis and Vita Zelce, or "historical actors who are challenges to dominant memory narratives ... [which are] configured to reflect and reproduce a social order that benefits politically and socially powerful groups or institutions in society."[76] By sharing their experiences, these Romani women challenge the silencing of their history, offering a counter-narrative to replace the dominant one in Romania, and arguably elsewhere, which has yet to fully incorporate their sufferings in Holocaust research, commemoration, and education.[77]

As case studies, the testimonies of Melentina and Silvia function in two key ways: firstly as narratives illustrating that Romani women employed various survival measures in reaction to the genocide, including relying on Romani cultural markers and knowledge to resist perpetrator policies; and secondly as narratives demonstrating that women were also victimized due to their gender as well as their ethnicity. By providing a deeper reading of narratives and avoiding isolating incidents of sexual violence, through contextualization of their experiences, I offer a more holistic view of what these women endured. I do so as a means of addressing the concerns of feminist scholars like Janet Jacobs who fear the gender stereotyping of women as merely helpless victims of sexual assault during the Holocaust and in collective memory and memorialization of it.[78]

In exploring the first function of the testimonies in conveying the reactions of individual women, both narratives provide accounts of women confronting various aspects of the genocide (starvation, forced labour, violence, death) by drawing upon their cultural inheritances to thwart death. In the face of unrelenting hunger, both women engaged in trade with locals to survive. For instance, Melentina drew upon an ethnic marker, Romani women as fortune tellers, well-reputed and sought out by non-Roma in the region, to circumvent the starvation policy of the regime. Melentina learned Russian, cultivating relationships with local women who exchanged food for card readings. In turning to Silvia's narrative, there are also mentions of cultural customs that saved her family. The intricate, hand-embroidered blouses and shirts worn by traditional Roma like Silvia's family were traded for food, as were the women's amber beads, so prized for bringing prosperity. The *căldărari* tradition of women wearing wealth, stored in gold and silver coins braided into their hair, was also advantageous in Silvia's case, as she bartered coins for food. Thus their Romani ethnic background, which condemned these women to death under the Antonescu regime, also proved advantageous because they drew upon Romani culture for their survival.

Both testimonies reveal that acts of resistance against the established orders of the Romanian administration were risky but necessary reactions for survival. Melentina strategized a work stoppage, understanding that hard labour, compounded with malnutrition, hastened death. In her words, she acted "completely crazy," evading backbreaking fieldwork. Time and energy conserved through resisting work details freed her to search for food. Melentina characterized her rule-breaking thefts as life-saving, noting that those who followed the perpetrators' rules died. Silvia's family also clandestinely refused to comply with Romanian gendarmes' orders to hand over all their wealth upon crossing over into Transnistria, a rule imposed by the Romanian regime in their robbing of Roma and Jews. The deviant act of hiding gold, for which they risked bodily harm or death at the border crossing into Transnistria in 1942, meant they kept valuable resources with which to trade later for daily needs. Silvia credited the family's survival to the hidden gold. Like Melentina, Silvia also regularly broke camp rules by sneaking out to trade with local women. Although these exchanges were essential, she received beatings when caught, though she managed to avoid getting killed, as sometimes guards shot Roma who left the camps.[79] Examples of Romani women's resistance are comparable to Jewish women's resistance as well.[80] They also move away from the dominant template of masculine resistance toward what Lenore J. Weitzman proposed as a gendered view of resistance.[81]

The second function of the Romani testimonies allows for a contextualized exploration of sexual violence. As Joan Ringelheim noted, rape and sexual assault were minimized or even denied in Holocaust studies, often because they were "considered peculiar or specific to women from what has been designated as the proper collective memory."[82] While gender has become a more explored topic in Holocaust studies, a male paradigm of Holocaust experiences yet dominates.[83] Further, academic discussions of rape during the Holocaust may inadvertently misrepresent the extent of sexual violence during the Holocaust by miring it in ideology rather than praxis, as did Helen Fein's analysis, which can then minimize or omit sexual crimes.[84] More recent texts, such as Hedgepeth and Seidel's 2010 edited collection, concentrate on sexualized violence against Jewish women during the Holocaust, but neglect to include Romani women other than in a few mentions.[85] This is further compounded by a dearth of survivor testimonies that are forthcoming about rape, often due to cultural associations of shame in speaking of such acts.[86] In cultures where women's modesty and purity are direct reflections on a family's reputation and honour, rape is viewed as shameful.[87] For traditional Roma, discussions of rape are shameful, involving potential ramifications for the victim because the relations happened with a man who was not the woman's husband, which is culturally prohibited.[88]

Thus the case studies of Melentina and Silvia, who both spoke of multiple rapes of Romani women (Melentina and her niece, Silvia and her sisters) in incidents with German soldiers, provide some insight into the ways in which Romani women were treated differently than Romani men, indicating that gender was at times no less salient than ethnicity in structuring experiences in the Transnistrian space. Both women spoke of resisting persecution, and losing loved ones in the process. The rape narratives also reveal that women do not necessarily remember and view a gender separation in the tragedy of sexual violence, which I believe is an important distinction not always highlighted in academic discourses of sexual violence. In widening the perspectives of the rape incidents to the larger narrative of genocide, we find that both women tell of their experiences from an individual yet collective viewpoint.

The accounts of Melentina and Silvia also broaden the perspective of sexual violence from gender-based to family-based. In both narratives, sexual assaults endangered men as well as women. While pregnancy, disease, psychological and physical trauma, stigmatization, and even death were consequences for women, some men (and women) who tried to protect them also faced physical and psychological trauma, and even death, as a consequence. In trying to protect Melentina, both her brother and her father were killed. Silvia's husband was badly burned and her father beaten while attempting to ward off her attackers. Both accounts reveal that extended families were present when women were assaulted. Historian Jean Ancel noted that any resistance by Romani women in Transnistria was met with suffering and death, and if the women's male relatives attempted to intervene, as sexual assaults were sometimes committed in front of women's families, these men would also be killed.[89] Ancel wrote that Romani women, marked for death by the regime, were raped en masse because perpetrators no longer viewed them as humans.

He called the sexual violence against Romani women "a collective crime committed by all nationalities" operating in Transnistria, noting that Romanian gendarmes, local Ukrainian and German guards, and Russian as well as German soldiers all raped with impunity.[90]

Ancel's analysis and the lived experiences captured in the two case studies indicate that a more nuanced accounting of sexual violence may be necessary to fully grasp the traumas as well as to comprehend the definitions of victims during or even outside of a genocide. Ancel unequivocally categorized the rape of Romani women as gender- and ethnic-based, as part and parcel of the genocide. More recent genocides in Bosnia and Rwanda have provoked a focus on rape of women as a gender-multiplied effect of genocide, where the intersection of gender and ethnicity compounds victimization.[91] How do we define victims of sexual violence in genocides? Legal systems have sometimes defined sexual violence differently than scholars have, and more recent genocides have pushed courts to more fully examine rape and sexual violence as genocidal acts.[92] For instance, the International Criminal Court (ICC) defines sexual violence as "an act of sexual nature against one or more persons or caused such person or persons to engage in an act of sexual nature by force, or by threat of force or coercion."[93] Yet, are definitions like this sufficient? If applied to the case of the Roma in Transnistria, only Romani women would meet the definition of victims of sexual violence. How then do we classify the beatings, maimings, and killings of men attempting to assist women who were being sexually assaulted? And, how do we then classify those who were forced to witness sexual violence?

There seems too clear a separation of sexual violence against individuals and other acts of violence during genocides. I suggest that further conceptualizations of sexual violence are needed to better understand the complexity of sexual crimes during genocides. I would like to push the categorization of victims, based on the Romani case, much further. As suggested by Elisa von Joeden-Forgey, violence unleashed upon families and communities becomes muted as a central element of genocides.[94] I would offer a more layered approach to understanding sexual violence in extending categories of victims to (1) primary victims, or those were forced into unwanted sexual attentions and acts; (2) secondary victims, or those who were physically assaulted during the process of sexual violence but who were not recipients of unwanted sexual attentions and acts; and (3) tertiary victims, or those who were forced to witness sexual violence, but who were not recipients of unwanted sexual attentions and acts. The three classifications address levels of physical and psychological harm inflicted upon a community present during sexual violence during genocide. The layering thus also approaches how Romani women recount their lived experiences of sexual violence as part of familial and communal assaults during their persecution by the Antonescu regime, while also accounting for destruction of individuals as part of the destruction of designated groups in genocides.

Conclusion

Some Holocaust scholars have called for a deeper investigation into women's experiences.[95] Others approach the separation of women's experiences from men's with caution for the potential moral stickiness that could derive from these types of analyses.[96] The case studies of the Romani women's narratives presented here illustrate that a gendered analysis of the Holocaust can be essential in revealing not only what individual women experienced but also what their families experienced. By examining sexual violence, these two Romani women told of their own pain, but also of family trauma, which highlights an essential element of genocide in perpetrators' attempts to destroy a group. Romani women were dually targeted because of their gender and their ethnicity. Their responses to genocide indicate that Romani women, like Romani men, participated in resistance against the Antonescu regime's annihilation policy. Further, an examination of the suffering of Roma at the hands of the Nazi-allied Romanian regime expands our conceptualization of the Holocaust by widening the lens of perpetration and victimhood, bringing a better understanding of the bio-racial policies that sought to kill millions.

Questions

1. How do Roma remember their experiences during the genocide? How do these reflections on the past then enter into the present?

If gender signified differing experiences, how then are gendered experiences passed down?

2. How do we contextualize Romani experiences alongside those of other victims of Nazism? How does the present-day social status of Roma either inhibit or enhance our understanding of their experiences during the Holocaust?

3. In commemorations, such as International Holocaust Remembrance Day and national remembrance days, Roma are often excluded. While numerous entities, from the Council of Europe to the US State Department, state that more attention needs to be paid to Romani rights as human rights, how does this exclusion perpetuate long-standing anti-Romani sentiment?

Notes

1. Radu Ioanid, Michelle Kelso, and Luminița Cioabă, eds., *Tragedia Romilor Deporțati in Transnistria 1942–1945* (Iași: Polirom, 2009), 165–182.

2. Michelle Kelso, introduction to *Tragedia Romilor Deporțati in Transnistria 1942–1945*, ed., Radu Ioanid, Michelle Kelso, and Luminița Cioabă (Iași: Polirom, 2009), 25.

3. Randolph Braham, ed., *The Destruction of Romanian and Ukrainian Jews During the Antonescu Era* (New York: Columbia University Press, 1997); Radu Ioanid, *The Holocaust in Romania: The Destruction of Jews and Gypsies under the Antonescu Regime, 1940–1944* (Chicago: Ivan Dee, 2000).

4. Roland Clark, "New Models, New Questions: Historiographical Approaches to the Romanian Holocaust," *European Review of History-revue europeenne d'histoire* 19, no. 2 (2012): 303–320.

5. Donald Kenrick and Grattan Puxon, *The Destiny of Europe's Gypsies* (New York: Basic Books, 1973). This was the only text widely available when I began researching in 1994.

6. Michel-Rolph Trouillot, *Silencing the Past: Power and the Production of History* (Boston: Beacon Press, 1995).

7. Zoltan Barany, *The East European Gypsies: Regime Change, Marginality, and Ethnopolitics* (Cambridge: Cambridge University Press, 2002); Janos Ladanyi and Ivan Szelenyi, *Patterns of Exclusion: Constructing Gypsy Ethnicity and the Making of an Underclass in Transitional Societies of Europe* (New York: Columbia University Press, 2006).

8. Michael Stewart, "The 'Gypsy Problem': An Invisible Genocide," in *Forgotten Genocides: Oblivion, Denial, and Memory*, ed. R. Lemarchand (Philadelphia: University of Pennsylvania Press, 2011), 137–156.

9. Until 2003, Romania had an official policy of denying that its wartime regime had a role in the Holocaust. After Nazi Germany, its wartime ally, the Antonescu regime perpetrated the largest massacres during the Holocaust, a well-concealed and horrible distinction that few know about, even in academia. Since 2004, however, the country's administrations have undergone major attitudinal shifts in recognizing past atrocities, a development that has had a vital impact on memory work in public institutions and especially in the field of education, where Holocaust history is now mandatory.

10. In 1995, when I first applied for a permit from the Romanian State Archives in Bucharest, archivists told me that there were no files about Transnistria, claiming they had all burned. Instead, they brought me folders concerning the emancipation of Roma from slavery a century before. Only after a chance meeting with Dr. Radu Ioanid of the United States Holocaust Memorial Museum, who was also working on collecting documents relating to the Holocaust, did I learn that the police and ministry files not only existed but also detailed the state's policy of destruction toward Roma.

11. In 2009, I was also a Charles H. Revson fellow at the United States Holocaust Memorial Museum in Washington, DC. There I consulted archival and library collections on the Romani Holocaust.

12. See Peter Wogan, "Deep Hanging Out: Reflections on Fieldwork and Multisited Andean Ethnography," *Identities: Global Studies in Culture and Power* 1, vol. 11 (2004): 129–139.

13. Michelle Kelso, "Holocaust-era Compensation and the Case of the Roma," *Studia Hebraica* 8 (2008): 298–334. From 1998 to 2001, I was a volunteer on the Swiss Fund for Needy Victims of the Holocaust/Shoah and the German Humanitarian Fund for Victims of Nazi Persecution. In 2001, I was a consultant on two compensation campaigns—the German Forced Labor Compensation Programme and the Swiss Banks Settlement.

14. Annette Wieviorka, *The Era of the Witness* (Ithaca: Cornell University Press, 2006), 143.

15. See *Hidden Sorrows: The Persecution of Romanian Gypsies During WWII*, directed by Michelle Kelso (Bucharest: In the Shadow Productions, 2005), DVD.

16. Sybil Milton, "Hidden Lives: Sinti and Roma Women" in *Experience and Expression: Women, the Nazis, and the Holocaust*, ed. Elizabeth R. Baer and Myrna Goldenberg (Detroit: Wayne State University Press, 2003), 69.

17. Dalia Ofer and Lenore J. Weitzman, eds., *Women in the Holocaust* (New Haven: Yale University Press, 1998).

18. Monica Flaschka, "'Only Pretty Women Were Raped': The Effect of Sexual Violence on Gender Identities in the Concentration Camps" in *Sexual Violence Against Jewish Women During the Holocaust*, ed. Sonja M. Hedgepeth and Rochelle G. Saidel (Lebanon: Brandeis University Press, 2010), 77–93; Helene Sinnreich, "The Rape of Jewish Women During the Holocaust" in *Sexual Violence Against Jewish Women During the Holocaust*, ed. Sonja M. Hedgepeth and Rochelle G. Saidel (Lebanon: Brandeis University Press, 2010), 108–123.

19. Milton, "Hidden Lives."

20. Judith Gerson and Diane Wolfe, introduction to *Sociology Confronts the Holocaust: Memories and Identities in Jewish Diasporas*, ed. Judith Gerson and Diane Wolfe (Durham: Duke University Press, 2007), 29.

21. Henry Friedlander, *The Origins of Nazi Genocide: From Euthanasia to the Final Solution* (Chapel Hill: University of North Carolina Press, 1995); Milton, "Hidden Lives"; Sybil Milton, "Gypsies and the Holocaust," *The History Teacher* 24, no. 4 (1991): 375–387; Sybil Milton, "Nazi Policies Toward Roma and Sinti, 1933–1945," *Journal of the Gypsy Lore Society* 2, no. 1 (1992): 1–18.

22. This extends further than Ofer and Weitzman's book. Although camps are contextualized in the treatment of women during the Holocaust, there is a pervasiveness of generalization to how women suffered under the Holocaust, rather than how women in a particular camp suffered in the Holocaust.

23. Zvi Y. Gitelman, *Bitter Legacy: Confronting the Holocaust in the USSR* (Bloomington: Indiana University Press, 1997); James Mark, *The Unfinished Revolution: Making Sense of the Communist Past in Central-Eastern Europe* (New Haven: Yale University Press, 2010).

24. See Timothy Snyder, *Bloodlands: Europe between Hitler and Stalin* (London: Bodley Head, 2010); and Charles King, *Odessa: Genius and Death in a City of Dreams* (New York: W. W. Norton & Co., 2011).

25. Dan Stone, "'Beyond the 'Auschwitz Syndrome': Holocaust Historiography after the Cold War," *Patterns of Prejudice* 44, no. 5 (2010): 454–468.

26. For more on King Carol II's reign, see Paul D. Quinlan, *The Playboy King: Carol II of Romania* (Westport: Greenword Press, 1995).

27. Elie Wiesel, Tuvia Friling, Radu Ioanid, Mihail E. Ionescu, and L. Benjamin, "Final Report of the International Commission on the Holocaust in Romania" (Iași: Polirom, 2005), 120.

28. International Commission on the Holocaust in Romania, 177.

29. King, *Odessa.*

30. For more on the Romanian occupation of Odessa, see King, *Odessa.*

31. Julius S. Fisher, *Transnistria: The Forgotten Cemetery* (South Brunswick: T. Yoseloff, 1969).

32. Viorel Achim, *The Roma in Romanian History* (Budapest: Central European University Press, 2004); Viorel Achim and Constantin Iordache, eds., *Romania si Transnistria: Problema Holocaustului: Perspective Istorice si Comparative* (Bucharest: Curtea Veche, 2004); Vladimir Solonari, "An Important New Document on the Romanian Policy of Ethnic Cleansing During World War II," *Holocaust and Genocide Studies* 21, no. 2 (2007): 268–297.

33. Stefan C. Ionescu, *Jewish Resistance to Romanianization: 1940–1944* (Basingstoke: Palgrave Macmillan, 2015).

34. For more on the Holocaust in Ukraine, see John Paul Himka, *Ukrainians, Jews and the Holocaust: Divergent Memories* (Saskatoon: Heritage Press, 2009).

35. International Commission on the Holocaust in Romania.

36. Michelle Kelso, "The Deportation of Gypsies from Romania to Transnistria 1942–44," in *The Gypsies During the Second World War: In the Shadow of the Swastika,* ed. Donald Kenrick (Hatfield: University of Hertfordshire Press, 1999), 98.

37. See Ben M. Thorne, "Assimilation, Invisibility, and the Eugenic Turn in the 'Gypsy Question' in Romanian Society, 1938–1942," *Romani Studies* 21, no. 2 (2011): 177–205.

38. They may or may not have identified with the categories imposed upon them first by former slave owners and then by government officials, such as census takers, who sorted them into categories based on residency (i.e., settled or nomadic), mother tongue, and religious affiliations. One example of this is the *căldărari,* or coppersmiths. Non-Roma also indentified them, and they may have identified themselves by the Romanian language identifier given to them, *corturari,* or tent dwellers. But among Roma, they would have identified as *căldărari.*

39. Radu Ioanid, introductive study to *Tragedia Romilor Deportati in Transnistria 1942–1945*, ed. Radu Ioanid, Michelle Kelso, and Luminita Cioabă (Iași: Polirom, 2009).

40. Thorne, "Assimilation, Invisibility, and the Eugenic Turn."

41. Ioanid et al., *Tragedia Romilor*, 277–278.

42. Ibid., 278–279.

43. Thorne, "Assimilation, Invisibility, and the Eugenic Turn."

44. Kelso, "Gypsy Deportations."

45. Kelso, "Gypsy Deportations," 109.

46. Lucian Nastasa and Andrea Varga, eds., *Minoritati Ethnoculturale Marturii Documentare. Tiganii din Romania (1919–1944)* (Cluj-Napoca: Centrul de Resurse Pentru Diversitate Ethnoculturala, 2001), 435.

47. Romanian National Archives: File IGJ, 126/1942, 209.

48. Nastasa and Varga, *Minoritati Ethnoculturale*, 435.

49. Ioanid, introductive study to *Tragedia Romilor*.

50. Ioanid et al., *Tragedia Romilor*, 83–103.

51. Nastasa and Varga, *Minoritati Ethnoculturale*, 488.

52. Ibid., 496.

53. Kelso, "Gypsy Deportations," 116.

54. *Hidden Sorrows*, directed by Michelle Kelso.

55. Ioanid et al., *Tragedia Romilor*, 111–142.

56. *Hidden Sorrows*, directed by Michelle Kelso.

57. Margareta Zizea (retired seamstress), in discussion with author, July 1999.

58. Ioanid et al., *Tragedia Romilor*, 111–142.

59. Kelso, "Gypsy Deportations," 116.

60. Ibid., 83–102.

61. Ibid., 112–113.

62. Romanian National Archives, File 43/1943, 260–262.

63. *Hidden Sorrows*, directed by Michelle Kelso.

64. Radu Ioanid, *Evreii sub regimul Antonescu* (Bucharest: Editura Hasefer, 1997), 316–321.

65. Romanian National Archives, File IGJ, 60/1943, 116.

66. Romanian National Archives, File IGJ, 59/1942, 305.

67. Nastasa and Varga, *Minoritati Ethnoculturale*, 570.

68. Ibid., 572.

69. Kelso, "Gypsy Deportations," 121.

70. Wiesel, Friling, Ioanid, Ionescu, and Benjamin, "Final Report" (Iași: Polirom, 2005).

71. *Hidden Sorrows*, directed by Michelle Kelso.

72. Henry Greenspan, *On Listening to Holocaust Survivors: Recounting and Life History* (Westport: Praeger, 1998), 9.

73. Ioanid et al., *Tragedia Romilor*, 165–182.

74. Lawrence Langer, "Gendered Suffering? Women in Holocaust Testimonies" in *Women in the Holocaust*, ed. Dalia Ofer and Lenore J. Weitzman (New Haven: Yale University Press, 1998), 360.

75. Michelle Kelso, "'And Roma Were Victims, too.' The Romani Genocide and Holocaust Education in Romania," *Intercultural Education* 24, nos. 1/2 (2013): 61–78.

76. Daina S. Eglitis and Vita Zelce, "Unruly Actors: Latvian Women of the Red Army in Post-War Historical Memory," *Nationalities Papers* 41, no. 6 (2013): 987–1007.

77. Stewart, "The 'Gypsy Problem'"; Michelle Kelso and Daina Eglitis, "Holocaust Commemoration in Romania: Roma and the Contested Politics of Memory and Memorialization," *Journal of Genocide Research* 16, no. 4 (2014): 487–511.

78. Janet L. Jacobs, *Memorializing the Holocaust: Gender, Genocide and Collective Memory* (London: I. B. Tauris, 2010), 44–45.

79. Kelso, "Gypsy Deportations."

80. Ofer and Weitzman, *Women in the Holocaust*; Hannah Sara Rigler, "Interview with Hannah Sara Rigler by Joni Sue Blinderman," *Mothers, Sisters, Resisters; Oral Histories of Women Who Survived the Holocaust*, ed. Brana Gurewitsch (Tuscaloosa: The University of Alabama Press, 1998).

81. Lenore J. Weitzman, "Living on the Aryan Side in Poland: Gender, Passing and the Nature of Resistance," in *Women in the Holocaust*, ed. Dalia Ofer and Lenore J. Weitzman (New Haven: Yale University Press, 1998), 187–222.

82. Joan Ringelheim, "The Split Between Gender and the Holocaust," in *Women in the Holocaust*, ed. Dalia Ofer and Lenore J. Weitzman (New Haven: Yale University Press, 1998), 344.

83. Debra Renee Kaufman, "Renaming Violence," *American Behavioral Scientist* 45, no. 4 (2001): 654–667.

84. Helen Fein, "Genocide and Gender: The Uses of Women and Group Destiny," *Journal of Genocide Research* 1, no. 1 (1999): 43–63.

85. Sonja M. Hedgepeth and Rochelle G. Saidel, eds., *Sexual Violence Against Jewish Women During the Holocaust* (Lebanon: Brandeis University Press, 2010).

86. For volumes with testimony from Roma mentioning rape, see Ioanid et al., 2009, *Tragedia Romilor Deportați*; Luminița Mihai Cioabă, ed. *Lacrimi Rome* (Bucharest: Ro Media, 2006).

87. Karen G. Weiss, "Too Ashamed to Report: Deconstructing the Shame of Sexual Victimization," *Feminist Criminology* 5, no. 286 (2010): 286–310.

88. Marioara Trancă (Roma mediator), in discussion with author, May 2014.

89. Jean Ancel, "Tragedia Romilor și Tragedia evreilor din România: Asemănări și deosebiri" in *Lacrimi Rome*, ed. Luminița Mihai Cioabă (Bucharest: Ro Media, 2006), 17.

90. Ibid.

91. Weiss, "Too Ashamed to Report"; Robin Schott, "War Rape, Natality and Genocide," *Journal of Genocide Research* 13, nos. 1/2 (2011): 5–21.

92. Schott, "War Rape, Natality and Genocide," 5–21.

93. "Definitions of Crimes of Sexual Violence in the ICC," International Criminal Court, accessed September 10, 2014, www.iccwomen.org/resources/crimesdefinition.htm.

94. Elisa von Joeden-Forgey, "The Devil in the Details: 'Life Force Atrocities' and the Assault on the Family in Times of Conflict," *Genocide Studies and Prevention* 5, no. 1 (2010): 1–19.

95. Ofer and Weitzman, *Women in the Holocaust*; Hedgepeth and Saidel, *Sexual Violence Against Jewish Women*; Ringelheim, "The Split Between Gender."

96. Langer, "Gendered Suffering?"

CHAPTER 3

The Gender Dimension of the Holocaust in France

Carol Mann

Introduction

The planned assassination of six million Jews in Europe, organized and carried out by Nazi Germany and its allies, constitutes a landmark in the study of genocides. In this chapter, much to my regret, I use the word *Holocaust*—a fallacious and even morally reprehensible term—as it refers to burnt offerings, that is, animals burned as a sacrifice to gods. There can be nothing divine about mass murder. The particularity of women's experiences in the Holocaust was not studied until the mid-1980s when a new gendered perspective emerged, spearheaded by Joan Ringelheim. Major works have followed, especially in the United States and Israel, with studies authored by Dalia Ofer and Lenore J. Weitzman, Marion Kaplan, and Sonja M. Hedgepeth and Rochelle G. Saidel.[1] Among these, Marion Kaplan alone has researched the daily life of women in this period in her fascinating work on Germany. Kaplan's scholarship has provided me with a precedent for my own research on women in France, where no gendered studies have as yet been published. Even Renée Poznanski's groundbreaking opus does not mention the specificity of the female predicament.[2]

The Holocaust presents a practically unique aspect concerning the treatment of gender. In other genocides, such as that of the Armenians (1915) or the Bosnians (1992–1995), women were generally raped for different reasons, including forcible impregnation. As sexual slaves, women lost their identity as well as their humanity, to become passive vessels of new generations of Turks and Serbs. Through the notion of *Rassenschande* (racial defilement), the Nazis took up the Hispanic ideology of *limpieza de sangre* (blood purity) used in the Spanish Inquisition, which necessarily excluded any possibility of survival for women. As Hedgepeth and Saidel have shown, rapes did occur, especially in concentration camps, but not as a collective war tactic.[3]

Thus at the heart of the mass annihilation of the Jews, a specific fate awaited women—especially mothers. In a 1943 speech to a select group of officers in Poznań, Poland, SS Reichsführer and general overseer of the concentration camps Heinrich Himmler made this clear:

> The question has been asked: What should we do about the women and children. I thought about it and found an obvious answer. I felt that I did not have the right to exterminate the men (if you like kill them and have them killed) and allow children to grow up who would seek revenge against our own children and their descendants. We had to take the grave decision to eliminate these people from the face of the earth.[4]

Women and girls, as potential or actual mothers of avengers, were to be exterminated as such, just as so-called Aryan women and girls were to be coerced into becoming breeders of a superhuman Germanic race. The symmetry was remarkable.

This particular genocidal scheme serves as the mainstay in attempting to understand both the Nazi tactics deployed and the struggles and coping mechanisms of Jewish women in France under threat. The latter have to be viewed in the context of a traditional distribution of gender roles in the conservative pre-war society. France was somewhat unique because issues of class and origin were more important than any form of Jewish solidarity when examining the differences between the privileged Israélites and their migrant contemporaries from Eastern Europe. Gender behaviour is completely subservient to these essential notions of identity.

Culturally Defined Roles of Jewish Women in France

Those whose lives I document are primarily mothers. These women married early, and their capacity for agency was enacted within the social parameters of the time.[5] The care, protection, and safeguarding of families—especially children—and financial autonomy were their priorities, to which some added political and militant resistance, for which they paid with their lives. Women's daily lives are largely untold. Apart from self-published memoirs, there are few documents that express ordinary Jewish women's points of view either before the war or during. What emerges has to be read between the lines of the letters I examined in the unique archives of the Centre de Documentation Juive Contemporaine (CDJC) in Paris, and in the silences that punctuate interviews I have recorded. I consider the strategies of survival put in place by women, often intuitively, to save and maintain their families despite impossible odds, to be true acts of resistance against genocide. Their fears and interpretation of a situation were translated into immediate action that included sending food to husbands in the internment camps, hiding children, or even attempting to salvage some element of Jewish tradition. This has been insufficiently documented—not just in this case but in every war, for the simple reason that their actions were taken for granted and seemed insufficiently heroic. The homefront, a repository of picturesque folklore, has always been relegated to the subaltern nether regions, yet this is where survival was made possible.

It can be said that seeking out the specificity of women's experience in war and genocide is akin to pearl-diving in the sense that Hannah Arendt uses this metaphor in her essay on Walter Benjamin "to select (his) precious fragments from a pile of debris."[6] In this chapter I attempt to salvage some of those hidden treasures.[7]

Jewish Men and Women in Pre-War France

In 1939 the Jewish population of France—estimated at about 350,000, of whom 200,000 lived in the Paris area—consisted of three distinct groups, with two subgroups. The first group (one-third of the total) considered themselves indigenous. These Jews had been in France for more than a hundred years, if not several centuries. They included the ancient communities from southeast France, many of whom had fled Spain during the Inquisition, and with those hailing from the east, mainly Alsace and Lorraine, where Jews had settled from the Middle Ages onward.[8] The French Revolution granted full citizen rights to Jews, and both communities managed to integrate successfully into French society. They moved up the social ladder to enter the world of politics and finance, as well as the arts, where women such as Sarah Bernhardt became some of the great divas of the 19th century. These frequently assimilated and often atheist Jews referred to themselves as Israélites.[9] That is, they identifed as French citizens of increasingly diluted Jewish faith who believed they were protected by the state, and considered themselves above any kind of threat despite the recurring antisemitism in France—especially in the aftermath of the infamous Dreyfus Affair.[10] In terms of self-representation, they identified with French interests and modelled themselves on the ruling bourgeoisie, where women took on obstensibly passive roles centred on the home but nevertheless studied far more than their Gentile counterparts. Like their contemporaries in Vienna, they despised the hordes of impoverished, ill-educated Jews flocking from Eastern Europe, and blamed what they considered this group's uncouth visibility for the renewal of antisemitism in the 1930s.

During World War I, France lost nearly one and a half million of its young workforce on the battlefields. After the armistice the country actively encouraged immigration, and by 1930 France had become the world's leading destination for foreign migrants, who by then numbered more than two million, of which Jews represented 10 percent.[11] Those who came prior to 1914 were motivated to do so by pogroms, cholera outbreaks, and systemic antisemitism in lands beyond France. Afterward, poverty and lack of opportunity in their home states encouraged those who arrived in the 1920s to begin a new life in France. These included mostly Yiddish-speaking Poles, Russians, and Romanians who had an awareness of potential calamity; however, they still placed their trust in France, the country that had drafted the Declaration of the Rights of Man.

Similarly, francophile, Ladino-speaking Sephardi Jews who hailed from the Ottoman Empire made up nearly 10 percent of the Parisian Jewish population, as did those who came from North Africa.[12]

As in London's East End or New York's Lower East Side, the majority of these migrants worked in the "rag trade," at home or in family enterprises, or otherwise serviced their own communities. Women were a vital part of this workforce, as they had always been among the poor. Further, women's work was honourable, given the tradition of women acting as economic supporters in families where males were Talmud scholars.[13] Women toiled, as well as looking after homes and offspring with the occasional assistance of an aged mother or mother-in-law, who generally never learned to speak French. Despite real poverty, all encouraged their children, girls as well as boys, to study in secular schools and integrate into a much-idealized society as equal citizens. Many of these Jews acquired French nationality and the Yiddish proverb *as happy as God in France* defined the day.

If Britain was often considered a stepping stone for further migration to the United States, coming to France, for Eastern European Jews, was frequently an ambition in itself. This was especially relevant among the younger, more politically aware socialist working-class migrants for whom religion had lost its importance, though they might observe kosher dietary laws at home. They congregated in tenements in specific areas on the right bank of Paris, traditional *shtetls*, here reinvented around the rue des Rosiers, and known as the *Pletzl*. Principally populated by the 19th- and 20th-century first arrivals, the *arrondissements* (namely Belleville) became home to the more secular younger migrants, and the La Roquette area, near the Bastille, was inhabited by Ottoman Jews.[14]

Two subsections of this migration were made up of artists on one side and students on the other. The influx of artists, which included Chagall, Modigliani, Lipchitz, Orloff, and others, flocked to France before World War I because they were attracted to Paris as the capital of avant-garde art. They kept within the bounds of the artistic community and were never sponsored by the rich Israélites who strove to ingratiate themselves with the establishment by collecting conservative art.[15] The second group of immigrants was composed of francophile middle-class students from Eastern and Central Europe who came to study in France, as the *numerus clausus* in their own countries blocked their entrance to university.[16] They lived near the universities, be it in the provinces or in the Latin Quarter of the capital. The numerous female students and scholars led extremely independent lives, like their artistic contemporaries, with little contact with their working-class compatriots in the rag trade. Their political consciousness and contacts would help some of them to later escape and subsequently join the resistance.

The third broad category of immigrants consisted of Jews who had fled Nazi Germany and Austria after 1933—usually intellectuals who tried, albeit unsuccessfully, to alert public opinion about Hitler's ambitions. In 1939 they represented about 19 percent of the total community. Members of this group were soon to become the first victims of Vichy France, simultaneously as aliens, Jews, and opponents of the Nazi regime.

The fragmentation of the Jewish community in Paris along social and class lines was extreme. This created a hierarchy that placed the Israélites at the top and Polish migrants at the bottom, with the animosity between them at times coming close to the rantings of the antisemitic press. Even Jewish writer Irène Nemirovsky (1903–1942), herself of Russian origin, portrays the eponymous character in her 1929 novel, *David Golder*, as a Ukrainian rag merchant turned evil Parisian businessman, thereby contributing to the stereotype antisemites thrived on.[17] Despite her conversion to Catholicism and her articles, which appeared in the most virulently racist publications (*Candide* and *Gringoire*), Nemirovsky could not escape deportatation to Auschwitz. The lack of solidarity and contact among the different strata of the Jewish community contributed to their collective vulnerability in the face of looming annihilation.

Anticipatory Reactions of Women to the Genocide: From Self-Delusion to Active Awareness

The extent to which the Jews of France were conscious of the threat posed to them by Nazi Germany in the 1930s is hard to fathom. In the aftermath, it was easy for many to say that they had felt threatened, but obviously no mass Jewish exodus took place. Certainly those who could both evaluate the danger and afford to leave the country did so, but only when the Nazi army marched on Paris. The vast majority, it has to be said, stayed put until it was too late to do anything, and in the best of cases, went into hiding.

Jews in France were exceptionally patriotic. Their trust in the government was immense and, in retrospect, colossally naive. After all, France had voted for a Jewish prime minister, Léon Blum, who led the Popular Front in 1936–1937, a short-lived progressive-socialist coalition that included women in the government at a time when they did not even have the vote. Among them was Cécile Brunschvicg (1877–1946), a Jewish feminist who came from an old family from Alsace, as did Léon Blum.[18] Like all Israélites, she considered herself primarily French, never taking a stand on issues concerning Jews. Brunschvicg's virulence against the Nazis, as expressed in her articles in *La Française*, principally centred on their treatment of German feminists. Yet after the Kristallnacht pogrom of 1938, she sought to aid Jewish-German refugees in France, but did not openly criticize antisemitism. A shift of focus seems to have occurred, from apparent indifference—stemming from the notion that she and her class were not concerned by Hitler—to one in which Brunschvicg may well have moved to an unspoken fear of drawing attention to herself as a Jew.

The fact is that, for various reasons, most Jews refused to consider themselves threatened by Nazi Germany and underestimated the political consequences of home-grown antisemitism, taking it for granted as one of the unfortunate options of everyday life, just as they had in Eastern Europe. The animosity between the bourgeois Israélites and the migrant working-class (frequently communist) Jews impeded any collective reaction and active strategy against impending tragedy. Only those who lived in the east of the country, in Alsace and Lorraine, close to the German frontier, had a more realistic idea of what could befall them.

Whatever the trust in the Popular Front, Zionism nevertheless remained a political option for Eastern European Jewish migrants, who perceived the move to Palestine as a possible (but seldom enacted) option against antisemitism. Native French Israélites considered this a form of treason against France as well as a form of religious nationalism, which increased their animosity against the Zionists.[19] They held a similar opinion concerning the newly founded League Against Anti-Semitism (LICA), launched by Bernard Lecache, a communist Jew of Russian origin.[20] These well-read and well-heeled, politically aware

Israélites who interacted with French society at large were often the most self-delusional. Of the different Jewish communities in France, it was certainly this one—the most privileged—that was the least prepared and the most deeply hurt by the Vichy government's participation in the Nazi genocide.[21]

The inward-looking life of their Polish contemporaries in the tenements on the other side of town offers an extreme contrast, even though the result, in terms of mass murder, was to be the same. Migrant Jews from Poland lived and worked in the selfsame areas, concentrated in three arrondissements. This restricted their world view, unless they belonged to a political group such as the Communist party or a trade union—truly male-dominated institutions. Most of them generally went from work to home via cafés, *landsmanshaftn* (benefit societies linked to their area of origin), and synagogues, many of which remained open throughout the war. Male socialization was mainly contained within their own group, in which most spoke mainly Yiddish, Polish, and at best heavily accented French. In contrast, when no one spoke French at home, wives and teen-age daughters were the true interface with society at large, because they had to deal with landlords, schools, doctors, and bureaucracy generally, as well as the neighbourhood. Their privileged sisters had no such menial experience, leaving such tasks to men or intermediaries. As a result, the women of the Israélites were less versed than their Polish counterparts in practical aspects of survival, especially in difficult conditions, and they also experienced increased animosity based on class and envy.

Migrant Polish mothers were often very ambitious for their children. The aim of the poor was to push their offspring out of the home environment, to go beyond the parental experience. The Israélites were equally ambitious, but with the goal of maintaining and developing their privileges for the next generation in what they thought was a stable social structure. The rarefied politicized feminist circle around Cécile Brunschvicg saw social evolution as occurring within their own privileged and educated circles centred in Paris.

In my own research, I have met women who remember their mothers stopping their husbands from declaring themselves to the police. These were often uneducated migrant women who had already learned to survive the antisemitism of Eastern Europe, and somehow transferred their street sense to urban Paris. Unlike the men, they nurtured no idealistic faith in French politics. The links between the working-class Jewish women with their immediate Gentile neighbours were to prove invaluable when it came to saving children from the roundups.

Yet, the overall capacity for direct agency was extremely limited for women, whatever their background. In these deeply traditional and patriarchal families, men represented authority. In the case of the working and lower-middle classes, the men had been the ones to initiate immigration and then progressively bring over their families. Even though women laboured for inferior wages, husbands and fathers were the official breadwinners, recognized by the state as the "chief of the household."[22] Among the privileged Israélites, men were often civil servants, lawyers, doctors, professors, and scholars who enjoyed (or so they thought) the confidence of the government and its institutions. Wives and especially daughters might study or even work, but they did not hold the power to make decisions governing the destiny of their families. Whether these wives and daughters were given a chance to express fears and apprehension is hard to fathom, as they left no memoirs, and no research was undertaken on this specific theme while that generation was still alive. In between not knowing and choosing to ignore, every shade of awareness or blindness can be charted.

When France declared war on Germany on September 3, 1939, like other French citizens, young Jewish men went to war, and although figures vary, around 12,000 non-national Jews joined on a voluntary basis, which lulled them into a false sense of security by creating a fictitious feeling of belonging.[23] When Germany defeated France and the German army goose-stepped down the Champs Élysées on June 14, 1940, the patriotism that had been displayed by young Jewish men fighting for France instantly became devalued and made irrelevant, in addition to becoming a supplementary cause of oppression. It could be said that the luckier ones became prisoners of war—and, therefore, never persecuted for being Jewish. Yet many kept their faith in France.

Even when the German occupation tightened its grip, most persisted in thinking that the French government would protect them to the very end. The renowned synagogue in the rue Pavée in the centre of the main Jewish quarter of Paris had a notice posted stating that talking about politics on the premises was forbidden.[24] The first decree of the new pro-Nazi regime on September 27, 1940, required Jews to register, something unheard of for any religious community in France.[25] The majority—whether French-born or foreign—diligently marched off to the police, and only a handful of Jews saw the danger in officially being listed. Rabbis advised congregations to obey; the famous philosopher Henri Bergson, despite being practically an invalid, made a point of going to the local commissariat to register. The following month, all Jews were ordered to have *Juif* or *Juive* (Jew/Jewess) stamped in bold red capital letters on their identity cards. Naturally, when the deportations started a few months later, the French militia had all the information they needed. Likewise, most Jews showed a comparable compliance when, in August 1941, they were ordered to bring in their radios to the police stations. The Israélites especially believed that following the rules implied state protection. On May 29, 1942, the Vichy government commanded all Jews above the age of six to wear a yellow star firmly sewn on their coats. It has been estimated that about 15 to 18 percent of French Jews refused to wear it.[26]

Can one imagine a gendered perspective in such circumstances? Any initiative remained above all personal, even though women collectively thought of imaginative ways of rendering the star invisible. For example, they would sew it behind a lapel or just above a breast pocket in which it could be inserted when necessary.

By mid-1942, similar laws governed all Jewish populations in every country under Nazi rule. If an increasing segment of the population surmised that this was part of a greater, more sinister plan, by then it was practically impossible to leave. Only when the arrests began did Jews try to use their contacts to get forged baptismal certificates and papers that would, they hoped, ensure them the deliverance of "a certificate of not belonging to the Jewish race," which were given out piecemeal by the Bureau of Jewish Affairs.[27] But their efforts usually proved fruitless—the implacable racial laws rendered conversions useless.

Who knew what? Declassified intelligence material shows that Western governments were aware of what was happening in the concentration camps in Poland as early as March 1942.[28] Reports from the underground eyewitness accounts from Jews who escaped the ghettos, and resistance fighters such as Jan Karski, all gave precise accounts of the genocide in progress. Articles appeared in the daily press in Great Britain and the United States. Even 13-year-old Anne Frank, in her famous diary, wrote on October 9, 1942, "What must it be like in those faraway and uncivilized places where the Germans are sending [Jews]. We assume that most of them are being murdered. The English radio says they're being gassed. Maybe that's the quickest way to die."[29]

Why the West did not react is beyond the scope of this chapter. Many Jews in France must have had the same information but perhaps considered it too difficult to reconcile with their daily reality. A genocide of this scale was, in every sense of the word, inconceivable. Jews' immediate responses to given situations may have helped to stifle anxiety, but in actuality probably impeded a more holistic perspective that could have pushed people to flee early on, at the cost of abandoning every form of material security and reassurance.

In the transit camps—especially Drancy—doubts, fears, and hope remained for many until the last moment. Perhaps because the Nazis made a point of not killing their victims openly before they arrived in Auschwitz, such ambiguous feelings could still be entertained, and rendered potential victims all the more vulnerable. For the Armenians in 1915 or the Rwandan Tutsis in 1994, murder took place before their very eyes, so doubt was not an option. Retrospectively, the history of the Jews in wartime France can be said to be that of the most extreme manifestation of denial and delusion.

France under Nazi Occupation

In June 1940, the Germans defeated the French army at record speed, which took the whole country by surprise. Prime Minister Philippe Pétain (1856–1951), an 84-year-old World War I hero, immediately ordered an armistice that meant total subservience to the occupying forces and compliance with Nazi legislation. As the German armies swept through Europe, the greater part of civilian populations fell under occupation and endured the consequences produced by the conditions of the war itself, and not because of Nazi ideology. In itself, this was not new, as wars have always been a part of European history. At the start of World War II, an entire generation of French men and women had already experienced at least five wars in their own lifetime (Crimea, 1853–1856; the Franco-Prussian War, 1870–1871; the Paris Commune, 1871; World War I 1914–1918; and various colonial wars in North Africa). From 1870 to 1871, Prussian forces besieged and starved Paris, and Parisians famously devoured rats and cats.

From May 1940 on, the civilian population of France, as in all German-occupied lands, suffered from the classic consequences of war; that is to say, on purely practical grounds. They experienced having their normal, familiar environment violated by the presence of a foreign and indeed alien military presence coupled with the ensuing all-engulfing restrictions that consistently destroyed the fabric of everyday life. France was divided in two parts until November 1942.[30] The north was officially occupied and the south was theoretically non-occupied, being controlled by Italian troops in the south, who were considered far more easygoing than the Germans. Families were divided, travel was exceedingly difficult, and work of any kind demanded special permits. Pétain held absolute power, beyond anything that had ever been experienced in France, and he implemented extreme reactionary policies influenced by fascist thinkers and politicians who at last found themselves in favour. Civil liberties and freedom of speech were revoked, refugees and opponents imprisoned, and antisemitism institutionalized. Yet the majority of the French population found ways and means to compromise and survive. Their pain was primarily material rather than moral.

Because the Germans plundered vast quantities of industrial, mineral, and agricultural production in France, from leatherwear to coal, blankets, furniture, shoes, and even frying pans, the shortages were considerable.[31] As in other parts of Europe, rationing had to be instituted and food tickets distributed, a system that became ineffective after 1943.[32] Survival became impossible without recourse to the black market. Young non-Jewish men, and to a lesser extent women, were sent off to work in German factories to replace soldiers who were fighting on the front. Others continued their lives under the new far-right regime, with varying degrees of submission and compliance to the new ruling class, which actively supported the Nazi overseers and diligently implemented their policies.[33] This new collaborationist elite often attained considerable wealth and recognition in the process. From this point of view, World War II was a classist war. The much-lauded French resistance, it has to be said, concerned only a tiny fraction of the population. The Jews of France experienced the same reality as the resistance fighters, but this was made immeasurably worse by the fact that genocide lay at the centre of this war and they, along with the Roma, were the designated victims.

Difference in Treatment of Women and Men

During the Holocaust two patterns emerged, often as sequences in a single individual's life. One pattern, something that could be termed crisis management, emerged in the occupied countries once the anti-Jewish laws based on the decrees of Nuremberg were promulgated. On top of the restrictions faced by the rest of the population, this meant instant loss of employment and therefore resources. In particular, men experienced this more acutely because they were the main breadwinners in these traditional families, whether they were Gentile or Jewish. By 1941, at least 50 percent of the Jewish population had lost their means of survival.[34] Women who were engaged in professions such as education and medicine found themselves immediately laid off without any compensation. Frustration, constant humiliation, and psychological damage ensued, as well as the severance of every vital link to everyday society. When the Nazi plan became clear, a feeling of terror engulfed Jewish communities, and women were, more often than not, those who truly coped with these consequences, as we shall see.

Another pattern was that of the Polish ghettos where the Nazis deported a considerable portion of the Jewish population from various parts of Europe, as well as most of the three and a half million Polish Jews. In France, the nearest equivalent—but by no means anywhere as tragic— were the internment camps, such as Pithiviers, Compiègne, and especially Drancy, which were the last dwelling places of many before their deportation to Auschwitz. The Nazis established a number of camps in non-occupied France, primarily in the southwest, where Jews who were arrested were temporarily imprisoned on their way to death (with a pos-sible stop at Drancy).[35] My research into the French archives reveals signif-icant social and gendered differences of behaviour and survival strategies within these camps. What awaited the victim in Poland or Germany was the logical culmination of this carefully crafted Nazi genocide, aided on French soil by the zeal of the newly empowered racist demagogues under the Vichy government.[36] Other lifestyle possibilities existed in occupied France as elsewhere, but they were marginal and included female resis-tants or those who chose not to declare themselves as Jews and survive under the constant threat of denunciation.

France was divided in two halves, but the same antisemitic legislation prevailed everywhere. The main difference, which was considerable, was that Jews were relatively safe from deportation in the south, at least until November 1942. As in all countries that came under Nazi rule, a local version of the 1935 Nuremberg Laws was implemented on French soil. The lethal combination of German racism and homegrown French anti-semitism produced innovations that went even beyond Nazi intentions.[37] This began with the overturning of naturalization, whereby anyone who had been granted French citizenship after 1927 was, in 1940, considered a stateless alien.[38] This affected approximately half of the immigrant popu-lation, especially the refugees who had earlier fled Nazi Germany.

The first antisemitic law implemented, the decree of October 3, 1940, expelled Jews from civil service—starting with education, which employed a number of young women.[39] This was also the case for medicine, law, and research. This is how Déborah Lifschitz (1907–1942), a renowned anthro-pologist and African specialist, found herself removed from her post at the Musée de l'Homme and deported to Auschwitz, where she was mur-dered.[40] Her case was typical of many young researchers who had come from Russia and Poland in the late 1920s and early 1930s to study in Paris. Lifschitz had been granted French nationality and pursued a brilliant career until she found herself bereft of any national, social, or professional status because of the Vichy ordinances. Similarly, France Bloch-Sérazin (1913–1943), from a typical French Alsatian assimilated family, lost her job as a chemist in a university research laboratory and resorted to giving private lessons to survive until she became an active resistant, and was subsequently arrested and executed in Hamburg.[41] Paulette Feldman's (1914–2006) husband ran a major cosmetics company. When he went into hiding, she took over and kept the business going throughout the war by selling products to hairdressers and beauticians who she had known previously and who catered to the new class of war profiteers.[42] She came from a previously affluent Russian-Jewish family ruined by the Kichinev pogrom (1903), and had arrived in France at the age of four. Her impeccable French as well as her social and business acumen afforded her a measure of ease and confidence. Cécile Brunschvicg, who had been Undersecretary of State in the Blum government, fled to southern unoccupied France with her husband.[43] She taught under an assumed name (and forged papers) in a school in Valence while her daughter joined the Gaullist resistance in London. None of these women wore the ignominious yellow star.[44]

Through successive decrees, Jews employed in journalism, cinema, theatre, radio, performing arts, and finance found themselves out of work, as did company directors and small business owners. About 50,000 businesses became "Aryanized," that is, forcibly taken over by non-Jewish managers appointed by the authorities, who often managed to bankrupt Jewish owners.[45] In many cases the less-profitable businesses were liquidated and the staff, which was frequently family, were left without any form of compensation. Universities expelled Jewish professors and the number of Jewish students was severely limited. The Nuremberg Laws implemented a quota system that applied to medical professions, including doctors, pharmacists, and midwives. When a number of highly educated career women lost their comparatively well-paid posts, they attempted to find means of survival linked to their education and, more often than not, what domestic skills they had in managing a household. Low-level clerical work, stock-taking, accounting, translation, or primary school teaching allowed entire families to survive. Most of their migrant female contemporaries had been employed in modest workshops, mainly in the garment industry, and frequently worked in family businesses. Because their jobs were frequently unregulated, many managed to find work and ended up supporting their families. Seamstresses found ways of bartering their skills, such as sewing clothes in lieu of rent, in rural parts of the non-occupied zones where many families went into hiding. Because of their greater contacts with the outside world, women often spoke better French than their husbands, and in the case of couples in which men could manufacture articles such as galoshes or slippers, wives went out to sell them. Indeed, alternative commerce was also a resource for the quick-witted and often for teenage girls, who found themselves contributing to family finances when their fathers were deported. In the Warsaw Ghetto, Jewish women showed themselves to be equally inventive in far more dramatic circumstances, as Cecilia Slepak's study, undertaken in 1941 for Emanuel Ringelblum's archives, has demonstrated.[46] Nevertheless, the problems that women had to face were practically insurmountable.

Jews were forbidden to go to theatres, cinemas, museums, parks, swimming pools, certain department stores, phone booths, the subway (except for the last coach), and markets. This meant that segregation worked on multiple levels, first by branding bodies with bright yellow stars, and then by creating areas of spatial exclusion. Once work disappeared, men were confined to the home, and frequently found hiding places in order to avoid arrest. Women, who until July 1942 were safe from deportations, took over entirely, organizing every aspect of survival for children and the elderly.[47] Hygiene became an issue. Tenements were equipped at best with a cold-water tap, so inhabitants would go to public baths to wash, but these became forbidden to Jews. "Aryan" doctors could no longer treat their Jewish patients, and Jewish doctors were impeded from working, which, when looked at with hindsight, is consistent with genocide. Shopping for food in markets, where non-rationed goods, such as some root vegetables hitherto reserved to cattle, could be obtained was permitted for Jews after 4 p.m., by which time there was little or nothing left.[48] Keeping kosher for many observant families, especially in the East European communities, was difficult, since traditional slaughtering was outlawed. Vegetarianism became a valid alternative for some. In non-occupied France where, until November 1942, Gestapo surveillance was not yet as efficient as it would become, kosher butchers still operated in Limoges and a few other places, killing chickens (if not cattle) in the traditional way.[49] *Matsos* continued to be manufactured throughout the war and traditional foods such as *kneidlach* and *kreplech* were improvised with whatever was at hand. Preserving such traditions represents a form of unacknowledged resistance, typical of Jewish women at the time. Likewise, many of those who went into hiding continued to light a tiny candle on Friday night. Newborn male babies were still ritually circumcised even though the Gestapo and the French militia would order men to lower their trousers to see if they were Jewish. In my own family, my grandmother and her sister set up a secret kosher canteen in the city of Clermont-Ferrand for refugees from Alsace and Lorraine, where they had been living until the forced exodus of 1940.[50] In retrospect, such behaviour sounds bewildering in the face of danger. But the fact was that for these pious working-class Polish women, the reality of the genocide had not impressed itself on their consciousness, even though in early childhood, they had experienced a pogrom where the priority was dignified survival. Another undocumented tragedy concerns wartime pregnancies. These caused heartbreaking dilemmas when women had to evaluate the danger of bringing new life into a perilous world. Resorting to clandestine abortion—which a number of women did—was fraught with danger, as the Vichy government made it punishable by death.[51] Pregnant women in Drancy were sent to the Rothschild hospital—the only one open to Jews—but then after the birth, were ordered back into the camp before being deported with their newborn babies to Auschwitz.

The first mass arrests of men took place on May 14, 1941, and continued afterward at a steady pace. Whereas the initial roundup concerned 4,000 foreign Jews—poor migrants—later the distinguished Israélites were also arrested and sent mainly to Drancy on their way to Auschwitz.[52] The Israélites' first reaction was to claim that this was a mistake and to try to get their wives to find some form of official document to get them out of what they believed was a temporary incarceration. The quest usually proved fruitless, but their wives spent much time seeking help, including pleading with the official Jewish organization, the Union Générale des Israélites de France (UGIF). The next phase involved sending food and clothing parcels to the camps and retrieving laundry parcels, all of which was complicated by continually changing regulations. These urgent necessities helped initiate innovative ways of communicating, since letter-writing was restricted to small weekly postcards that were inevitably censored. Yiddish was forbidden and all correspondence had to be in French.

When not even phonetic French could be managed, prisoners resorted to those who set themselves up as scribes.[33] In the meantime, despite rationing and restrictions, women did their best to send voluminous food parcels—the contents mostly obtained on the black market. This was undertaken at considerable personal cost and deprivation. These sacrifices were sometimes acknowledged by more thoughtful husbands, but frequently ignored by angry and frustrated men whose demands seemed endless. Since Drancy was in the vicinity of Paris, women would attempt to visit with, or at least briefly see, their husbands and sons from a distance behind the barbed wire.

Paying rent on a single diminished income became practically impossible. Women, already overwrought, took on the responsibility of moving goods and hiding valuables such as jewellery and books for some, yards of fabric or simply foodstuffs for others. Additionally, women dispatched children to various relations, and wives moved in with in-laws, all of which was a cause of additional stress. The restrictions of everyday life were the hardest to manage for mothers of young children and teenagers for whom every place of entertainment and leisure was now out of bounds. This meant that social interaction in public meeting places—such as parks and theatres—disappeared, isolating families even more and forcing them to stay within the bounds of their narrow lodgings. If they could, women sent their younger children (under the age of six) to play with their neighbours' children when they took them to the park. Otherwise, the older ones—left unattended—would run along the larger avenues while their mothers looked on from park benches.

The loneliness and terror for many young women was harrowing. A series of letters written over a period of several weeks, from July 16, 1942, to September 9, 1942, by a young Romanian-born Jewish woman to her brothers in the United States is preserved in the CDJC archives. They are exceptional in that they describe events and emotions as they occur in the appalling summer and autumn of 1942 when 42,500 Jews were sent to Auschwitz. Lea Horer describes her life throughout this period. We are given to understand that she and her husband, David, came from Romania to France. When the war started, her brothers fled to the United States. This configuration is typical of migrants of the period. She writes that David was arrested the previous year and sent off to an unknown destination, and the food parcels she sent were returned. The couple had a five-year-old daughter, Suzanne.

> After David's arrest, I wanted to work, earn a living, my child is my only solace, my life. I took on hard jobs, such as carrying heavy parcels, my life is so tough.... I did everything I could so that my child had what she needed: she is well dressed, so pretty with her blonde curls. She is so talented, so intelligent, if she weren't Jewish, how happy and proud I would be, but now what for?[54]

Lea describes the infamous mass arrest, the *Rafle du Vel d'Hiv*, on July 16 and 17, 1942, as she is experiencing it, hidden in her room. Rumours had circulated across town, but no one had imagined women would be arrested, which sent shock waves throughout the community. One-quarter of the Parisian Jewish population—13,152 victims, including 415 children and babies—were rounded up and placed in the airless velodrome in Paris; they were then sent to various transit camps—mainly Drancy—before being rerouted to Auschwitz.

> Today, since four in the morning, they have been arresting men, women and children. They haven't been here yet, I'm hiding behind the locked door, they'll have to break it down. Some French people have brought me food. The child is full of life and wants to sing and jump about. I beat her to make her stop and we both weep. If only I could put an end to our lives, hers and mine![55]

She takes up her pen three days later, on July 19, 1942:

> For the time being, I am still here, they haven't come for me yet. I went out today for the first time. The disaster is indescribable. So many suicides. Children thrown out of windows, mothers gone mad, it's a disaster such as the world has never known. I used to know some people but they've all been arrested or have fled. I am alone and forsaken like a stone. The child is so nervous and anxious having been

locked up for days on end. She asks why she has to suffer, I answer "because you are Jewish," she asks me to explain why she has to be Jewish. What can I tell her? I am going out of my mind....[56]

Lea refers to rumours of new arrests and the fact that they have to flee from one hiding place to the next, sustaining their hope of going to America: "my sweet little girl says she wants to go and live with Uncle Maurice. Over there, she says, they surely let Jews into parks."[57]

The final letter is dated September 14, 1942. Lea gives her brothers a neighbour's address where she hopes to hide Suzanne as she awaits imminent arrest. This was one of the heart-wrenching decisions mothers frequently had to make. The police had already come for her, and she concludes her letter in haste: "Like my child, my dear child, I too want to live. I am still young, I have not yet known the beauty of life, punished as I am for the crime of being Jewish. You (in America) who will surely survive this, you must avenge all these innocent young lives. So dear brothers, I will do my utmost to save myself and my child. But who knows?"[58]

We do not know what befell the unfortunate Lea and her daughter, but it is probable that they were both gassed at Auschwitz. Lea refers to the separation of mothers and children and their deportation as the most terrible experience. Indeed this policy was a French specificity that the Germans originally had not foreseen. At first, the Nazi authorities had intended to arrest only Jews above the age of 16. Yet Vichy Premier Pierre Laval, in July 1942, asked for specific permission to extend this to children in order to achieve the quotas Berlin demanded. Adolf Eichmann approved, and the French took over the organization of what now qualified as a full-fledged genocide, as 6,000 children and infants were expedited from France to Auschwitz, where none survived.[59] The deportation of children was greeted by protests all over the world levelled against the otherwise paternalistic Vichy government, which theoretically posed as the protector of families. Initially even babies were wrenched away from mothers after their arrest in the camps of Pithiviers and Beaune-la-Rolande in August 1942, where French police intervened with unprecedented cruelty. When Berlin sent orders that infants should not be sent to Auschwitz unaccompanied, the French authorities simply chose random adult prisoners in Drancy to fill the convoys.

In a move presented as humanitarian, Laval decreed that henceforth children would always be deported with their parents, so as to preserve family units. The real reason, as Michael Marrus explains, was that orphaned children created a serious administrative problem as well as a political embarrassment.[60] French public opinion, the clergy, and a number of foreign legations tried to intervene, mostly in vain. Laval pretended to agree to let some children go to the United States, on the condition that there would be no public criticism of French policies in the media and elsewhere, but bureaucratic delays kept the children in France, thereby demonstrating the French ideological and logistical involvement in the Nazi project.[61] Genocide does not allow for the smallest measure of clemency.

Reactions of Jewish Women in France to their Experiences during the Genocide

Holocaust survivors I have interviewed in recent years, who were children at the time, frequently recall the resourcefulness of their mothers. Jewish households often became monoparental from summer 1940 on, as fathers—believing themselves the only ones threatened—fled to the unoccupied zone or further. At a time when marriage typically occurred before the age of 20, this meant that these women were still young and energetic, with the insolence and *chutzpah* youth affords. Tales abound about mothers using their charm and forcefulness to negotiate with smugglers and middlemen to bring their families to safety and dodge the omnipresent Gestapo. They were often torn between aiding their hidden spouses and fighting for the survival of their children and elders. For the first time, they handled finances (usually and legally the preserve of husbands) and pawned their jewellery, argued with banks and creditors, battled their way onto crowded trains, and talked their way through arrests. Many found ways and means to leave their children with friendly neighbours. Despite the near-perfect collaboration of the Vichy French government with the Nazi rulers, a considerable number of French Jews—especially children— were saved because of local solidarity.[62]

Women were obsessed with the well-being of their families, and this is evident in the thousands of letters, preserved by the CDJC, that were written by inmates in the transit camps. Men shared their anxiety, but in contrast appeared to be far more worried about their own present state and comfort. Their letters were often filled with long lists of demands, which display infantile regression and barely suppressed anger at not being able to assist their families in times of need.

In a letter dated February 14, 1942, Avram S. writes from Drancy to his wife, "I received the meatballs, tell me the truth did you really make them yourself, in that case you can send me more but put more garlic.... I received the underwear and the jacket, but that's not what I wanted, you should have sent the blue one."[63] In another letter, Avram demands pastries, sugar, salt, jam, and much else. At the time of his correspondence to his wife, weekly meat rations were down to under 200 grams, and sugar rations were 17 grams (a teaspoonful) for an adult male, which meant that his unfortunate wife had to deprive the rest of the family in order to feed him.

Simon S.'s letter to his wife, dated May 7, 1942, is typical of the recurring sexual jealousy:

> For nothing on earth would I like to find out unsavoury things about you on my return. You know that I shall be very strict about these matters. Even though I know you are loyal, I find it hard to escape those annoying thoughts which run through my head each time I reread your letter. So you went to the pond with the children, you who are usually so afraid of being cold, you actually put a swimsuit on and made Jackie and Bobbie go into the water. Honestly, you've changed completely and I bitterly regret how you opposed me when I was by your side.[64]

Most wives did their best to comply with their husbands' wishes, but sometimes that became impossible. In a letter from Madame Heftmann to her husband on July 8, 1942, she writes,

> Now you write to tell me you want a sports jacket, but it's impossible to find one. You also want a cap with a vizor, that's just as impossible so I'll send you a beret, don't worry you won't look like a

tramp; you write that you want shirts with soft collars, are you going to a wedding or something? Please try to hold on to the matsos I sent you because they keep.[65]

Of course, there are numerous letters of men who display decidedly nobler feelings. Young men were often afraid of alarming their mothers, and young Armand, on the eve of being deported to an unknown destination on June 27, 1942, writes from the camp of Beaune-la-Rolande, "Please don't say anything to Mama, you know how sensitive she is, console her immediately. We have to go on suffering because we are Jews, but this can't last, soon we will be freed, I implore you once again to keep calm, don't panic and don't say a word to Mama, you know how she will react."[66]

Women, once incarcerated, seemed to make far fewer demands—mainly soap, shampoo, a comb for lice, and sanitary towels. The younger ones might ask for cosmetics, the older ones for knitting and warm clothes; but more often than not, their letters express anxiety about those they left behind—especially if their husband was a POW or had already been deported. Chaya W.'s letter to her sister sent on July 24, 1942 is typical:

> I left a lot of food with Madame Arves, take the lot for winter. In the toilet under the window, I've hidden flour, and Madame Arves has another 5 kg which you must also take. She has a box full of fabric from which you can make a coat for little René, I am leaving my little darling in good hands, you'll look after him like your own, won't you.... In the kitchen you'll find some clarified butter in the oil box, a little bit of wine, go to the grocer, he owes me oil and eggs, if you can't go, phone Lulu.[67]

A few days later Chaya sent a note saying that they were leaving for Poland: "[We shall travel] four or five days in sealed freight cars. I'm really glad to leave René in France, especially not to inflict more misery and hunger on the poor child, at least that's something he won't have experienced."[68]

Jewish Women in the Resistance

Some of the most notable female figures in the French resistance were Jewish and belonged to separate, though mainly socialist and communist, political parties. Women as different as France Bloch-Sérazin, Romanian-born Olga Bancic, and Antoinette Feuerwerker—the wife of a rabbi—were united by angry despair and readiness to take extreme risks, though they all had young children.[69] Surely it was their awareness and acknowledgement of the reality of their situation, and their refusal to be deluded that motivated them as members of a community that knew themselves to be sentenced to death. After the mass arrests at the Vel' d'Hiv, a number of young girls—especially those who had lost close relatives and parental control—joined Jewish resistance movements.[70] Their priority was to smuggle children to safety, either with peasant families in remote rural areas, in makeshift safe houses, or—in the best of cases—in Switzerland. Many of these girls had belonged to the Jewish Scout movement (*Scouts Israélites de France*), where they received basic survival training that would prove invaluable.[71]

The case of Marianne Cohn (1922–1944) is typical of these young resistance activists. She fled Nazi Germany with her family in the 1930s. Her parents were imprisoned in the internment camp of Gurs, while Marianne and her sister were taken in by the Jewish Scouts. She soon went underground, initially as a liaison agent working on forged identity papers, and finally smuggling groups of children over the border into Switzerland.[72] At one point she was incarcerated and tortured, but she remained silent throughout, an experience Marianne admirably describes in a poem that begins with the following lines:

I shall betray tomorrow, not today

Today, you can tear my nails out

I shall not betray

You do not know how far my courage will go

I do ... [73]

Marianne was arrested with 28 children, aged 4 to 15 years, in Annemasse, France. She was given the option to escape, but refused to do so, fearing the Germans' revenge on her charges. The children were saved by the local mayor, but Marianne's body was found later—raped and mutilated.[74] In the official French history of World War II, the contribution of female resistants is barely recognized, and that of the Jewish ones practically unacknowledged.

Conclusion

One can ask if the survival strategies—or lack of them in some cases—of Jewish women in France fit in with those of other women in other conditions of genocide. The theoretical framework that unites all the essays in the present work are evolutions of the structural sources identified by Ofer and Weitzman[75] and further investigated by Marian Kaplan.[76] This methodology seeks to evaluate a balance between capacities inherited or acquired before the onset of the war, and gendered reactions to extreme discrimination and danger. It has to be said that women in France were not treated differently from men during the Holocaust—if they were temporarily spared the worst for a time, it was clear that their total annihilation was planned, and that the plan also included children. This holistic concept of total genocide largely excluded sexual abuse, which, when it occurred, was not systemic.

Any form of spontaneous behaviour is a reflection of character and personal circumstances, but filtered through social conditioning and expectations. This was true of Jewish women in the Holocaust as well as their Armenian, Tutsi, or Bosnian equivalents. The stress on the family is certainly true in all configurations where heteronormative structures dominate—as in countries where wars take place today. Female agency, as everywhere, was exercised according to cultural background and social class. The same situations elicited comparable reactions for differing reasons.

Thus, working-class Jewish women from pious Eastern European families may have well had powerful female role models of previous generations who saw their families through hardship and pogroms. This would have encouraged resourcefulness and independence of thought when it came to dealing with the survival of children and elders in dire circumstances, whether in Paris or once in the camps on their way to Auschwitz. Their more-educated contemporaries, born and bred in France, would have been able to study and use acquired professional skills and social connections profitably. Yet the comfort in which these women grew up generally made them less adaptable to the brutal reversal of fortune. In every case, political awareness would have been in conformity with their environment, but the women's approach might have been less theoretical and more grounded on the street-level reality they encountered on a daily basis. In practice, working-class migrants were ultimately less trusting of the French authorities than their over-confident *Israélite* contemporaries were.

The gender dimension in the Holocaust revealed itself through largely unconscious individual acts of bravery performed by women who had their social and historical heritage as a reference point, and their sense of loyalty to their loved ones as a motivation. Yet, despite the vast scholarship of the Holocaust, much of their story remains to be written.

Questions

1. Where and how do gender issues intersect with genocide?
2. What are the differences in how Nazi ideology considers German "Aryan" women and Jewish women?
3. What were the factors that played into the lack of solidarity among Jewish women in France? What social, religious, economic, and political constructs prevented Jewish and non-Jewish women in France from helping each other?

Notes

1. Dalia Ofer and Lenore J. Weitzman, eds., *Women in the Holocaust* (New Haven: Yale University Press, 1998); Marion Kaplan, *Between Dignity and Despair: Jewish Life in Nazi Germany* (New York: Oxford University Press, 1999); Sonja M. Hedgepeth and Rochelle G. Saidel, eds., *Sexual Violence Against Jewish Women During the Holocaust* (Lebanon: Brandeis University Press, 2010).
2. Renee Poznanski, *Être Juif en France pendant la Seconde Guerre Mondiale* (Paris: Hachette, 1994).
3. Hedgepeth and Saidel, *Sexual Violence Against Jewish Women.*

4. Trials of War Criminals Before the Nuernberg Military Tribunals, Washington, US Government Printing Office, 1949–1953, vol. XIII, 323.

5. Carol Mann, *Femmes dans la Guerre 1914–1945* (Paris: Pygmalion/Flammarion, 2010); Carol Mann, *Chérubins et Morveux: Bébés et Layette à Travers le Temps* (Paris: Pygmalion/Flammarion, 2012).

6. Hannah Arendt, ed., *Walter Benjamin: Essays and Reflections* (New York: Random House, 1968), 45.

7. The reader will find that I frequently refer to personal interviews in my notes. I grew up in a family that experienced the Holocaust mainly in France (though its members hailed from Poland, Hungary, and Romania). The majority of this vast family were deported and murdered in Auschwitz, but a number of women survived. I was brought up, like so many of my generation, by parents, grandmothers, aunts, and the occasional uncle who spoke about their experiences; they did not speak of the worst part—that was shrouded in silence—but of their everyday lives. It was much later, by the time most had passed away, that I realized the importance of what I had passively heard as a child. The numerous people I interviewed subsequently corroborated their tales. As astounding as it sounds, there are practically no published references for many of the incidents linked to personal details about survival. Academic writing has to have an original source to generate references and this essay will be part of those sources. The reader will have to bear with me, as much is the result of primary research I have been conducting over the years. I am thankful for my grandmothers, Hella Mangel and Frieda Zysmann; my uncles, André, Marcel, Alain, and Simon; and my aunts, Fanny, Elsa, Sécha, and Thérèse, for their amazing courage and what they taught me about this under-researched area of history.

8. For more information see, among others, Michel Winock, *La France et les Juifs de 1989 à Nos Jours* (Paris: Éditions de Seuil, 2004), 11.

9. The term *Israélite* was first coined officially under Napoleon I, who allowed Jews to practise their religion in a state-supervised structure known as *Le Consistoire central israélite de France*, and it came to refer, in popular parlance within the community, to French-born Jews and their descendants, as opposed to migrants coming from Eastern Europe after World War I.

10. Winock, *La France et les Juifs*, 105.

11. Gérard Noiriel, *Immigration, Antisémitisme et Racisme en France: (XIXe–XXe Siècle) Discours Publics, Humiliations Privées* (Paris: Fayard, Pluriel, 2014), 305.

12. Jérémy Guedj, "Les Juifs Français Face aux Juifs Étrangers dans la France de l'Entre-Deux-Guerres," *Cahiers de la Méditerranée* 78 (2009): 43–73, cdlm. revues.org/4637.

13. Paula Hyman, *From Dreyfus to Vichy: The Remaking of French Jewry, 1906– 1939* (New York: Columbia University Press, 1979), 32.

14. André Kaspi, *Les Juifs pendant l'Occupation* (Seuil: Pris, 1997), 28.

15. This became obvious in my own research for a biography on the French artist Modigliani. Carol Mann, *Modigliani* (London: Thames and Hudson, 1980).

16. This was the case for my own uncle (who subsequently married my maternal aunt), who came to Strasburt in Eastern France from Oradea in Transylvania. My mother, aunt, and numerous other members of the family had friends in this community of students who frequently rented rooms in Jewish homes.

17. Irène Némirovsky, *David Golder*, trans. Sandra Smith (New York: Vintage Books, 2007).

18. Muriel Pichon, "Cécile Brunschvicg née Kahn, Féministe et Ministre du Front Populaire," Archives Juives 2012/1 (vol. 45).

19. Hyman, *From Dreyfus to Vichy*, 64.

20. Guedj, "Les Juifs Français."

21. Kaspi, *Le Juifs pendant l'Occupation*, 77.

22. There are at least 15 instances in the French Civil Code dating back from the French Revolution that refer to the responsibilities of the *honus pater familias*, all of which were finally removed from official legislative texts in 2014.

23. Jean-Louis Crémieux-Brilhac, "Engagés Volontaires et Prestataires," in *De l'Exil à la Résistance, Réfugiés et Immigrés d'Europe Central en France 1933– 1945*, ed. Karel Bartosek, René Gallissot, and Denis Peschanski (Saint-Denis, France: Presses Universitaires de Vincennes, 1989), 1–283 .

24. Poznanksi, *Être Juif en France*, 57.

25. Kaspi, *Les Juifs pendant l'Occupation*, 54.

26. Poznanksi, *Être Juif en France*, 64.

27. *Certificate de non-appartenance à la race Juive*.

28. See the comprehensive study in Robert J. Hanyok, *Eavesdropping on Hell: Historical Guide to Western Communications Intelligence and the Holocaust 1939–1945* (Minneola: Dover Publications, 2013).

29. Excerpt from Anne Frank's diary, online from the Anne Frank Center, accessed October 13, 2014, annefrank.com/about-anne-frank/diary-excerpts.

30. Kaspi, *Les Juifs pendant l'Occupation*, 87.

31. Henri Amouroux, *La Vie des Français sous l'Occupation*, vol. I: *Les Années Grises* (Paris: Fayard, Livre de Poche, 1961), 195.
32. Ibid., 163.
33. Henri Michel, *Paris Allemand* (Paris: Albin Michel, 1981), 93.
34. Poznanksi, *Être juif en France*, 70.
35. Ibid., 216.
36. Michael Marrus and Robert O. Paxton, *Vichy France and the Jews* (Redwood City: Stanford University Press, 1995).
37. Michel Winock, *Nationalisme, Antisémitisme et Fascisme en France* (Paris: Points Seuil, 2004), 218.
38. Kaspi, *Les Juifs pendant l'Occupation*, 94.
39. Poznanksi, *Être Juif en France*, 151.
40. Based on my own research, including primary documents for a book on Déborah Lifschitz that I am currently working on.
41. Mann, *Femmes dans la Guerre*, 304.
42. Paulette Feldman, interview by the author.
43. Pichon, "Cécile Brunschvicg née Kahn."
44. Mann, *Femmes dans la Guerre*, 307.
45. Jacques Sémelin, *Persécution et Entre-Aide en France Occupée* (Paris: Edition du Seuil/Arénes, 2013), 252.
46. Mann, *Femmes dans la Guerre*, 203; Dalia Ofer, "Gender Issues in Ghetto Diaries and Interviews: The Case of Warsaw," in *Women in the Holocaust*, ed. Dalia Ofer and Lenore J. Weitzman (New Haven: Yale University Press, 1998), 143–167.
47. Poznanski, *Être Juif en France*, 319.
48. Based on the author's personal interviews with survivors as well as letters from the Centre de Documentation Juive Contemporaine related to trafficking of counterfeit cards.
49. Based on the author's personal interviews, letters from the Centre de Documentation Juive Contemporaine, and also the author's family stories. My uncle Charles actually ran a kosher butcher shop in Limoges, despite restrictions imposed by the Gestapo. He and his brother were subsequently deported and murdered in Auschwitz, but his actions were relayed through surviving relatives.
50. Based on information passed down by the author's family.
51. Jacqueline Lang, *La Rose et la Bleue, une Jeune Femme sous l'Occupation: Témoignage, 1942–1945* (Paris: Logomotif, 2004),100.
52. Poznanski, *Être Juif en France*, 307.

53. Based on the author's review of hundreds of letters at the Centre de Documentation Juive Contemporaine sent from Drancy, in which the person writing the correspondence often mentioned that they had someone write the letter in French, since they did not know the language. Authorities required that all correspondence be written in French.

54. Lea Horer's letters, July 16 to September 9, 1942, located at Centre de Documentation Juive Contemporaine, Paris, France.

55. Ibid.

56. Ibid.

57. Ibid.

58. Ibid.

59. Serge Klarsfeld, *La Shoah en France*, vol. 4: *Mémorial des Enfants Juifs Déportés de France* (Paris: Fayard, 2001).

60. Michael Marrus and Robert O. Paxton, *Vichy France and the Jews* (Redwood City: Stanford University Press, 1995), 265.

61. Poznanski, *Être Juif en France*, 319.

62. Based on personal interviews, letters from the Centre de Documentation Juive Contemporaine, and conclusions I have come to during my research.

63. Letter from Avram S. dated February 14, 1942, located at Centre de Documentation Juive Contemporaine, Paris, France.

64. Letter from Simon S. dated May 7, 1942, located at Centre de Documentation Juive Contemporaine, Paris, France.

65. Letter from Mme. Heftmann dated July 8, 1942, located at Centre de Documentation Juive Contemporaine, Paris, France.

66. Letter from Armand dated June 27, 1942, located at Centre de Documentation Juive Contemporaine, Paris, France.

67. Letter from Chaya W. dated July 24, 1942, located at Centre de Documentation Juive Contemporaine, Paris, France.

68. Letter from Chaya W. dated July 27, 1942, located at Centre de Documentation Juive Contemporaine, Paris, France.

69. Mann, *Femmes dans la Guerre*, 306.

70. Ibid., 306.

71. Ibid., 306 and following, including chapter "Juives et Résistantes en France."

72. Ibid., 306 and following, including chapter "Juives et Résistantes en France."

73. Ibid., 317.

74. Ibid., 318.

75. Ofer and Weitzman, *Women in the Holocaust*.

76. Kaplan, *Between Dignity and Despair*.

CHAPTER 4

Silencing the Women:
Violence through Rape in the 1971 War of Liberation

Farah Ishtiyaque

Introduction

It is a well-established fact that war necessitates violence. The text-book definition of violence as a method of war includes both corporeal and psychological "damages" meted out to the conflicting parties fighting the war. Imprinted in the history of South Asia are two bloody dates. The first is the 1947 partition of the Indian sub-continent into India and Pakistan and the further partitioning of Pakistan into East and West Pakistan. The second was the 1971 creation of the new independent nation-state of Bangladesh, which was partitioned out of East Pakistan. Both partitions involved a common methodology of violence that included rampant killing, plundering, looting, carnage, and rape.[1]

One of the darkest moments in the 20th century was the Holocaust, which has become a baseline for genocide. It is irrefutable that all Jews, irrespective of their gender, were targeted for annihilation during the Holocaust. In contrast, in Bangladesh (East Pakistan), there were two groups of enemies targeted for mass annihilation. First, the Bengali Muslims were the primary enemy of the nation-state of Pakistan, as they were rebelling against the western Pakistani wing, demanding complete autonomy for the eastern half of the state. Second, the Bihari Muslims were seen as collaborators of the West Pakistan Army, and the Mukti Bahinis (Bengali Freedom Fighters) saw them as a threat to their vision of independent Bangladesh.

The migration that ensued during 1947 was colossal in scale, and Indian Muslims (from North and East India) started their pilgrimage to either East or West Pakistan. Such migrants were called *muhajirs*. The *muhajirs* who travelled to the eastern wing of Pakistan, however, became known as Bihari Muslims. The original meaning of the term *muhajir* was a religious one. *Muhajirs* accompanied the Prophet Muhammad from Mecca to Medina during the holy month of Ramadan, and were received by the welcoming hosts, the Medina *ansars*. However, the Indian Urdu-speaking Muslims who left India in 1947 for the east wing of Pakistan, and who came to be known as Bihari Muslims, did not receive the same warm welcome as their counterparts who spoke Bangla. The linguistic divide between Urdu and Bangla was too wide, and Bihari Muslims came to be seen as outsiders, aliens. The 1971 Liberation War furthered the rift between these two linguistically different communities. The differences were not only linguistic, but also political in nature. The Bihari Muslim *muhajirs* supported the Pakistani government during the Liberation War, while the opposing group, the Mukti Bahini, wanted an independent Pakistan. The Bihari Muslim population became outsiders within the newly established country of Bangladesh. They approached Pakistan asking to be repatriated, but West Pakistan remained silent on their request. These stranded Bihari Muslims became a stateless and forgotten people—living in 60 refugee camps within the borders of Bangladesh. Some were able to relocate to the United Kingdom, Australia, or Gulf countries, while others were able to successfully integrate with the Bangladeshis. As of today, some Bihari Muslims continue to live in the refugee camps in cramped and hopeless conditions.

The subhuman treatment of Bihari Urdu-speaking women during the Liberation War does not mean that the violence they experienced was any more or any less than that of Bengali-speaking women. Both dealt with the trauma of rape and the war in similar ways; however, the Bihari women had to cope with the additional trauma of victimization and being identified as an "other" among their eastern-wing neighbours.

Through several literary texts—Aquila Ismail's *Of Martyrs and Marigolds*, and Tahmima Anam's *A Golden Age* and its sequel *A Good Muslim*—I analyze the silence that surrounds both the act of rape and rape victims.[2] I have deliberately chosen the works of these two writers, since this chapter engages itself with women and various negotiations carried forward by them vis-à-vis the nation during the Liberation War of 1971. Anam and Ismail write about the role of women, and in particular the role of Bihari Muslim women, both during and after the war. The authors focus on the family unit, and are able to use this unit in their fiction to recount the broader historical events of 1971 and the making of independent Bangladesh. The microcosmic families become the focal point of the writers through which they comment on the macrocosm of Bangladeshi society. The authors give women the centre stage and celebrate their heroism. Both also show the atrocities meted out to the marginalized Bihari Muslim community, accused of being collaborators with the West Pakistan Army. These novels are important in debunking the dominant Bihari Muslim narrative, and help illustrate that despite linguistic differences, Urdu-speaking families believed in and sympathized with the Bangladeshi cause, yet were alienated and persecuted. It is interesting to note that both novels were written by female writers and featured women as central characters who negotiate their liminal identity in the creation of the new nation-state. Anam and Ismail narrate the events of the war and its aftermath through the use of strong female characters. The protagonists in these works negotiate their way through the events from a position of disempowerment on three distinct levels: their fringe ethnic status, their gender, and their nationality.

Understanding that rape connects women, irrespective of the different partitions (1947, 1971), ethnicity (Bengali, Urdu-speaking), and wars (the Liberation War of 1971), I attempt to read a broader ethos of humanity and female bonding.[3] If wartime rape was a tool of subjugation used by men, for women it had deeper and much more damaging meanings. For women, forceful penetration "defiled," "smeared," and "stained" the virtuousness of the female self. The rape victim's character and integrity was questioned because of this act of aggression, and a woman was now considered to be "corrupt" and "loose." Women associated rape with dishonour. Impurity was considered to be the benchmark of a rape victim and her chastity was compromised with this act. The silence around rape reinforces the taboo attached to it in a patriarchal society.

The character of the illegitimate violent behaviour during and after the Liberation War, also referred to as the partition of Pakistan, was similar to the First Partition of India (1947). Gyanendra Pandey's *Remembering Partition* argues that nationalism and nationalist historiography draws a line separating "partition" and "violence," which is misguided.[4] For most survivors "partition was violence" and it is this division that this chapter addresses.[5]

I examine violence as a quintessential part of the Liberation War, as opposed to being an irrational, disorganized, and often chaotic appendage of wartime. I am interested in locating the particularities of violence inscribed on the female body in recounting and dismantling the gender violence in the Liberation War. By doing so, I investigate the complicated relationship between history, nation, and women, although not necessarily in that order. As Dalia Ofer and Lenore J. Weitzman write about Jewish women during the Holocaust,

> To use gender as a framework for analysis is simply to become more attentive to the possible consequences of one of the major axes of all social organization—along with age, class, and religion ... once we are alert to and begin to ask questions about the social expectations and behaviors of men and women, a variety of assumptions, decisions, and social patterns become more noticeable and take added meaning.[6]

The official state-sponsored narrative anointed as the "national history" is remembered by all citizens of the nation. Screened, selected, and privileged memories contribute to the making of the "usable history" to be consumed by the nation and the world at large. Yet silences and gaps pervade this nation's history. The official national history of 1971, much like earlier scholarship on Holocaust memorialization, obliterated women's experience of violence. By attempting to relocate the lost voices of women, particularly the doubly disempowered Bihari Muslim women in East

Pakistan/Bangladesh, this chapter attempts, in the words of Joan Kelly, "to restore women to history and to restore our history to women."[7]

I delve into the mechanism of gender violence meted out to women—both Bengali and Bihari—focusing on rape as an aggressive apparatus of mass annihilation. I attempt to re-inscribe the rarely discussed Bihari Muslim women into the historical landscape of Bangladesh. Their silenced, muffled voices are important in ensuring a nuanced understanding of both nation formation and their position as citizens in the newly formed nation. Apart from generating a peoples' narrative of 1971, which is inclusive of all voices irrespective of gender, age, and ethnicity, women's experiences of genocidal wartime crimes and violence shed light upon the sheer barbarity and loss of humanity. The genocide of 1971 was, as Yasmin Saikia calls it, a loss of *insaniyat* (humanity).[8] Unearthing the women's muffled voices is important because, as Saikia notes,

> they enable our understanding of the experiences of the collective and show the scars that individual women endure. More importantly, women's memories make us deeply aware of their resilience to come to terms with the past to move forward and engender a new future. Women's truth telling questions our own culpability in enforcing a dehumanizing silence upon them. We need to know their stories in order to know ourselves in postcolonial South Asia.[9]

Historical Overview of the 1971 War

The 1971 Liberation War lasted nine months, during which the freedom fighters (the Mukti Bahinis), under the leadership of Sheikh Mujibur Rahman, rebelled against the oppressive West Pakistan Army. The tenuous terrain of the two-nation theory on which Pakistan was founded started crumbling when there was a clash of interests between the two wings. The imposition of the language of Urdu resulted in an internal rift between the Bengali-speaking and the Urdu-speaking Muslims who had come from India to settle in the eastern wing of Pakistan. The subsequent language riots of the 1950s, along with unequal allocation of national assets, economic exploitation, and the lack of political representation in the country's national parliament resulted in East Pakistan's open rebellion. Sheikh Mujibur Rahman of the Awami League won a sweeping victory in the 1970 general election. His party won 160 seats of the total 162 in East Pakistan. Zulfikar Ali Bhutto of the Pakistan People's Party (PPP) won in West Pakistan with a majority of 81 seats out of 138. With the support of the West Pakistan Army, Bhutto delayed the formation of the National Assembly. The postponement of the assembly session was the final blow to East Pakistan, which forcefully revolted against West Pakistan. Nine months of intense civil strife brought about the freedom of East Pakistan from its western counterpart. Thus began a repetitive cycle of mindless killing, rape, plunder, and shuffling of human lives. India launched a frontal attack against the West Pakistan Army on November 26, 1971, thereby advocating the cause of liberation for Bangladesh. By December 16, 1971, the war was over and history witnessed the creation of the independent state of Bangladesh.

Bihari Muslim is considered a derogatory name for the *muhajirs* in East Pakistan. They are deemed enemies of Bangladesh, as they were suspected of collaboration with the West Pakistan Army. Yasmin Saikia explains,

> In particular, during the civil war the Biharis were targeted as the "enemy" of the Bengalis.... The cleavages between the Bengalis and Biharis in speech, livelihood and living arrangements enabled the transformation of the Biharis into an "outcast" group by the Bengali nationalists and they targeted them for violence. The majority of the ethnic attacks happened in towns where the Bengalis and the Biharis worked and lived side by side as neighbours, before the violence broke out.[10]

Women's Culturally Defined Roles among the Bihari Muslims

Women, regardless of language or ethnicity, were responsible for the home and hearth before and after the 1971 Liberation War. They were custodians of the emotional well-being of the family unit, as illustrated by Rehana, a character in the novel *A Good Muslim* who helps her son recover from post-traumatic stress disorder brought about by the war, by encouraging him to read the Quran.

Women were responsible for maintaining the cultural ethos of their community and were entrusted with bringing up daughters who would be obedient and submissive to their husbands. The benchmark of a good woman was viewed in terms of her chastity and virtuousness.

Anticipatory Reactions

Men and women dealt with the internal strife between the two wings of Pakistan differently. The thought of being raped instilled so much fear in women that hiding and guarding their chastity became their chief agenda. We see an example of this in the novel *A Golden Age*, during Operation Searchlight (March 25, 1971) wherein the Pakistan Army cracked down on East Pakistan, indulging in rampant killings of intellectuals and potential revolutionaries at Dhaka University. Mrs. Chowdhry, mother of a young woman named Silvi, is afraid and worried about her daughter's safety and protection. The anticipation of rape—"what if they come for her?"—forces Mrs. Chowdhry to marry Silvi off to Sabeer, a soldier in the Pakistan Army.[11] Mrs. Chowdhry's self-assurance that marriage would provide safety to unmarried girls was, of course, wrong; many married women, such as the unnamed young bride from the novel *Of Martyrs and Marigolds*, were sexually assaulted by the Mukti Bahini soldiers. Also in *Of Martyrs and Marigolds*, we see that the mother of Haseena, upon realizing that the Muktijuddho soldiers had come "late in the night," ran to her daughter and "ordered Haseena to get under the bed and not come out until she was told to do so."[12] These examples show that the Bangladeshi people—primarily the mothers—realized the danger to their daughters. They took pre-emptive measures to try to ward off anticipated violence toward or rape of their daughters, such as marrying them off to Pakistani men for protection, or putting them in hiding.

Difference in Treatment of Women and Men

The 1971 Liberation War was between groups of men who used the bodies of women to combat and fight each other. Obviously, individuals of both sexes suffered during the Liberation War, but the processes of suffering and violence incurred by their bodies were of a different kind and nature.

The violence meted out to the female body was of a unique kind, differing from that of the men, as men used their penises as a dangerous weapon to promulgate violence. Rape was used as a strategic weapon of war. Rape victims were exclusively women, and rape was and still is used by men as a decisive instrument to demonstrate their power over an enemy.

Wartime strategy co-opts wartime rape and uses it as a war tactic for a number of reasons, highlighting the matrix of power relations. Wartime rape is an international trend and women, from the Armenian genocide to Kosovo, Rwanda, and Darfur, among others, have been subjected to this private invasion. Sexual harassment and rape was a rare occurrence during the Holocaust but women were certainly "terrorized by rumors of rape."[13] It is interesting to note that the Nazi policy condemned its soldiers who raped Jewish women, calling the act a "racial shame." In contrast, during the Liberation War, the concept of "racial shame" was co-opted by the warring factions to bring shame to the opposing side by defiling its women and future lineage.

In the novel *Of Martyrs and Marigolds*, a newly wed Bihari Muslim bride and a young Bengali Muslim woman, held captive at the desolate house in Chittagong, are ravaged by the Mukti Bahini soldiers who desecrate their bodies, violating and defiling them. Once the soldiers are done, the women return "dishevelled and dirty ... pieces of grass and twigs stuck to their clothes and hair ... the qameez stained with blood."[14] These two defiled women are symptomatic of the larger defilement of the nation. The orgy of violence extended to sheer pornography, as accounts by Bhasin and Menon, in *Borders and Boundaries: Women in India's Partition*, explain:

> [S]tripping; parading naked, mutilating and disfiguring; tattoo-ing or branding the breasts and genitalia with triumphal slogans; amputating breasts; knifing open the womb; raping, of course; killing fetuses is shocking not only for its savagery, but for what it tells us about women as objects in male constructions of their honour. Women's sexuality symbolizes "manhood"; its desecration is a matter of such shame and dishonour that *it has to be avenged*.[15]

Through the landscape of war and using the woman's body, men in effect abuse each other, violating and vandalizing the nation at large. Brownmiller states that "[r]ape became not only a male prerogative, but man's basic weapon of force against woman, the principal agent of his will and fear. His forcible entry into her body, despite her physical protestations and struggle, became the vehicle of his victorious conquest over her being, the ultimate test of his superior strength, the triumph of his manhood."[16]

The Bihari Muslim woman is the doubly disempowered subaltern buried in the shadows of pain and endless suffering. Her gender and ethnicity positions her in dual positions of inferiority and power play. Bengali-speaking women were complicit in making the Bihari Muslim women pariahs. Apart from belonging to the suspicious "othered" community of *muhajirs*, they were also treated as enemies due to their affiliation with the West Pakistan Army. They were stereotyped as being against the Liberation Front of Bangladesh and were seen as possible collaborators with the enemy, Pakistan. In addition to this, there was a rupture within the female community. Saikia examines the rupture between the women speaking different languages and writes the following:

> The voices and experiences of minority women such as the Biharis, even today, are not included within the efforts to remember. Bengali women have co-opted to the Bengali men's will to construct meanings of nationalism and feminism within culturally and ethnically specific contexts today. The construction of the Bihari women as the "other" makes it possible to imagine such an identity. Hence, instead of challenging patriarchal values and authority, Bengali women have become subject-accomplices in dehumanizing "others."[17]

Women suffered differently during the war. Many women offered their bodies for rape in order to protect their family and children. In *Of Martyrs and Marigolds*, Sekina offers her body to be ravaged by the Mukti Bahini soldiers to "save" her baby, whom the soldiers would have surely killed otherwise.[18]

One of the most important functions of wartime rape was forcible impregnation; martial rape was a tool of, as Claudia Card identifies it, "genetic imperialism."[19] The perpetrators raped women and used the womb to signify literal and symbolic occupied territory. Children of such incidents were, of course, identified by the biological father and shunned by society. The aim of impregnation was intergenerational defilement. Card explains, "Martial rape can undermine national, political, and cultural solidarity, changing the next generation's identity, confusing the loyalties of all victimized survivors."[20] Being silent about wartime rape was also a strategy used by women to be able to later live a normal life, without being "othered," secluded, and ostracized, as the knowledge of rape would lead to family members rejecting both them and their children altogether.

Humiliation of the female self and the symbolic male self was one of the biggest effects of rape. Women lived under the constant fear of being raped and consequently "spoiled." Their hidden genitals being made public through the very act of rape, and their identification as survivors of rape, soiled their *ijjot* (honour). Suri, the protagonist in *Of Martyrs and Marigolds*, is repeatedly humiliated by the Mukti Bahinis who frisk her by checking the face and "other things that defined womanhood," since some Urdu-speaking men were trying to escape by posing as women.[21] The screening of her body further humiliates Suri: "the soldier tapped first one bosom and then another with his bayonet, nodded, and smiled as he proclaimed that Suri was indeed not a man."[22] Apart from the physical intrusion, which jeopardized the dignity of the women, constant slurs and verbal abuses dehumanized them. *Whore* was a common term of abuse hurled at them, which shows a significant understanding of rape. Once raped, a woman's body was no longer hers; it was a public property and she was considered a prostitute, giving sexual pleasures to men.

The Different Reactions of Men and Women in Their Everyday Lives

Wartime rape, as a method of breaching women's dignity and the nation at large, throws light upon the relationship between memory and history. Preserving the chastity of the female body reflects the symbolic honour of the nation. Victims of wartime rape are unable to talk about the multi-layered moment of rape, as it shames their human selves and is an attack on their very existence. All too often, they teach themselves to forget the episode of brutal invasion or intrusion, as the trauma is too painful to deal with. Raped women forcefully forget their personal and collective memories in order to be accepted back into society. History frequently strategically erases such mention of sexual abuse, since it ruptures the masculine notion of nationalism, bringing shame and disrespect to men—and by extension, the nation. History further glosses over the already forgotten episodes of wartime rape in order to restore a nation's dignity and integrity.

Wartime rape is an accepted global phenomenon, and addressing it is not a unique revelation. However, feminist research on the wartime crimes of 1971 has managed to gloss over the condition of Bihari Muslim women. Media coverage on Bangladeshi war crimes has given prime focus, and rightly so, to the Bengali women; but it has neglected the destitute and hapless condition of the marginalized Bihari Muslim women. The stateless refugee position of the Bihari Muslims provoked them to seek help and protection from the nation-state of Bangladesh, as they considered the state to be their *mai-baap* (mother-father). Bangladesh has a peculiar and interesting procedure for dealing with rape and rape victims. The state, under the reign of Sheikh Mujibur, conferred the title of *birangona* (war heroine) to women raped during the Liberation War. By doing so—by identifying rape victims as heroines—the state hoped to provide them with dignity, honour, and certain economic benefits in order to integrate them into the rubric of the new society. Needless to say, this benefit was exclusively for the Bengali-speaking women, completely ignoring the Bihari Muslim women, and victimizing them further. Urvashi Butalia states, "This relationship [parent-child] was to change over time, as refugee [Bihari Muslim women] began to mobilize on questions of their rights as citizens and began to make demands of the state."[23] Bihari women were treated as disposable entities, and were tragically orphaned by both their Bengali-speaking counterparts and by the state.

Nur Jahan, a Bihari Muslim victim of the 1971 war does not wish to "talk" about her suffering, and pleads for a "human life." She says, "What happened to me or my children, or to the women here, who will tell their stories?... I don't want to talk. Tell me, can you help us? We want to live a human life, we are human beings, is it possible for us to have a human life? What is the point in telling all this now? We will go to the graveyard but no one will deliver us from here."[24] Women like Nur Jahan find themselves unable to express the degree of violence meted out to them and so prefer to remain silent.

The act of forceful penetration was unimaginable for the women. The silence that surrounds the naming of the event is symptomatic of the silenced or muffled voices of the women and their histories in the nation-building project. Saikia explores the unavailability of an apt term to describe the event of rape. She writes, "Cultural unease is expressed in the lack of an equivalent word for rape in Urdu. In Bangla, although there is a word for rape, *dharshan*, it is never used in women's testimony of war experiences."[25]

This inability to name rape as rape and substituting it with names like *izzat lootna* (honour lost), *osohay* (helplessness), *bhoi* (fear), and *nirjatika* (brutalized), shows the intricate silence and confusion around the experience. Each term further alienates the woman from the actual episode, making her vulnerable and disempowered in society, thereby creating a serious problem of historical accountability. Veena Das, while interviewing women who suffered during the partition of 1947 explains, "A zone of silence [was] around the event. This silence was achieved either by the use of language that was general and metaphoric [*osohay, bhoi, nirjatika*] but that evaded the specific descriptor of any events so as to capture the particularity of their experience or by describing the surrounding events but leaving the actual episode of abduction and rape unstated."[26]

This evasive but pregnant silence is seen in victims' recounting of traumatic episodes through testimonies, and also in literary fiction based on the 1971 partition. The actual act of rape or sexual abuse is erased or often blurred by the victims due to loss of consciousnesses. Saikia, in her interview with a rape survivor (Taslima's mother), underlines the pervasive silence around the episode when she relays how the woman remembered the event: "It was mid-day, after lunch. I was on the other side of the pond, and they came from behind me. I was facing south, and they came from the north, hence I could not see them.... I shouted and I *fainted*!

I became *unconscious*. When I woke up I saw that I was in my house. I came back to my senses after four or five hours. *It* all happened near the pond" (emphasis added).[27] The woman's denial of being aware of the act shows how women tried and still try to hide the act of rape, thereby keeping the honour of their self, men, family, and society at large intact. A similar occurrence takes place in the novel *Of Martyrs and Marigolds* when a Bangladeshi soldier attempts to rape a young woman, Suri: "He brought his face close to Suri's. She could smell stale *bidhi* tobacco in his breath. He laid one hand on her thighs and he edged closer to her pressing his body to hers. Suri began to shake with fear; and her legs gave way. The man held her tight pushing her down.... Suri felt a heavy weight descend on her, and then *darkness enveloped her mind*" (emphasis added).[28]

These two cases highlight the "darkness" that surrounds the very idea of rape. Silence about the act is poignantly described in the novel *A Golden Age* when Maya's university friend Sharmeen is abducted from Rokeya Hall, and "could not be found,"[29] and there was "still no sign of her."[30] It is important to note the vagueness surrounding the abduction of Sharmeen; the silence that envelops her is indicative of a bigger secret—the secret of her sexual abuse. The unwillingness to accept and vocalize the event pushes it into the realm of oblivion.

The silence around rape in both testimonies and the novels is haunting and charged with multiple understandings of the patriarchal society. The reasons for silence regarding rape include the lack of responsibility taken by the nation-state (here Bangladesh) of allowing the rape of both Bihari and Bengali women during the war. The silence is reflective of the ethical irresponsibility and acceptance of the loss of *insaniyat* (humanity). The nation's effort to forget the barbarity meted out to women is indicative of the condition of official history that suffers from partial amnesia, only remembering episodes and events that valorize the nation-state and boost the patriotism of its citizens.

Rape during wartime becomes a yardstick to measure men's manliness, virility, and patriotism. However, the trauma of wartime rape circumscribes itself on the victim, her relatives, and her family in different ways. In *A Golden Age*, Maya, on hearing that her friend Sharmeen had been abducted, becomes "silent" and "drifted through the house like a cloud of dust."[31] If Maya could not comprehend the violence Sharmeen was subjected to, Rehana, Maya's mother, could not console her daughter. "She could not find a way into her daughter's grief, drawn so tightly around her."[32] Rehana's primary concern is for the safety of her children, who are now slowly becoming alienated from each other. Maya actively indulges in politics by supporting the freedom struggle, spending time at the university, and wearing white, which is customary for mourning. After realizing that Sharmeen has been subjected to rape, Maya is unable to live in the same country, and in fear of being raped, moves to Calcutta.

As noted earlier, rape, abduction, and forcible prostitution during the nine-month war only proved to be the first round of humiliation for the women. During the reign of Mujibur, Bangladesh recognized rape victims as *birangona*, or "brave women." The government hoped that through the process of recognition, not only would the "soiled" women come forward, but the nation would also be able to eradicate the "enemy seeds" in their wombs. The offer was to reintegrate them into society and give them a normalized life. This did not happen, however, since the women were further scorned and rebuked, treated as prostitutes and whores. In the novel *A Good Muslim*, Piya, a Bengali woman who is abducted and repeatedly raped in the army camps, is identified as a *birangona* and forced by the state to abort the war child. The trauma of killing her unborn child forces Piya to run away from Maya and Sohail, who had become her protectors.

Despite Bangladesh's attempts to restore women to society, and consequently the nation, through various outreach programs such as conferring of the title *birangona*, it fervently pushed the envelope of forgetting. The newly created nation of Bangladesh glossed over the brutal violence meted out to its women—the forceful rapes and subsequent impregnation.

The Role of mother/Mother

The chosen iconography for many nations has been the female form, with a specific societal role designed for her—that of a Mother.[33] The idea of a nation can become elusive for many, but when an image is associated with the nation, it is easy for us to attribute qualities and make sense of the abstract term *nation*. The figure or icon of the Mother, the ever-sustaining, ever-nurturing, ever-caring, selfless female, then becomes a metonymy for the nation-state.

Veena Das, in the essay "Language and Body: Transactions in the Construction of Pain," writes,

> The desire for icons allows the nation as an object to be made magically visible through an investment in this magnified sexuality. The potential for violence is written in this construction.... In the modern project of building a nation the image [of Mother] is not diminished, but enlarged. Its dramatization means that bodies of women are violently appropriated for the cause as nationalism gives birth to its double-communalism. If one deified women so that the nation could be imagined as the beloved, the other makes visible the dark side of the project by making the bodies of women the surfaces on which their text of the nation is written.[34]

The figure of the Mother, infused with abundant sexuality, is also invoked in the narrative of nation-building. The body of the female becomes the tabula rasa wherein the topography and the boundaries of nations are mapped. The violence done to the body highlights the various procedures or processes of the nation-building project. Das further observes that the nation is imagined in feminine terms.[35] India is addressed as *Bharat-Mata* (Mother India). Bangladesh and Pakistan are also conceived as caregiving mothers who protect and ensure the well-being of their citizens. Woman's biggest and most powerful role is that of being a mother. It is ironic to note that the mother becomes the iconic figure of the nation as the Mother, and is subsumed in its grand narrative so much so that other markers of identity, such as religion and ethnicity, become less significant, yet her body is brutally attacked because of these different identity markers.

The newly created Islamic nation of Bangladesh constructed itself on the model of Bibi Fatima—the daughter of the Prophet. "She is constructed as a quiet and obedient wife who achieves motherhood through piety rather than sexuality. She is often compared to Aisha, the dynamic, forceful, and childless favourite wife of the Prophet."[36] The iconic figure of Bibi Fatima is reflected in the real life heroes—the mothers who in their own little

ways contributed towards war and freedom. Official history has obliterated their sacrifices and contributions; hence it is important to understand
their role during the war in order to get a composite history of the nation-
state of Bangladesh.

The character of Rehana in *A Golden Age* is the quintessential mother,
looking after her children, Sohail and Maya, providing care and support to
them. She reminds herself, "I'm a mother. Above all things, a mother. Not
a widow, certainly not a wife. Not a thief. A mother."[37] Her world revolves
around her two children, who are both actively involved in the politics
of 1971, supporting the Awami League and aligning themselves with the
Mukti Bahinis. Her children encourage her to be a part of the rallies and
get-togethers, but she does not have the "proper trappings of a nationalist."[38] Rehana is not well read and does not understand the meaning
of unfamiliar words like *comrade, proletariat*, and *revolution*. Moreover,
"Rehana had ambiguous feelings about her country she had adopted."[39] A
Bihari Muslim who moved to the eastern wing of Pakistan from India during 1947, she still loves her Urdu and cannot "replace her mixed tongue
with a pure Bengali one."[40]

Nationalism sweeps itself with a certain seduction, and Rehana is enam-
oured by the idea of nation, and of contributing toward the Liberation War.
From being a biological mother, her transformation to the metaphorical
Mother begins. She attends a rally wherein Sheikh Mujib addresses the
crowd. "Rehana watched as he waved his arms to quiet and reassure his
people. His. They belonged to him now; they were his charge, his children. They called him father."[41] Consumed by the rhetoric of patriotism
and pro-nationalistic zeal, Rehana finds herself shouting "*Joy Bangla, Joy
Bangla, Joy Bangla*" with the crowd.[42] She realizes that she needs to be part
of the struggle in order for the country to keep "being her home, and the
children ... being her children."[43]

After Operation Searchlight, refugees start appearing near her home,
and Rehana, representing both the mother and Mother figure, takes the
mantle of responsibility, looking after them by providing them food and
blankets. Like Bibi Fatima, who practised piety and humility, Rehana
donates her beautiful silk sarees to be used as blankets for the freedom fighters. Rehana single-handedly mobilizes other women from the

quarter to begin "Operation Rooftop." The women sew blankets out of sarees, old and new, for freedom fighters, as Rehana reasons, "We're at war, and my daughter says I have to do something. To prove I belong here. So I'm doing something."[44] Unsatisfied with her contributions toward the war, Rehana breaks down, saying, "I'm not doing enough. I want to do my part. Maybe it's not for my son—maybe it's something else.... I can love something other than my children. I can. I can love other things."[45] Rehana actively engages in social work, and in the sequel, *A Good Muslim*, we see her assisting widows and elderly women, counselling them in various women's rehabilitation centres.

The nation of Bangladesh placed the iconic figure of Mother on a pedestal and everyone bestowed reverence on her. Yet, it is interesting to note that Bangladesh also defiled potential mothers by snatching away the agency of choice from them. Raped women had hyphenated subjectivities within the national framework of a liberated Bangladesh. There were two types of women—"pure" women (not raped) and "impure" (raped) women. Women's experiences were not just uncared for, but their position was relegated to an absent subject in public history. Saikia investigates the absence of women in the public history of Bangladesh by writing, "This national political memorializing was creating a text of 1971 without a serious investigation of the historical events and outcomes. In this seemingly fluid stage of historical text production, women were tellingly absent and whenever inserted appeared as victims."[46]

Birangonas were the sexually violated women, the victims of the Liberation War, and considered a liability to the nation. The title was conferred upon them in the hope of integrating them into the matrix of the newly freed society. The nation, through the introduction of the title of war heroine, aimed to erase the act of rape, since the people believed it brought shame to their women. By relabelling the women as war heroines, the state hoped to erase the unspeakable violence from the memory of the general public. Bangladesh flew in medical specialists from other countries to perform massive numbers of abortions on these "war heroines" who were carrying the children of the enemy, the Pakistanis. Saikia notes the following:

Despite the legitimization of this process by the government as a face-saving device for women's benefit to enable them to regain their lost honour, the truth is harsher. At the very moment of the birth of the nation, both the Bangladesh State and Bangladeshi society failed their women by taking away women's agency and, by transgressing their humanity, transforming them into bodies that were manipulated so that men would not have to deal with the unhappy reminders of the past.[47]

Mass abortions are not an uncommon phenomena in the landscape of any post-war society. Ofer and Weitzman write that during the Holocaust, pregnancy was an urgent concern in the concentration camps.[48] Similar to the infamous German policy under which pregnant women who refused to abort their children were transported to the concentration camps for their immediate extermination, so too were the wombs of *birangonas* monitored and regulated by the state, to cleanse itself from any odious presence.

Nira Yuval-Davis and Floya Anthias have put forward the view that women have tended to participate in ethnic and national processes and, in relation to state practices, as biological reproducers of members of ethnic collectivities and as reproducers of the boundaries of ethnic/national groups.[49] Wartime rape was used by the enemy to propagate "genetic imperialism," marking the enemy women's wombs as occupied territory. The womb contained the fetus of the enemy state and the child born out of such forceful impregnation potentially defiled the homogenous ethnicity of the nation-state of Bangladesh. Pregnant *birangonas* were seen as impending threats, as they could potentially pollute the nation-state by producing offspring who would be hybrid, having both Bangladeshi and Pakistani origins. This was in direct contrast to the participatory roles of women as biological reproducers of an unadulterated ethnic race of Bengali Muslims. The intervention by abortion was introduced to get rid of any "enemy seeds" that posed a threat to the purity of the liberated nation. Bangladesh was proud of its pure Bengali lineage and did not want to risk introducing a generation of mixed origins, which would destabilize the homogeneity of the nation-state.

National honour was a driving force behind rehabilitating women in Bangladesh through the title of *birangona* and introducing intervention by abortion. The morality of Bangladesh rested on ethical, righteous, political, social, and human responsibility and ownership. In 1971, Bihari Muslim women were stripped of any agency during the genocide, as well as after. Women did not have a say in the decision making, and the nation-state did not distinguish between "the human angle, the political angle and the women's angle."

Bangladesh, like Pakistan, was designing itself on the basis of Islam. Aisha, the strong, pious, childless favourite wife of the Prophet, was a role model. *Birangonas* were encouraged to give up their children by constantly reminding them of Aisha, who was also childless. Once abortions were carried out, the *birangonas* were given economic empowerment through women's rehabilitation centres, where they were taught sewing, stitching, and cooking, among other domestic skills, to sustain themselves and earn a livelihood. Men were also encouraged to marry such women. Bangladeshi society treated its brave women as commodities, as items, and put price tags of monetary benefit on them. Men who agreed to marry the *birangonas* were promised permanent employment along with housing facilities from the government.

But there are several important questions that need to be asked. How were the raped women recognized as *birangonas*? Was the policy of restoring *birangonas* implemented at the grassroots level? Were the sexually violated women integrated into the society? Did they get married? Were they accepted in the newly liberated country? Did the golden land of Bengal welcome them and treat them equally as true heroines of war—as they considered the Mukti Bahini soldiers to be heroes?

Nayanika Mookherjee explains the efforts by the state to locate women who had been raped during the genocide:

> In the 1990s the international recognition of rape as a war crime also made it imperative for various Bangladeshi feminist and human rights activists to document histories of sexual violence committed during the 1971 war so as to provide supporting evidence to enable the trials of the collaborators. This entailed a search

for "grassroots," "subaltern" "war heroines" and the recording of their testimonies of rape by various left-liberal journalists, feminists, NGO activists, and human rights lawyers.[50]

It is because of this warrant of search, issued by the government of Bangladesh, that defiled women were located and interviewed. *Birangonas* were encouraged to speak up and give their testimonies, narrating their experiences in Gono Adalat (the People's Tribunal). The women were assured by the state that they would be given full protection and assistance as a reward for their brave act of testifying.

The state sanctioned various ways in which the women could lead a life of normalcy. However, the efforts proved counterproductive. Women were not taken care of by the government of Bangladesh. The women who were identified as *birangonas* recount that they were shunned and further ostracized by the society and labelled "fallen" and "loose." They were deemed to be "corrupt" women, equivalent to prostitutes. Ferdousi Priyabhashini is one of the most recognized women to speak out about her sexual assault during the 1971 War of Liberation. In an interview with Saikia, Priyabhasani claims that "[a]fter 1971, I was considered 'number one' prostitute in Bangladesh ... the first time I came out publically about my victimization in 1971 was in 1999. It took me 20 years to regain some sense of self-respect and be able to talk about it. People didn't like to hear about it initially. Strangers used to call and insult me asking me the price of my service."[51]

Instead of garnering any respect from society, *birangonas* were additionally forced to the periphery, as the nation looked down upon them as "pariahs," "untouchables," or worse—like prostitutes, sex-workers. The women were scorned by men and women alike, isolated or even disowned by their families. Rape—a very intimate act—was expected to be hidden from public knowledge, as it brought shame and dishonour to the society and its men. The fact that women would talk openly about their brutal rape experiences in the hope of employment and economic stability made them appear to symbolically sell their bodies, like prostitutes. They were objects of ridicule and were forced to constantly live in a state of disgrace and guilt.

Bangladesh, as an Islamic country, is conservative about women's sexuality. *Birangonas* choosing to come out into the open and accept the title along with the monetary benefits, made the Bengali men uncomfortable. Despite being the nation's chosen modus operandi, the conferring of the title of *birangonas* backfired. The Bangladeshi state failed its women, because it was not just the people but also the state who could not forgive them for the shame they brought to the golden land. The state failed to see that it was not the women's fault; they had been forced to have sexual intercourse with the enemy. They were innocent.

Saikia maintains that the state failed women like the war heroine Nur Begum by not living up to its promise of providing job opportunities. The state further humiliated them by removing their existence from the official history of the country. They were war heroines but were not valorized like the Mukti Bahinis. Those soldiers who fought for Bangladesh were seen as patriotic, strong, nationalistic, and courageous, whereas the *birangonas* like Begum were seen as a liability. On paper and in theory they were considered to be war heroines, while in reality they were not treated as such because of their gender and their defilement. As Begum claims,

I am an original *birangona*. My name is not included in any gazette. I don't have any record. All my papers and documents have been destroyed. A fake freedom fighter promised to marry me, to create a family with me. They got us married and he was given a government job, which he continues to enjoy. He is happily living with his wife and children, but I couldn't enjoy the same benefits or have a family with him. My child has suffered. Tell me what kind of country is this? People laugh at me, they jeer at me. Where can I get peace? It would have been better if I had died then. It is fruitless to live in this Bangladesh. Has it produced any result for people like us? I am asking you. Do you think this country will do any good for us? I am expressing my inner sorrows to people like you ... do they understand what a *birangona* is? Why she became a *birangona*? To fight for our freedom, to protect our country I became a *birangona*.[32]

The golden land of Bangladesh did not recognize these women as agents of change. It did not see them as contributing toward the freedom struggle. Instead, they were mocked, ridiculed, and further isolated. The title *birangona*, which had the positive connotation of war heroine, was distorted to *barangana*, referring to "penetration" and "women penetrated." This further put the burden of shame and responsibility on women, making them seem perpetually guilty.

In the novel *A Good Muslim,* we come across the character of Piya, who is sexually ravaged during the Liberation War. She is taken to the army camps along with many other women. Their hair is shaved off so they cannot strangle themselves; and they are brutally assaulted by as many as 20 or 30 soldiers, one after the other. The "bracelet-shaped scar" on her wrist testifies to the sheer violence meted out to her for nine consecutive months.[53]

The character of Maya is training to be a surgeon, and chooses to serve in various makeshift hospitals, carrying out the state-mandated procedure of abortion on the raped women. In the novel, Maya represents the voice of liberated Bangladesh who is critical of all the lies that the state made to its women. The author, Anam, ironically gives the voice of reason to this character who, despite carrying out her duties toward the nation-state, is critical of its policies:

Maya saw women like Piya every day at the rehabilitation center; they had been pouring into the city for weeks. Some had been raped in their villages, in front of their husbands and fathers; others kidnapped and held in the army barracks for the duration of the war. Maya was tasked with telling these women that their *lives would soon return to normal,* that they *would go home* and their *families would embrace them as heroes of the war.* She said this to their faces every day *knowing it was a lie,* and they listened silently, staring into their laps and willing it to be true. (emphasis added)[54]

Yet these women were not accepted back into their homes; their families and society at large did not accept them. In order to lead a life of normalcy some women chose to go back to Pakistan with their captors as they did not "want to be heroines" of the new nation-state. They were "ashamed." They wanted "to leave their shame behind, start again."[55]

The silence around rape and the victims of rape becomes evident in Anam's book when both Sohail and Maya discourage Piya from speaking out about her experiences—to hide the fact that she is pregnant. "Something had rippled within her, demanded to get out, and they had silenced it."[56] Society's silencing of the many Piyas further perpetuated the notion of guilt and shame. *Birangonas* like Piya, at a moment of utmost vulnerability, felt defeated and let down by society and the nation-state at large, which was compelling them to further hide away and obscure themselves from the world.

Rehana, who represents the iconic figure of the Mother, compels Maya to understand that women like Piya had no agency in choosing their lives. The state of Bangladesh decided for them, and "they forced her. And she is not the only one."[57] Maya, like her country, believes that in order to usher in new beginnings one needs to forget the past. Rehana reminds her that being a mother is the fundamental responsibility of the woman, and the nation-state of Bangladesh denied the *birangonas* the choice of motherhood.

Maya initially believes that the state is extending kindness to women like Piya by aborting the fetuses, as their wombs were "defiled by the enemy," "a vial of poison," and that they are carrying the "seeds of the enemy."[58] Women do not need to give birth to children who are "bastard" Pakistanis. It is only in due time that Maya's nationalistic fervour gains critical reasoning. She joins a group that discusses the war, and the post-war society of Bangladesh. It is at this moment that Maya realizes how women suffered during the war, and that the trial for the collaborators is the need of the hour. It is through the discussions held in the meetings that she sees the other side of nationalism—how the nation-state used women like her, indoctrinating them with a spirit of nationalism in order to carry out mass abortions. They used her to kill unborn babies and snatch away the agency of women, all in the name of nationalism and patriotism for the country. She then recognizes her own role as a perpetrator of the post-war violence against women like Piya. Maya realizes that "[t]hey had comforted her [Piya] and told her it was over, that she was safe; but they had not made it possible for her to speak. It was an act of kindness that had led to the end of everything—Maya knew that now."⁵⁹

Women are often seen as victims of the war—as inevitable casualties. However, it is important to see that the women of Bangladesh had more roles than just rape victim and *birangona*. They were potential aggressive agents during and after the Liberation War. They were passionate about their country and contributed to creating a better society, which had humanity or *insaniyat* as its core value.

In *A Golden Age*, Maya, from the beginning, is engaged in student politics. Despite being an Urdu-speaker and having no historic space for herself in the nation-state of Bangladesh, she creates a space for herself to contribute toward the rebellion movement against the Pakistan Army. Through the character of Maya, Anam highlights the importance and presence of women in the making of Bangladesh. The female characters Maya and Rehana are active contributors to the war. The author brings in the mystic relationship between women-sexuality-nation through Maya and Rehana. If Rehana is the iconic Mother figure, her daughter is the iconic female participant in the war who goes missing in the official narrative of Bangladesh. Maya wants to be actively involved in each and every step of the movement. She wants to experience for herself the events, and not simply be informed about them. She wants a physical, bodily marker to identify herself as bleeding for the cause of Bangladesh. Her absence from Rokeya Hall during Operation Searchlight makes her feel isolated and left out from the nation-making process. "At first Maya was vaguely irritated she'd missed everything. All her friends had stories of that night, and while she slept saying, 'Good thing I wasn't on campus,' there was a slight regret at having been sidelined. She wanted some mark, some sign that the thing had happened to her. A bruise on the cheek. A tear in her blouse."⁶⁰

Anam's character of Maya from *A Golden Age* and *A Good Muslim*, as well the character of Suri, the young woman from *Of Martyrs and Marigolds*, epitomize women being appropriated with the landscape of Bangladesh. Maya remembers, in *A Good Muslim*, "all through the movement, [she] had walked barefoot from Elephant Road to Shaheed Minar in red-and-white saris, greeting one another with the national salutation, *Joy Bangla*.

Victory to Bengal,"[61] while Suri adorns herself with orange and yellow marigolds to commemorate the death of the six Bengali martyrs during the Language Riots of 1952. Women like Maya and Suri decorate their bodies in celebration of the newly created nation-state of Bangladesh. The act of wearing marigolds and walking barefoot become symptomatic of the larger nation-state of Bangladesh celebrating its newly acquired freedom.

Maya, throughout Anam's two novels, is invested in the making of the golden land of Bangladesh. Aspiring to be a surgeon, she trains instead to be a country doctor, as the need of the hour demands it from her. Country doctors like Maya are important since "that's what people need out there, someone to help them deliver babies."[62] Maya carries an immense burden of guilt within her because of the many abortions she willingly performs after the war. It is the guilt of killing so many babies and snatching away the agency of the women that forces Maya to become the mouthpiece for all *birangonas*. Maya wants to write a short editorial on the war criminal trial. Inspired by Jahanara Imam, who has called for a trial, Maya wants people to remember the war—especially to assure the women that people have not forgotten them. Maya wants to stand up for the rights of the raped women, the *birangonas*, as she believes that "calling them heroines erases what really happened to them. They didn't charge into the battlefield and ask to be given medals. They were just the damage, the war trophies. They deserve for us to remember."[63]

In *A Good Muslim*, Piya becomes a catalyst to ignite the spark of realization within Maya to chronicle the violence inflicted on women and the state's failure of its war heroines. Maya cannot get the image of Piya out of her mind: "Piya squatting on the verandah, the words bubbling at her lips. She and Sohail had conspired against her that night. They had comforted her and told her it was over, that she was safe—but they had not made it possible for her to speak. It was an act of kindness that had led to the end of everything—Maya knew that now. And there was only one way to make it right."[64] Maya cleanses her guilt by writing an article calling the dictator a war criminal, for which she is arrested. Her act of speaking up on behalf of the *birangonas* comes full circle when the trial takes place and Piya steps forward to give her testimony:

I was captured by the Pakistan Army on 26 July, 1971. They came to raid my village; someone had told them we were hiding the guerrillas. My father was killed ... I was put on a truck, our neighbour's daughter was with me; she was only fourteen ... we were chained to the wall. Someone had been there before us—we saw her name scratched into the wall. She had hanged herself, so they shaved our hair and took our saris ... twenty, thirty. They took turns. After the other girl died, it was just me.[65]

Piya, unlike most other *birangonas*, practises her personal agency and does not abort her child. She raises the child and names him Sohail—dedicating her child to the man who saved her life, Sohail, Maya's brother. Maya is proud of Piya's bravery and her decision to testify against the war criminals. It is through Piya that Maya recognizes that the history of Bangladesh carries the wounds of many women like Piya, and that these wounds have not been addressed. The only way they can be healed is to recognize women not just as victims but also as real human beings with a right to dignity, choice, and life.

Yet, women like Maya and Rehana, who helped in rehabilitating women back into society, were not seen as brave heroes. Suri's mother in the novel *Of Martyrs and Marigolds*, despite her Urdu-speaking ethnicity, is actively involved in the rehabilitation process. She joins the Women's Association to help set up relief camps in Mirpur for the rescued Urdu-speaking women and children. "The Women's Association collected as much food, clothing, and utensils as it could."[66] However, women's contributions toward the war were limited to providing domestic help and lending emotional support. Saikia, on interviewing women who provided their services during the war, notes the following:

Women who were introduced to me as "important social workers" they could not tell me about their work; it was difficult for them to talk about it. They did not see their activities during the war as particularly meaningful or their post-war contributions as part of the healing process of the nation. Sometimes, they described difficult situations that they encountered and the immediate and intuitive assistance that they provided. For them these were not heroic acts but were "small gestures" owed to family and friends. They talked about them as routine work—to care for others—and did not claim special status as heroes because they responded to the need of another person. Precisely because they did not talk of the work as conscious acts of bravado but presented them as "duty," the work that individual women did during and after the war has gone largely unnoticed in the national register.[67]

The process of nation-making deliberately obliterated women's services, as women themselves became complicit in undervaluing their roles and responsibilities. Their contribution toward the war was only a personal, emotional response that stemmed from their deep care and affection for others. I argue that the gender roles imposed on their identity made them perhaps internalize themselves as care providers and not freedom fighters. The character of Piya becomes an important signifier denoting the glaring absence of Bihari Muslim women from the official history of Bangladesh. The title of *birangona* was exclusive and did not cover the "world's forgotten lost," failing to unite these women within the framework of the nation-making process. Novelists Anam and Ismail debunk the missing subjectivities from the national history of Bangladesh by sketching characters like Maya, Rehana, Piya, Suri, Sharmeen, and others who were involved to the best of their capacity in the making of the nation-state of Bangladesh.

Conclusion

Genocide under the cover of war can be convoluted. The genocidal activity that occurred during the 1971 War of Liberation, which spawned the new nation-state of Bangladesh, was no exception. During the war, the West Pakistan Army targeted and killed not only Bengali Muslims, but also Bihari Muslims. The Bengali Muslims and Bihari Muslims also attacked each other over long-simmering grievances related to political, social, and linguistic differences. The violent carnage by the Pakistan Army against the Bengali population during the war is well researched and documented; however, little is known or written about the suffering of the Bihari Muslims who were torn between the two countries of Pakistan and Bangladesh. The plight of the Bihari Muslims, rendered "stateless refugees," and the privations of their community during and after the Liberation War has been left out of the official history of Bangladesh.

Rounaq Jahan identifies the "systematic and organized rape" of women by the Pakistanis as one of several distinct stages of genocidal activity during the 1971 war.[68] Yet this violence against women—both Bengali and Bihari—during the Liberation War has largely been left out of much of the narrative regarding the war. The organized history of Bangladesh strategically mentions women as necessary casualties—collateral damage in the midst of the new nation's birth. But this birth of a new nation-state was painful for the women forced to endure it. It is estimated that approximately 200,000 young girls or women were raped. Rape became an effective part of the toolbox used by men within the war.

Women's lives were shattered, with no guilt or remorse, by the states of Bangladesh and Pakistan. The voices of the sexually exploited, brutally terrorized, and mostly silent women give us an understanding of the loss of humanity during the war. Their identity as women made them viable targets for unfathomable cruelty, violence, and humiliation. In this chapter, I have attempted to erase the distinction between the violence against women and the Liberation War. Instead, the violence that accompanied the war should be seen as a building block on which the community and nation at large was built. By doing so, I have attempted to investigate the complicated relationship among history, nation, and women. Wartime rape has been studied as a singular event that brought Bengali- and Urdu-speaking women together and united them in bonds of humanity and shared experiences. The bodies of women were used to subjugate, defile, and humiliate the other side. Yet the plight of Urdu-speaking Bihari Muslim women during the war remains overlooked and understudied. The nation-state of Bangladesh failed the Bihari Muslim women after the Liberation War by displacing them in the newly formed land of Bangladesh, by calling them Biharis, by omitting the violence that was meted out to them, and by denying them the right to fair trials to punish the perpetrators.

Perceiving gendered experiences is important in understanding the social, economic, political, and cultural matrix of women and genocide. Just as Ofer and Weitzman identified the missing voices of Jewish women within Holocaust studies, the Bihari Muslim women are the invisible subjects in the history of Bangladesh. These women were exploited and violated during the Liberation War, but the atrocities and crimes committed against them are rarely mentioned. The past as well as present-day suffering of Bihari Muslim women is distanced and not considered part of the history of Bangladesh. Finally, a cross-cultural and comparative framework of women's experiences can give voice to these forgotten women.

Questions

1. How does orchestrated gender violence and victimization of women aid in the nation-building process?
2. What are the different factors that contributed toward the invisible identity of Bihari Muslim women during and after the 1971 War of Liberation?
3. What constitutes "home" for women? Can a monolithic concept of "home" be applicable to Bihari Muslims, especially when they negotiate their existence vis-à-vis their ethnicity and diasporic sensibility?
4. How do women contribute in making and narrating the nation-state?

Notes

1. For further information on the history of India, Pakistan, Bangladesh, and the partition, see Rounaq Jahan, "Genocide in Bangladesh," in *Centuries of Genocide: Essays and Eyewitness Accounts*, ed. Samuel Totten and William S. Parsons (New York: Routledge, 2013), 249–276. See also Anthony Mascarenes, *The Rape of Bangladesh* (New Delhi: Vikas, 1971); S. Siddiq, *Witness to Surrender* (Karachi: Oxford University Press, 1977); G. W. Choudhury, *The Last Days of United Pakistan* (London: Hurst and Company, 1975); or R. Sisson and L. E. Rose, *War and Secession: Pakistan, India and the Creation of Bangladesh* (Berkeley: University of California Press, 1990).

2. Aquila Ismail, *Of Martyrs and Marigolds* (North Charleston: Createspace, 2011); Tahmima Anam, *A Golden Age* (New Delhi: Penguin Books, 2011); and Tahmima Anam, *A Good Muslim* (New Delhi: Penguin Books, 2012).

3. Female, with a capital "F," is used symbolically for all women irrespective of caste, religion, or ethnicity.

4. Gyanendra Pandey, *Remembering Partition* (New Delhi: Cambridge University Press, 2001).

5. Ibid., 7.

6. Dalia Ofer and Lenore J. Weitzman, eds., *Women in the Holocaust* (New Haven: Yale University Press, 1998), 1.

7. Joan Kelly, *Women, History and Theory* (Chicago: University of Chicago Press, 1984), 2.

8. Yasmin Saikia, *Women, War and the Making of Bangladesh: Remembering 1971* (New Delhi: Women Unlimited, 2011).

9. Ibid., 11.

10. Ibid., 50–51.

11. Anam, *A Golden Age*, 66.

12. Ismail, *Of Martyrs and Marigolds*, 118.

13. Ofer and Weitzman, *Women in the Holocaust*, 8.

14. Ismail, *Of Martyrs and Marigolds*, 119.

15. Ritu Menon and Kamla Bhasin, *Borders and Boundaries: Women in India's Partition* (New Delhi: Kali for Women, 2007), 43 (emphasis in original).

16. Susan Brownmiller, *Against Our Will: Men, Women and Rape* (New York: Penguin Books, 1975), 14.

17. Saikia, *Women, War and the Making of Bangladesh*, 69.

18. Ismail, *Of Martyrs and Marigolds*, 194.

19. Claudia Card, "Rape as a Weapon of War," *Hypatia* 11, no. 4 (Autumn, 1996): 7.

20. Ibid., 8.

21. Ismail, *Of Martyrs and Marigolds*, 4.

22. Ibid., 5.

23. Urvashi Butalia, "An Archive with a Difference: Partition Letters," in *The Partitions of Memory: The Afterlife of the Division of India*, ed. Suvir Kaul (Ranikhet: Permanent Black, 2011), 125.

24. Saikia, *Women, War and the Making of Bangladesh*, 187.

25. Ibid., 126.

26. Veena Das, "Language and Body: Transactions in the Construction of Pain," *Daedalus* 125, no. 1 (Winter, 1996): 84.

27. Saikia, *Women, War and the Making of Bangladesh*, 173.

28. Ismail, *Of Martyrs and Marigolds*, 189.

29. Anam, *A Golden Age*, 81.

30. Ibid., 82.

31. Ibid., 86.

32. Ibid., 87.

33. *Mother* with a capital "M" is used as an iconic figure representing the nation-state, while mother with a small "m" is used to define one of the many roles of women laid down by society; for example, mother, daughter, sister, and wife. The iconic Mother figure is an image that stands for the various characteristics of motherhood. The characteristics of motherhood are then appropriated by the nation-state.

34. Das, "Language and Body," 74–75.

35. Ibid., 74–75.

36. Lynn Bennett, *Dangerous Wives and Sacred Sisters: Social and Symbolic Roles of Women in Nepal* (New York: Columbia University Press, 1983), 262–274. Nations have always been associated with female divine powers. A similar parallel exists in Hindu pantheon of the chaste warrior virgins in Durga and Kali and the erotic, feminine wife in Parvati.

37. Anam, *A Golden Age*, 162.

38. Ibid., 55.

39. Ibid., 55.

40. Ibid., 55.

41. Ibid., 57.

42. Ibid., 57.

43. Ibid., 58.

44. Ibid., 106.

45. Ibid., 211.

46. Saikia, *Women, War and the Making of Bangladesh*, 85.

47. Ibid., 202.

48. Ofer and Weitzman, *Women in the Holocaust*, 7.

49. Nira Yuval-Davis and Floya Anthias, eds., *Women-Nation-State* (London: Macmillan, 1989), 6–11.

50. Nayanika Mookherjee, "'Remembering to Forget': Public Secrecy and Memory of Sexual Violence in the Bangladesh War of 1971," *Journal of the Royal Anthropological Institute* 12, no. 2 (June 2006): 436.

51. Saikia, *Women, War and the Making of Bangladesh*, 165–166.

52. Ibid., 147.

53. Anam, *A Good Muslim*, 72.

54. Ibid., 69.

55. Ibid., 70.

56. Ibid., 76.

57. Ibid., 141.

58. Ibid., 244.

59. Ibid., 224.

60. Anam, *A Golden Age*, 118.

61. Anam, *A Good Muslim*, 43.

62. Ibid., 51.

63. Ibid., 223.

64. Ibid., 223–224.

65. Ibid., 292–293.

66. Ismail, *Of Martyrs and Marigolds*, 151.

67. Saikia, *Women, War and the Making of Bangladesh*, 192.

68. Rounaq Jahan, "Genocide in Bangladesh," 255.

CHAPTER 5

What Is Remembered?
Gendered Silence, Sexual Violence, and the Khmer Rouge Atrocity

Theresa de Langis

Introduction

Dalia Ofer and Lenore J. Weitzman's edited volume *Women in the Holocaust* represents a watershed moment in feminist genocide studies. In collecting a series of historical accounts of the Holocaust that "envision the specificity of everyday life and the different ways in which men and women responded to the Nazi onslaught," the volume demonstrates the imperative of a gender analysis to accomplish a "richer and more finely nuanced understanding" of atrocity.[1] By attending to the structural sources of gender difference—the specific social positions of power and influence occupied by men and women, and wherein most often women are subordinated to men—genocide scholars "begin to ask questions about the social expectations and behaviors of men and women" that allow "social patterns [to] become more noticeable and [to] take on added meaning" within and across atrocity scenarios.[2] Such analysis exposes our received "master narratives" as partial and insufficient precisely for their lack of perception around women's lived experiences, their agency, and their survival choices while occupying subordinate positions of power in the midst of state massacre.[3]

If women's experience generally is neglected in historical accounts of mass tragedy, then women's experience of sexual violence—deeply rooted in gendered power imbalances that serve to exert male domination and control over women—for too long has occupied the space of "blind spot" in received historical accounts of genocide and state atrocity. Shulamit Reinharz, in the foreword to another seminal text, *Sexual Violence Against Jewish Women During the Holocaust*, writes of just such an historical elision:

> It's as if the issue [sexual violence against Jewish women by Germans soldiers] was always there, but I didn't see it because no one had pointed it out and labeled it as such. I also did not notice sexual abuse because it was always part of the larger story such as deportation, camp life, and murder. I expect that after reading this volume, others will react as I did. The awareness will haunt them—they will see what was hidden but always there before their very eyes.[4]

The passage is extremely suggestive in pointing to how the silence surrounding sexual violations in times of atrocity is multivalent. Indeed, despite great gains over the past two decades to adjudicate conflict-related sexual crimes, such violence continues to be so normalized and pervasive that it may prove invisible ("I also did not notice sexual abuse because it was always part of the larger story").[5] Additionally, even when noticed, the passage intimates, such acts are often not assessed as violations ("no one had pointed it out and labeled it as such"). Significantly, the passage suggests, these crimes are not so much overlooked as they are actively suppressed ("hidden"). Indeed, the chapters of the volume present a myriad of suppressions of sexual-violence histories as linked to the genocide, silenced by direct and structural gender discrimination that serves to discount sexual violence claims by placing shame and blame on victims and ensuring impunity for perpetrators.

In regards to the rape of Jewish women by German state actors during the Holocaust, the accepted thesis has long held that it did not happen, based on the "mistaken belief about the unwavering German implementation of *Rassenschande*" and contrary to numerous sources that testify to rape as part of the genocidal tactics of the Holocaust.[6] When actual victims of Holocaust-related rape did come forward, they were told their experiences were isolated cases, "exceptions to the rule," and therefore insignificant to the scope of the full atrocity.[7] Scholars who attempted to rectify the elision of sexual violence as part of the Nazi atrocity (deemed a "feminist agenda") were seen to "trivialize or banalize" the totality of the Jewish tragedy.[8] Indeed, in light of the many suppressed narratives surrounding sexual violation during the Holocaust, an important question emerges: What is remembered about mass state violence and genocide, and how is it remembered? This is a matter of incomplete history, as well as incomplete justice.

Comparison with the Cambodian atrocity is a case in point, and parallels with the Holocaust in the treatment of sexual violence as part of the state massacre are uncanny—and could only have been meaningfully analyzed via the gender analysis approach advocated by Ofer and Weitzman.[9] In both the German and Cambodian instances, "political history" takes precedence over "social history"[10]: the "hard" evidence of a written official policy has been prioritized over and validated as more legitimate than personal accounts at the local domain of lived experience situated within a specific cultural context.[11] In virtually identical theses, sexual violence claims in both scenarios have been historically dismissed and largely divorced from the greater context of state mass violence. In Cambodia, the dominant historical narrative has asserted that due to an official policy—Code #6, or the rule against "immoral offences"—sexual violence under Pol Pot's ultra-Maoist Khmer Rouge regime (1975–1979) rarely occurred and was harshly punished when it did take place.[12] Yet as feminist and human rights scholars have begun to seriously examine personal accounts in both the Cambodian and German contexts, so too has a counter-narrative developed around the way Code #6 was operationalized as a lived reality: the "rule," historically assumed in either scenario as an anti-rape measure, did not protect women from abuse, but rather put them at greater risk of sexual violation, precisely by exploiting deeply entrenched gender stereotypes about women's (sexual) submission and subordination.[13]

In Cambodia, historical elision is made more urgent by the current hybrid tribunal, the Extraordinary Chambers in the Courts of Cambodia (ECCC), created in 2006 to bring those most responsible from Khmer Rouge leadership to justice for crimes committed under the regime. Its present trial, Case 002, is considered one of the most complex in scope and gravity since the Nuremberg Tribunal, reckoning with the highest death toll from mass atrocity since the Holocaust.[14] Jurisdiction covers the precise days of the Khmer Rouge regime—April 17, 1975, to January 7, 1979—and focuses on the catastrophic consequences of the regime's collectivist policies, from which an estimated quarter of the total population is calculated to have perished from starvation, overwork, illness, persecution, forced relocation, torture, and execution. To achieve its ideological aim of establishing a communist agrarian utopia, the regime—ominously referred to as Angkar, or the Organization—forcibly evacuated all cities (including the whole of Phnom Penh) and separated the country's population into "new" people (evacuees from urban centres suspected of capitalistic tendencies) and "old" people (an idealized, largely uneducated, rural farming class). The regime instituted a new calendar, beginning at Year Zero, and all individual human rights were suspended; private property and money were abolished; religion and the practice of cultural rites prohibited; and tens of thousands of people were arbitrarily executed for even the smallest infraction and without due process of law. Working as slave labour on farming and infrastructure projects, the population suffered from mass starvation, disallowed from eating the very rice they produced and harvested. Perhaps most dramatically, the private family itself was dismantled and all aspects of living were collectivized, including wet nursing, child-rearing, food preparation, and eating, with family members separated by age and sex into work units, most often mobile and with few visitation rights. As a means of increasing the labour pool and reproducing a pure revolutionary class, thousands of strangers were assigned spouses by Angkar and forced to marry, with penalty of punishment or death for refusal and no special provisions for work assignments or food rations for pregnant women.[15]

These elements of the atrocity have long been part of the established historical record.[16] What has proven a persistent blind spot in historical accounts is a gender analysis of differential treatment and impacts, including atrocity-related gender-based violence. This oversight is also evident in the proceedings of the ECCC, critiqued by feminist scholars for its "reluctant and narrow" approach in taking up sexual and gender-based crimes under the regime.[17] Indeed, while the policy implementation of forced marriage was widely noted in even the earliest historical accounts,[18] the *charge of the crime* of forced marriage was not brought against the accused by the ECCC until 2009—and then only after considerable advocacy from victims and their lawyers about how such marriages were a form of gender-based violence.[19] As for rape outside of forced marriages, and gender-based violence more broadly, the ECCC's investigations for Case 002 have determined the accused cannot be liable for such crimes, if they did occur, due to an official Khmer Rouge policy that served to prohibit rape and punish perpetrators, namely Code #6. Such a conclusion stands in stark contrast to a mounting body of research documenting acts of sexual violations by Khmer Rouge actors that include rape, gang rape, mass rape, rape as part of torture, sexual mutilation and humiliation, and rape of enemies prior to execution, among others.[20] Many surviving victims, meanwhile, continue to live with stigma and shame associated with sexual violations.

When it comes to genocide and mass atrocity, what is remembered and how? If the ECCC is "the official vessel for depositing memory" about the Khmer Rouge atrocity, then it by default "fails to offer a way for those outside its jurisdiction to express their narratives" about their distinct experience of atrocity.[21] Meanwhile, there exists generally a "desperation of survivors to tell the story, to communicate their experience ... to the world, and to be believed when they tell the story."[22] Such "desperation" to be heard and to be believed is especially salient for those whose narrative of the atrocity has been actively repressed, hidden from view, silent, and also silenced for decades.

Today, almost four decades since the fall of the regime, Cambodian women are coming forward to break the taboo around speaking their full experiences of gender-based violence under the Khmer Rouge. This chapter presents an interpretation of one such survivor's account, the life-story oral history narrative of Sok Samith, a female survivor of the regime and a witness to sexual and gender-based violence, including forced marriage and Code #6.[23] Her personal narrative is analyzed to explore the specificity of women's experience as embedded in gender ideologies across the lifespan—providing important context to the atrocity itself—and to examine "the cultural definitions and expectations of the two sexes" and their relative positions of power as a means to better understand the "differences in how men and women experience[d] their lives" under the Khmer Rouge regime.[24] The intent of the chapter is not to present new legal evidence for consideration by the ECCC, and the chapter's concern with sexualized violence may be a broader category than legal definitions would allow in a court of law. Indeed, one of the advantages of oral history methodology is its ability to provide a platform for female survivors of the Cambodian atrocity to have full authority over their own narratives about the wide-ranging nature of their experiences *as women*, including and outside of sexual violence and above and beyond adjudicative aims and strictures. To accomplish a gender analysis of mass atrocity that prioritizes women's agency within their specific socially circumscribed spheres of power and influence, the reading of Sok Samith's narrative is organized around the four-part framework provided by Ofer and Weitzman: (1) the culturally defined roles of proper Cambodian womanhood across Sok Samith's lifespan, from 1960 to the present; (2) the anticipatory responses she and other women deployed as strategies for survival during the armed conflict, atrocity, and genocide; (3) the extent to which women were treated differently than men as part of the atrocity; and (4) her reaction and those of other women to the physical and emotional circumstances of experiencing atrocity. In looking at the blind spots with a gendered lens, new interpretative space opens up around our understanding of the Khmer Rouge atrocity, especially in how the most widespread of violations (collective eating or the breakup of the family, for example) held unique significance for women due to their traditional gender roles, as well as how women's socio-cultural gender identities left them vulnerable to sexual exploitation and abuse directly related to the aims and purposes of the state's mass violence.

Biography

Sok Samith was born in 1960 in Phnom Penh, the youngest of seven siblings. In 1968, she moved with her parents to the family's paternal home village in Svay Rieng, a rural province on the Cambodian border with Vietnam. Sok Samith's parents, like virtually all residents of the countryside, primarily worked in some aspect of rice farming. In off-periods, her mother was a trader between Vietnam and Phnom Penh, and Sok Samith stayed alone with her abusive, alcoholic father for extended periods of time. As their village was situated on the Vietnam border, the area was greatly affected by the massive illegal carpet bombing by the United States between 1969 and 1970 that killed tens of thousands of Cambodian civilians, driving massive migration into Phnom Penh, and swelling the ranks of the extremist Khmer Rouge insurgency.[25] By 1970, the country was in a full-fledged civil war, greatly exacerbated by geopolitics, between Khmer Rouge fighters (backed by North Vietnam) and the government of General Lon Nol (backed by the United States and, consequently, South Vietnamese forces). That same year, Sok Samith and her parents fled back to Phnom Penh, and it was from there that she witnessed the fall of the government to the Khmer Rouge in 1975. In three days' time, the entire city was emptied of its population, and Sok Samith and her family were forcibly evacuated along with two million other residents into the countryside. She was 15 years old. The family was split up during the relocation, and Sok Samith was luckier than many to have remained nearby her mother and a sister for the duration of the regime over the next four years.

Following the Khmer Rouge's fall in 1979, Sok Samith returned to Phnom Penh to support herself and her mother, working primarily in the hospitality industry, burgeoning after the arrival of the United Nations (UN) and the opening of the country to the international community in the early 1990s. Like many Cambodian women in her cohort, she has accomplished only a few years of schooling in her lifetime, and her employment prospects have remained limited. Today, even as she continues to suffer from the economic, physical, and emotional effects of her Khmer Rouge experiences, Sok Samith is a frequent speaker on radio and in public forums on the importance of keeping the memory of the atrocity alive for future generations, especially in terms of violence against women, as an initial step in remediating root causes that make atrocity and genocide possible in the first place. It is with her permission that I use her full name and her narrative for this analysis.

The Impact of Culturally Defined Roles on Women: Mediated Identity

> We had the "woman's law." Women must know what is right and wrong, how to take care of the husband and the family and relatives, how to be honest and not to have love affairs. The woman must respect her husband in all things.... This is one reason my mother could not leave my father.

Understanding how gender identity is socially constructed in a particular context is imperative to opening interpretative space about what is "hidden but always in view" in terms of the distinct ways women and men experience genocide and atrocity. Sok Samith's passage opening this section refers to just such a socio-cultural construction in the Cambodian context, the *Chpab Srey*, or women's law, a prescriptive idealized gender ideology codified in a long Buddhist poem often attributed to King Ang Dong in the 19th century. *Chpab Srey* articulates women's appropriate behaviour as embedded in religious, cultural, and national identity, with her "purity" standing as sign and cipher of the honour and dignity of the nation writ large.[26] In a Buddhist context, the implications are far-reaching, with family harmony a signal of good karmic status in present and future lives.[27] As a deeply entrenched normative text (the poem was taught in the public schools until 2006), the conservative gender ideology of the poem has been noted to constitute a restrictive cultural stereotype that rationalizes discrimination against women and hinders their full realization of human rights.[28]

The ideal woman of *Chpab Srey* is a wife, and the poem is largely directed to women in this role. Her virginity at marriage (the sign of a dutiful daughter) and her fidelity within it (the sign of an obedient wife) are paramount to her social value and mark her as the sexual property of men.

A self-in-relation to the needs and interests of others (her parents, her husband, her children), she is assumed as submissive and subordinate to her husband: she must address him as senior (*bong*) even when he is younger; she must fulfill his sexual demands as part of her wifely obligations; and she must never talk badly about his abusive behaviour or sexual infidelities.[29] Indeed, in evoking women's purity, patience, and silence in relation to her husband, *Chpab Srey* likewise calls upon women to receive acts of violent abuse as normalized. Sok Samith describes the physical and violent inscription of male (sexual) appropriation of the female body as rationalized through *Chpab Srey* in describing her father's abuse of her mother: "I lived in a poor family. My father was always drinking and it made my mother suffer. He was a violent man, and he used violence on my mother. Yes, what he needed or what he wanted, he would take. I remember my mother crying when he forced her to have sex with him. She always, always, always was suffering."

Within the logic of *Chpab Srey*, to speak out about abuse amounts to self-incrimination, as blame is placed on the wife for not knowing (to use Sok Samith's words from the opening passage) "what is right and wrong," "how to take care of a husband," or how to "respect [the] husband in all things." This same exhortation for silence holds for victims of sexual abuse: as any sex outside marriage irreparably tarnishes the value of a woman, and in turn the honour of the family, speaking about such things leads to shame and stigma for victims, incentivizing silence and secrecy.[30] And, as *Chpab Srey* limits what can be spoken aloud about abuse, so too does it constrict the available options for escape. As Sok Samith says of the *Chpab Srey*, "This is one reason my mother could not leave my father."

As *Chpab Srey* rationalizes a male prerogative to use (sexualized) violence in exerting domination over women, such violence fundamentally serves to engender its victims. Rather than a personal or private violence, such abuse is part of the cultural fabric that designates gendered status and roles. Further, such abuse is maintained through structural violence, both in terms of the lack of social protections and legal recourse available to victims (most often suspended during states of emergency, if they exist at all), as well as in the complicity of communities in legitimizing the restrictive gender ideology of *Chpab Srey* through tolerance of abuse. Sok Samith links her mother's abuse to the culturally prescribed subordinate status of women generally, and the power wielded by men to exert dominance:

> I think violence in the family happened a lot at the time I was a child, and not only to my mother or in my family. A lot of women went through this.... The men had power over women, and they could beat, hurt, or rape their wives, and the neighbors didn't dare to get involved. So, after my father abused my mother, after my mother stopped crying, three or four or five days, my father would came back home and talk softly. My mother would forgive and agree he could return. And the abuse would begin again.

As Sok Samith describes, violence against women in her community, even when visible, remained hidden, repressed, and silenced—and as such serves to perpetuate patriarchal male privilege and sexual preroga-tive. The cyclical nature of the abuse ("My mother would forgive.... [T]he abuse would begin again") underscores the assumed dependency of wives on husbands that exceeds the economic (such as in this case, where the wife is the primary breadwinner for the family) and configures the ideal woman as an identity in relation to and mediated by men and (latent or actual) male violence.

This reading is not to suggest that all men are abusers and that all women are victims of abuse, before, during, or after the Khmer Rouge regime, due to the tenets of *Chpab Srey*. The code is an ideal, prescriptive rather than descriptive. Its applications are also variant, based on other identity markers, such as class and race. Nevertheless, such cultural codes of gendered identity influence and inform available expressions of iden-tity and agency, resulting in distinct consequences in the lived reality of women's lives as they struggled to survive atrocity.

Women's Anticipatory Responses: Mediated Agency and Survival Strategies

If *Chpab Srey* codifies a paradigm wherein an idealized woman's identity is mediated by (male) violence, so too does it impact her agency, or what Ofer and Weitzman call "anticipatory responses." Women are never subsumed completely as victims of their (violent) circumstances, but rather are also agents with options for action. Nevertheless, cultural definitions of womanhood, such as *Chpab Srey*, serve to delimit what acts constitute appropriate behaviour and what choices are available for action in a particular context. In times of armed conflict, genocide, and atrocity, such cultural norms—deeply embedded and culturally entrenched—are not simply suspended. They continue to operate at deep levels of identity and circumscribe women's available response options. Sok Samith gives an example of her mother's attempt to exert agency in the midst of intersecting personal and state violence during the outbreak of Cambodia's civil war:

> The war began in Svay Rieng province in 1970.[31] We lived outside the village, far from the other houses, and we had to run a far way to our neighbor's house for safety against the fighting. But at times my father refused to go. He said there would be no privacy and he would not be able to have sex with my mother. They fought loudly, accusing each other, and I was young, I was crying. I remember one time, the fighting around us was very bad and my mother wanted to leave for safety. [Cries.] My father violently forced my mother to have sex right then and there. We were under our house,[32] and I could see my mother and my father naked in the moonlight. He was happy with what he had done, smiling, and my mother was crying, crying.

Despite her mother's efforts to escape the violence—both the domestic abuse and the armed conflict—such agency is thwarted by her social status as a male-mediated subject—or, indeed, a male-owned (sexual) object, in a patriarchal framework of power. The passage points to the abusive tactics of control at the personal level: the isolation of the abused ("we lived outside the village"); possessive control of the abuser ("my father refused to go"); and the use of sexual violence to exert domination ("My father violently forced my mother"). As a lived reality, the partition between public and private violence dissolves in the scene, as they are experienced cyclically, accumulatively, and as a continuum. While the case of Sok Samith's mother may be extreme, her narrative warns not to dismiss it as exceptional as many women in the period were subjected to violent male control in alignment with the conservative gender ideology of *Chpab Srey*.

It is important to note the agency Sok Samith's mother does exert in the narrative: she shouts loudly at her husband despite his abuse; later in the narrative, she successfully relocates the family to Phnom Penh for safety. Yet such a power asymmetry, within a context of actual and latent multi-dimensional violence (personal, structural, and state), disciplines woman's behaviour and restricts her direct, unmediated agency. It is necessary, therefore, to look for women's responses in a different light: if to take overt action is to risk exposure to violence and condemnation, then the agency of the subordinate subject is more likely (and more safely) expressed as covert action. Such agency, precisely in seeming not to act, may be difficult to register, but it nevertheless carries efficacy and potency.

The Khmer Rouge regime, in its brutal totalitarian rule, is an adequate case to test such a thesis about women's covert agency under oppressive circumstances. The regime's forced marriage policy in particular is an instance where women, seemingly bereft of all possible options, managed to influence outcomes, at times not only covertly but subversively.

Sok Samith describes the forced marriage of her widowed sister, Rothana,[33] to a Khmer Rouge official more than twice her age:

> My sister was forced to marry by the Khmer Rouge after her husband died of malaria in 1977. She had two small children, one only eight months old, when she was told she would marry. She tried to refuse, saying she had two children already, one still a baby, and my father had recently died and she could not ask his permission. The cadre told her if she refused she would be killed. My sister thought mother was old and I was still young, so she agreed for the family.

The passage describes the double bind placed upon women when contending with competing patriarchies: on the one hand, to marry without the father's approval is an act of disobedience that carries negative social and karmic consequences; on the other hand, to refuse the patriarchal state is to risk death. The passage also explicitly links forced marriage to its reproductive aims and therefore appropriation of women's bodies ("She tried to refuse, saying she had two children already"). Indeed, the passage suggests, one of the immediate consequences of the Khmer Rouge dogma was Angkar's monopoly over women's bodies, and violence against these bodies, as state prerogative.

Sok Samith's description of Rothana's wedding procedure makes clear the utilitarian nature of the mass-produced unions forced by the regime, with women as the sexual object of exchange:

> She married along with thirty other couples, and when she entered the room she had no idea who her husband would be. Parents and relatives were not allowed to attend. The men sat in rows on one side of the room, the women in rows on the other side. At the front of the room were two empty chairs; they called the man, and then they called the woman to sit next to him. When he held her hand, she realized he was now her husband. My sister was twenty-three-years-old, and that man was sixty-years-old, older than our father had been. He was the cadre in charge of logistics for the district.

Recent research has contributed to a much deeper understanding of forced marriages. We have, in particular, much greater detail about the forced conjugal relations for the three days following the wedding procedure, often under the surveillance of Khmer Rouge spies.[34] Forced conjugal relations resulted in the rape of many women within forced marriages. Men, who were also victims of forced marriage, were sometimes both victims and perpetrators in terms of forced conjugal relations, as they were at times compelled to rape recalcitrant wives or face death themselves.[35] Yet the system also provided men with certain prerogatives, with many permitted to "request" wives for final approval by the patriarch, Angkar, mirroring traditional wedding proposals. Khmer Rouge actors may have been provided special dispensation to choose wives according to their rank and status, as Sok Samith's passage suggests. Women, in contrast, were not permitted to choose or request a spouse, and those women who refused marriage or sexual relations with forced-married husbands risked threatened and actual rape, with at least one documented case of sexual slavery.[36] While "consent" generally is made meaningless by the acutely coercive rule of the regime, women in particular were presented with an impossible choice in a zero-sum proposition, informed by the preoccupation of "purity" of *Chpab Srey*: to refuse was to chance rape by the state; to agree was to chance rape by an assigned husband.[37]

And yet women managed to exert agency even within this extreme paradigm. Indeed, Sok Samith's narrative suggests that at least some women (an identity-in-relation) agreed not simply for their own survival, but for the survival of their kin network. Many, like Rothana, also may have reduced the marriage to a transaction of survival sex—that is, exchanging sex for the materials and privileges needed to survive. Rothana's agreement to the marriage can be read, in this light, as covert subversion framed as gendered obedience ("My sister thought mother was old and I was still young, so she agreed for the family"). As forced marriage was a means to destroy the traditional privatized family and its loyalties, so Rothana's taking on the status of "wife" allows her access to the power needed for her own family's survival. Sok Samith describes the transactional arrangement of the marriage, leveraged not only by the wife but the family as a whole: "My mother was not satisfied with not being part of the wedding or the marriage, but she was happy that my sister's husband loved our relatives. He always gave us food. My sister and mother had a good house to live in with a well-equipped kitchen better than the old house." Sugar and salt, medicine and herbal remedies, shoes, a bicycle, leave privileges to visit family members—these were only some of the benefits conferred on Sok Samith and her family after the forced marriage to the logistics officer. These materials, and other privileges, most certainly contributed to their physical survival through the regime, even though they could never make up for the state's violation of human rights and fundamental freedom that forced marriage represented.

It is more than physical survival that concerns Sok Samith in her passage. Significantly, she points to the "well-equipped kitchen" as the signal of privilege—certainly a rarity during a time of starvation, food rationing, and forced collective food preparation and eating for the regular civilian population. Yet the kitchen is also symbolic space, the node of the mother's influence at the traditional family hearth, and precisely the sphere eliminated through the collectivist policies of the regime. Very few families were able to maintain any version of a normalized familial life, with forced-married couples divided into separate work camps after the three-day wedding and consummation period, and children likewise separated from parents. Rothana's marriage, in contrast, to a Khmer Rouge official, allowed for the mother and daughter to live as a family unit, to maintain control over a vital sphere of influence (providing family nourishment) and to preserve a modicum of human dignity.[38]

As the kitchen carries gendered symbolic and material meaning, especially for women, so does marriage itself, again evoking the role of mothers. Early researchers have pointed to how traditionally, marriage was the single-most significant source of power and prestige in Cambodia for women.[39] While accommodated, unmarried women were strongly pressured to be married, resulting in near universal female marriage prior to the Khmer Rouge regime.[40] Indeed, in colloquial Khmer the term *widow* refers to *all* unmarried women, even when divorced, abandoned, or never married (at a certain age), stressing again how women's identity is constructed as in-relation to men. Yet while family patriarchs provided final approval for traditional marriage unions, *in fact*, mothers played the central role in arranging the union and in serving as the prime advocate for the daughter in negotiations, with coerced marriages of daughters especially discouraged by custom.[41] Mothers also arranged and hosted the elaborate three-day traditional wedding ceremony, which involved 13 separate ritual acts (many to call forth ancestral spirits) that required the gathering of select family members and elders, cultural laymen, monks, and dozens of symbolic fruits and other symbolic objects. Prosperous weddings signalled auspicious marriages, which in turn signalled good karmic status.[42]

This system of cultural rites and customs, laden with gendered significance, was entirely eliminated as part of the Khmer Rouge forced marriage policy.[43] Sok Samith's narrative describes not only how the policy impacted women in particular because of their gender identities and roles as wives, but also how the policy itself was received as misogynistic in its attack on the sphere of influence conventionally relegated to women, and as Angkar took on the role of the omnipotent patriarch. Sok Samith describes the role and value of "mother" under the ultra-Maoist, ultra-patriarchal Khmer Rouge regime:

Only Angkar was the parent and could decide the future of the children. Angkar was the one to decide everything. Mothers meant nothing [during that regime]. Sometimes, children were told to murder their own mothers. My mother did not attend my sister's wedding. She found out about the marriage when she saw my sister follow her new husband into his house. The situation was very painful for my mother and sister.

Presenting murder on the same level of impact as a mother being excluded from a daughter's wedding gives a clue to the weight of customary the mother-daughter relation, in particular as regards marriage arrangements, even if it may seem hyperbolic to Western readers. The passage accentuates the utilitarian and objectifying valuation of women's (sexualized) bodies under the regime while stripped of the markers of status associated with traditional gender role assignments—ensuring the harmony of the family and performing acts associated with motherhood materially (food preparation), emotionally (love and loyalty), and culturally (tending to the karmic duties and cultural rites, including arranged marriages). It is not surprising, therefore, to hear Sok Samith claim, "I thought women suffered much more than men under the Khmer Rouge and it seemed men had more power than women. Women were never treated well or considered to be important at all." Women did in fact occupy positions of public power under the regime, including as cadre (though at much lower numbers than men), and in some of the highest political leadership positions of the state (though most likely through their relation to powerful men).[44] Yet what Sok Samith, as a young civilian woman, describes about the survival choices made in her small female kin network sheds light on how agency operated in a context of atrocity, from a fundamentally disempowered subject position gendered as woman.

In reducing women to their most utilitarian reproductive capacity as sexual objects of exchange, forced marriages and enforced conjugal relations resulted in countless pregnancies—endured above and beyond the other extreme conditions of the regime, such as hard labour and starvation. What in a traditional marriage context would have been a source of celebration was, during the atrocity, a source of terror and dread for women fighting for their own survival. It was also an opportunity for Rothana, and perhaps for other women, to express rebellion against the oppressive conditions of the regime. Sok Samith describes, "But my sister didn't love her husband at all. He was an old man. About two or three months after the wedding, she became pregnant. She threw herself down a hill until she miscarried. She told her husband she had fallen and the baby had died, but really it was an abortion."

The abortion may have saved Rothana's life, and certainly allowed her to exert some control over her own body. The abortion was also a subversive (and secretive) act that radically undermined the objective of reproduction in forced marriage. Therefore, it can be read as an act of resistance in an asymmetrical power paradigm, exerted by a disempowered gendered subject whose agency is mediated by multiple layers of real and latent patriarchal violence. That the forced marriage and the aborted pregnancy came at the cost of self-harm ("she threw herself down a hill") is indicative of the constricted possibility for unmediated and independent agency in a framework in which women's gendered identity, enforced by a continuum of violence, is reduced to sexual property.

Sok Samith's narrative exposes areas in which the Khmer Rouge regime was experienced as a fundamentally gendered atrocity—received differently by women and men, with distinct impacts, meanings, and options for available response and survival. Sok Samith, her sister, and her mother did all survive the Khmer Rouge regime. At its fall, Rothana's marriage was discovered to be polygamous, and her husband returned to his native village and his first wife, further underscoring male (sexual) prerogative. Rothana returned with her sister and mother to Phnom Penh, assuming again the title of widow and keeping the forced marriage a secret so as not to harm her prospects for remarriage.

Difference in Treatment of Women and Men

A gendered analysis of forced marriage demonstrates how an identical crime can be experienced by both men and women, and yet have radically different gendered consequences, impacts, and meaning. Forced marriage, in all of its elements, is a gender-based crime: committed against both women and men, it was specifically a form of gender discrimination that served to subjugate women as sexual property for exchange. Strategically, under the Khmer Rouge leadership, it resulted in the state's monopoly on the use and abuse of women's bodies and their reproductive labour, de facto establishing a state-sanctioned culture of rape within marriage. As forced marriage was a central policy of the regime, so gender-based violence can be said to have been a core element of the Khmer Rouge modus operandi. Women's options for agency were further constricted and distorted by gendered cultural codes of conduct that disallowed women's direct and independent action. Where women might exert influence under *Chpab Srey* (in the family, in the pagoda for ancestral rites, in the market as vendors to provide subsistence survival) were precisely those spheres eliminated and criminalized under the Khmer Rouge state. While historical accounts of the Khmer Rouge period most often take a "gender blind" approach to such issues, thereby masking the gendered nuances and variations of violence under the genocidal regime, an examination of the personal narrative of female survivors reveals that they were exposed to specific violations and treated differently than men under the regime. The rule against "immoral offences," or Code #6, exemplifies this point.

Code #6 was one of the 12 codes of conduct that applied to Khmer Rouge actors, with Code #6 extending to the population generally. Most commonly, Code #6 is translated in abbreviated form as "Do not abuse women."[45] International analysts, including the investigative offices of the ECCC, have almost universally interpreted the phrase to mean "Do not rape women." In contrast, Cambodian survivors describe the code as a prohibition against *any* sexual activity outside of marriage, frequently described as secret and consensual love affairs.[46] This second interpretation is consistent with *Chpab Srey*'s extreme preoccupation with women's purity and sexual subordination in marriage, and helps to reveal how Code #6 served to rationalize the policy on forced marriage; as each person was to be married according to Angkar's approval, so any sexual activity outside that framework was criminalized. Indeed, mounting research suggests that Code #6 was applied *most often* to consensual relations. In cases of rape (outside of forced marriage), it was applied to both victims and perpetrators, with victims punished *more often* than perpetrators. The code appears to have been applied most harshly to the civilian population; perpetrators of rapes are reported as almost exclusively Khmer Rouge actors who received little to no punishment.[47] Rather than acting as a protective measure, Code #6 put rape victims, especially civilians, at greater risk of punishment and further abuse, thereby incentivizing victim silence for survival.

Sok Samith describes her understanding of Code #6 from the perspective of a civilian woman:

> We were not allowed to love each other under the Khmer Rouge. There was a rule against "immoral offenses." If an unmarried man and unmarried woman were caught wasting time together and suspected of loving each other, the Khmer Rouge would kill them or send them to prison. We were not allowed to have girlfriends or boyfriends. It was very strict—there was no flirting allowed, you could not love each other even without touching, we were not allowed to look each other in the face. Women and men could only be assigned by Angkar to marry. If you were found to be in love, you were killed. Only those not afraid to die dared to love each other. For those afraid of dying, they dared not do so.

Sok Samith—focusing her attention on the very intimate, interpersonal impacts of Code #6 between consensual partners—humanizes what might otherwise be a broad and abstract policy. The code served to criminalize love outside of unwavering and unquestioning loyalty to Angkar, and, as Sok Samith suggests, it was implemented via strict surveillance of the population by Khmer Rouge spies and cadre. Sok Samith uses her own life—when she was 17 years old and shared a non-physical crush with a Khmer Rouge cadre—as an example. A few days after secretly sharing his rice with Sok Samith in the forest, he was found shot dead, and Sok Samith suspects he may have been murdered for their rendezvous under the provisions of Code #6.

Yet it is not Sok Samith's own experience that she retells in her oral history. Rather, her narrative is motivated by a need to tell the story of her Vietnamese friend, Ouk, raped and punished for "immoral offences" during the regime. Sok Samith describes, "Yes, in that regime, I myself saw the exact story as that of sister Ouk, raped until she was pregnant and then sent to the prison, tortured and beaten, her legs in chains for everyone to see. She had her baby in the prison." Ouk's Khmer husband had been sent as a foot soldier to the front lines. When he didn't return for his regular visits, Ouk decided to consult the local fortune teller, Ta So, who was also the District Officer for the regime. Sok Samith describes the exchange: "Ouk went to see Ta So and he said, 'If you want to know about your husband, you must agree to have sex with me so I can bring his soul here.'" The husband never returned, but the rapes continued for months until Ouk became pregnant, binding her belly tightly to prevent discovery. Ouk was seven months pregnant when she was arrested for "immoral offences."

Overall, the situation reminds us of how women's experiences are fundamentally mediated by men and male power—from accessing information to providing motivation for approaching a Khmer Rouge officer. *Ta*, or *grandfather*, is a title that denotes age as well as status. The power asymmetry between Ta So and Ouk—a woman, a wife without a husband present, a "new" person, and an ethnic Vietnamese (the Vietnamese state was the political enemy of the Khmer Rouge state)—puts Ouk at great risk. Her risk is further exacerbated by seeking to access a cultural practice banned by the regime, even as her perpetrator stands in the position of Khmer Rouge actor/fortune teller/rapist. In a context where gendered power differentials were so acute and where coercion a daily lived reality, consent in this scenario, as in forced marriage, is distorted to the point of meaninglessness ("you *must* agree" [emphasis added]). And, while it is possible that Ouk may have "agreed" to the initial transaction of sex for survival—in this case, information about her husband, upon whom she is existentially dependent—the deal certainly quickly dissolved into sexual exploitation; the rapes continued but the husband never returned. The gendered power asymmetry would have left her with no room for refusal once the deal was revealed as a trick, with Code #6 playing a role in driving the repeated rapes deeper underground, perhaps by the perpetrator, but certainly by Ouk.

Pregnancy resulting from rape put women at much greater risk of discovery, and therefore punishment, under the precepts of Code #6. Outside of the women-specific risk of pregnancy, Sok Samith also stresses the points of difference between women and men in terms of punishment:

> The woman was always punished more than the man for "immoral offenses." Ouk was sent to prison and then tortured so everyone could see she was seriously punished. They shackled her legs and forced her to dig the dike. She was allowed rice only once a day. She delivered the baby in the prison. She was released in 1977, but she was later killed as part of the regime's targeting of the Vietnamese population.[48] For the man, for Ta So, I didn't see any torture. They sent him away but we didn't know where; he disappeared. After the Khmer Rouge collapsed, he was back home as though nothing had ever happened.

That Ta So faced little punishment as a Khmer Rouge actor is consistent with other research, recounted above, and the general understanding of the abuse of power of the regime over the civilian population. Yet, in Sok Samith's passage, "more than" refers both to quantity and to quality—more women (largely reported as the vast share of victims) were subjected to punishment than men (largely reported as the vast majority of perpetrators); victims (overwhelmingly women) were punished more harshly than perpetrators (overwhelmingly men). "More harshly" has not been considered in most historical accounts, but the claim is consistent with how the deeply ingrained tenets of *Chpab Srey* continued to operate during the regime. That Ouk's punishment was public spectacle indicates that it was meant to serve as an object lesson for the population as a whole, both of Angkar's monopoly over women's sexual labour (with exceptions for punishment for its loyal actors), as well as its total control and domination over the civilian population (marked on the woman's body). Ouk's female, Vietnamese, pregnant, shackled, tortured body on display stood as sign and cipher for the sexually defiled enemy of a "pure" revolution. That Ouk was later killed in the purges against the Vietnamese casts a genocidal hue over the scenario, with her past exposure to sexual abuse putting her at high risk for continued sexual abuse as linked to the purges. Again, genocide, and even rape, may not meet the legal standards as described here, but rather the terms look to cue the multiple layers of intersecting oppressions Ouk was navigating in making decisions and formulating responses. Ouk's story, remembered and narrated by Sok Samith, opens interpretative space to consider how the Khmer Rouge state implemented a fundamentally gendered atrocity, with sexual violence against women not divorced from but deeply connected to its aims and purposes.

Women's Reactions and Processes in Responding to Genocide

If the ECCC is "the official vessel for depositing memory" about the Khmer Rouge atrocity, who will remember the story of Ouk? And, if cultural codes of conduct normalize and silence violence against women, how will such a story be heard? Indeed, if our histories of the atrocity neglect sexual violence accounts, then do they not also re-inscribe women's subordinate and devalued status as speaking, acting, historical subjects? For those women, such as Sok Samith, who come forward to share their stories, their truth-telling is an act of courage that calls for political and cultural defiance in rupturing the silence of the repressed sexual content of the "master narrative." Such speaking exposes the dominant discourse as woefully incomplete in depicting the atrocity as experienced by women, and it greatly contributes nuance and depth to our understanding of the atrocity as it was experienced on the margins of power and in the shadows of subordination.

Like all survivors of the Khmer Rouge genocide, Sok Samith today contends with the physical, psychological, and economic consequences from the Khmer Rouge period. She says of her life following the military collapse of the regime, "My life after the Khmer Rouge was zero." Until the present, she suffers vivid recurring nightmares and panic attacks from the trauma experienced decades ago. She also suffers from a myriad of physical ailments directly related to the hardships during the regime, but she is unable to afford treatment on her salary as a housekeeper. Her life has been directly impacted by the implementation of Code #6 and its prohibition against "loving each other." Of the young man she suspects was murdered for sharing his rice with her, she says, "That is why I remain unmarried even today, and I will love him forever."

As a single woman, Sok Samith represents the "excess" of women's status outside the self-in-relation to men and male violence endorsed by *Chpab Srey* and operationalized through a myriad of violations of fundamental rights and freedoms, including the right to truth. As *Chpab Srey* clusters (sexual) violence and silence, so too does it place restriction on what is permitted to be remembered—and vocalized—as informed by cultural constructions of gendered identity. Rather than challenge such repression, historical accounts may have subsumed it into the dominant narrative. Yet Sok Samith "cannot forget" precisely what she is expected to suppress as narrative, as the dutiful daughter. She comments specifically concerning the taboo of discussing her father's (sexual) abuse of her mother, "I am not supposed to talk badly about my father, and it is hard to share his story, but this is the truth and I remember it clearly. I wonder why I remember this story and never have forgotten it? The other stories I have forgotten, but this story I never forget."

Sok Samith, as post-atrocity subject, has asserted herself as a political speaker, most particularly in serving as a civil party to the ECCC, seeking justice for the 20 members of her family who perished under the regime. She is unique in this ambition among her surviving family members, and by implication survivors generally. She explains:

Yes, we suffered all together but many do not want to remember that regime. I on the other hand often talk in public forums and on radio about my story during the regime. The story of that regime is still in my memory and I cannot forget it. According to my observation, my brothers and sisters and relatives who survived, those who have children, no longer like to be reminded of the past. They just let it go and do not talk about it much. They say it is useless to revive such a sad story again and again and that remembering it is useless and no help at all. Past is past. They think the ECCC is nothing but a show, a pretend performance and they do not support me being involved. I am a civil party to the court for the death of my relatives.

Starvation, forced labour, arbitrary detention, forced movement, torture, and execution are stories that almost all survivors share, especially with their children. Forced marriage and other forms of sexual violence, on the other hand, are repressed narratives in the general discourse, especially for those victims who have children. Such crimes, it seems, hold a special category for the shame and stigma they carry, not on perpetrators, but on victims. Sok Samith's statement as a civil party will contribute to inserting this hidden reality into the dominant historical discourse being developed by the proceedings of the ECCC.

Yet when it comes to the story of Ouk—and indeed the entire arc of Sok Samith's oral history narrative and its account of multivalent violence—she must reach outside the purview of the ECCC. For her, the Khmer Rouge period is part of a longer personal history of state violence, resulting in crimes for which there is little hope of justice (the illegal U.S. bombing campaign, for example), and exacerbated by the personal abuse of her mother and other women that she witnessed while bombs fell. Sok Samith describes the chaotic cycle of armed conflict she experienced in her childhood:

> The fighting on both sides never seemed to stop. The South Vietnamese stockpiled their shells on the hill overlooking the village, and then in the early morning the North Vietnamese came to steal the artillery. At night, there were bombardments. We all, both young and old, were very familiar with bombardments by this time, so we hurried to find a safe place to hide. Almost every night I could see the airplanes, US airplanes that dropped bombs everywhere, the people fleeing and running away. It looked like a scene in the movies—everywhere people running and screaming and the noise of the airplanes bombarding us. Sometimes the airplanes would drop a parachute with food aid but the people were afraid it was a bomb and would not touch it.

From the perspective of civilians caught in the crosshairs of the fighting, political factions are redundant, as violence comes from all sides and even survival aid is taken to be a weapon in disguise. The scene described is precisely the one in which Sok Samith's mother was prevented from escaping, discussed above, adding yet another dimension to the cyclical continuum of violence experienced by women during times of conflict and atrocity.

Yet if Sok Samith disrupts the delimited dates of the Khmer Rouge regime to tell the story of its contributing factors and consequential results, so too do her accounts of sexual violence under the regime exceed the normative narrative frame, making her witnessing an overtly political act that subverts the silences that are so central to the subordination of sexual violence victims—and which, in turn, ensures impunity for perpetrators. Sok Samith comes back again and again in her narrative to the story of Ouk:

> I saw with my own eyes what happened to Ouk, a Vietnamese woman who lived in Tmor Reap. It was in 1976.... Yes, in that regime, I myself saw the exact story as that of sister Ouk, raped until she was pregnant and then sent to prison, tortured and beaten, her legs in chains for everyone to see. She had her baby in the prison.... But I believe I have to share my story, especially the story of my friend Ouk, which has never been revealed before. She was Vietnamese with a Khmer husband who fought in the Khmer Rouge army. She was raped and put in jail and tortured and then killed. Not many people would dare to speak this story out, and it is only me who knows what happened and can spread the information so everyone knows the truth about the Khmer Rouge regime. So at least if I speak out, Ouk can claim some of her rights as a human being who was seriously abused and deserves to be remembered.

Claiming herself as witness ("I saw with my own eyes what happened," "Yes, in that regime, I myself saw the exact story"), as a woman who remembers with specificity (the date, the place, the name, and the race of Ouk), Sok Samith claims narrative space to assert a counter-frame to what is remembered about *women's* experiences during the atrocity. In so doing, her narrative itself confers status to Ouk as a full "human being" who "deserves to be remembered." For Sok Samith, at least, Ouk's story of rape and genocide is not periphery to the atrocity, but rather serves as the (gendered) foundation of domination and mastery that makes atrocity possible in the first place. As Sok Samith takes on the role of remembering for the others who have perished, so too does she help us to see the blind spots of an historical discourse woefully incomplete in depicting state massacre as experienced by women and as inextricably related to the functions and consequences of gender-based violence. As she says, "If I don't tell this story, it will die with me. I tell it so we do not forget what happened to women like Ouk."

Sok Samith's narrative is personal, local, and intimate. Yet it provokes an important question about atrocity and genocide more broadly: Can we ever hope to eliminate state massacre if we do not speak its full contours as part of our histories? The result of probing the elision of sexual violence histories is not to argue that women suffer more or more acutely than men in any particular scene of mass violence. It is, rather, to emphasize that men and women, occupying different positions of power in society, experience and react to atrocity in distinct and unique ways, and that women's agency in particular may be driven deeply underground by cultural constructs of gendered identity. Understanding these nuances and variances provides a more sophisticated view as to the root cause of atrocity—as dominance, expressed as violence, often with women's bodies playing symbolic and central roles. Such understanding makes more meaningful our global commitment to non-repetition and accountability. We can no longer afford blind spots in what is remembered about genocide and atrocity, and it is time to "see what was hidden but always there before [our] very eyes."

Questions

1. How does understanding how gender identity is socially constructed in a particular context help to open interpretative space about what is hidden but always in view, in terms of the distinct ways women and men experience genocide and atrocity? What are some examples from this chapter or other genocides you have studied that point to gendered nuances and variations of genocidal violence?

2. The author points to the existence of the Khmer Rouge rule against "immoral offences," or Code #6, comparing it to a similar policy during the German Holocaust. Both policies were used to argue that sexual violence was not part of the greater atrocity, thereby missing the opportunity for judicial redress, and creating ellipses in historical accounts. How does the chapter illustrate the importance of testing official policy against the lived realities of women's lives? What new information and knowledge develops by attending to women's narratives of atrocity and taking their experiences seriously?

3. What does the author mean when she writes, "if our histories of the atrocity neglect sexual violence accounts, then do they not also re-inscribe women's subordinate and devalued status as speaking, acting, historical subjects?" How do reclaimed stories of sexual violence serve to expose the "(gendered) foundation of domination and mastery that makes atrocity possible in the first place"?

4. Oral history is a specific methodology with a unique ethical code of conduct. How does the chapter illustrate the special challenges of the oral history approach? Why does the author suggest that Sok Samith's use of her real name is a political act of resistance? What precautions must researchers take to make such a conclusion possible?

Notes

1. Dalia Ofer and Lenore J. Weitzman, eds., *Women in the Holocaust* (New Haven: Yale University Press, 1998), 1.
2. Ibid., 2.
3. Ibid., 16.
4. Shulamit Reinharz, foreword to *Sexual Violence Against Jewish Women During the Holocaust*, ed. Sonja M. Hedgepeth and Rochelle G. Saidel (Waltham: Brandeis University Press, 2010), x. The volume is the first interdisciplinary anthology of academic treatments on women and sexual abuse during the Holocaust.

5. See Morten Bergsmo, Alf Butenschon Skre, and Elisabeth J. Wood, eds., *Understanding and Proving International Sex Crimes* (Beijing: Torkel Opsahl Academic EPublisher, 2012). Gains in international criminal law include the adjudication of sexual crimes under the International Criminal Tribunal for the former Yugoslavia (ICTY), the International Criminal Tribunal for Rwanda (ICTR), and the Special Court for Sierra Leone (SCSL); the United Nations Security Council Resolutions 1325 and 1820 and following on women, peace, and security; and General Recommendation No. 30 on women's human rights in conflict by the Convention on the Elimination of All Forms of Discrimination Against Women (CEDAW).

6. Helene J. Sinnreich, "The Rape of Jewish Women During the Holocaust" in *Sexual Violence Against Jewish Women During the Holocaust*, ed. Sonja M. Hedgepeth and Rochelle G. Saidel (Waltham: Brandeis University Press, 2010), 117.

7. Nomi Levenkron, "'Prostitution,' Rape and Sexual Slavery During World War II" in *Sexual Violence Against Jewish Women During the Holocaust*, ed. Sonja M. Hedgepeth and Rochelle G. Saidel (Waltham: Brandeis University Press, 2010), 15.

8. Ofer and Weitzman, *Women in the Holocaust*, 14.

9. While the Khmer Rouge regime is alleged to have attempted genocide against religious and ethnic minority populations, the atrocity as a totality was directed at, and adversely impacted, the population as a whole. The term *atrocity* is used in the chapter to denote the larger context of offences, while *genocide* is used to denote its legal meaning. See, for the definition of genocide under international criminal law, Adam Jones, "Gender and Mass Violence" in *Gender Matters in Global Politics*, ed. Laura J. Shepard (New York: Routledge, 2010).

10. Ofer and Weitzman, *Women in the Holocaust*, 14.

11. Ibid., 2.

12. See Michael Vickery, who has argued that women were never safer from sexual abuse than when under the Khmer Rouge regime, in *Cambodia: 1975–1982* (Seattle: University of Washington Press, 2000).

13. See Brigitte Halbmayr, "Sexualized Violence Against Women During Nazi 'Racial' Persecution" in *Sexual Violence Against Jewish Women During the Holocaust*, ed. Sonja M. Hedgepeth and Rochelle G. Saidel (Waltham: Brandeis University Press, 2010); and Theresa de Langis, "'This Is Now the Most Important Trial in the World': A New Reading of Code #6, the Rule

against Immoral Offenses under the Khmer Rouge Regime," *Cambodian Law and Policy Journal* 3 (2014): 61–78.

14. For background, including protracted political negotiations on creating the ECCC, see John D. Ciorciari, ed., *The Khmer Rouge Tribunal* (Phnom Penh: Documentation Center of Cambodia, 2006).

15. For information on the Khmer Rouge period, see David Chandler, *A History of Cambodia*, 4th ed. (Chiang Mai: Silkworm Books, 2008); Ben Kiernan, *The Pol Pot Regime: Race, Power and Genocide in Cambodia under the Khmer Rouge, 1975–1979* (New Haven: Yale University Press, 1996); and Elizabeth Becker, *When the War Was Over: Cambodia and the Khmer Rouge Revolution* (New York: Public Affairs Press, 1998).

16. See Khamboly Dy, *A History of Democratic Kampuchea (1975–1979)* (Phnom Penh: Documentation Center of Cambodia, 2007). Though intended for high-school readers, it represents the first volume written by a Cambodian about the Cambodian genocide.

17. Theresa de Langis, "A Missed Opportunity, A Last Hope? Prosecuting Sexual Crimes under the Khmer Rouge Regime," *Cambodia Law and Policy Journal* 2 (2014): 40.

18. For example, see François Ponchand, *Cambodia: Year Zero*, trans. Nancy Ampous (New York: Holt, Rinehart and Winston, 1978).

19. Silke Studzinsky, "One Eye Blind? Is the ECCC a Model of How Sexual Violence Crimes Should Be Investigated and Treated?" Gerda Werner Institute: Feminism and Democracy, April 16, 2012, www.gwi-boell.de/ en/2012/04/16/blind-one-eye-icc-model-how-sexual-crimes-should-be-investigated-and-treated.

20. See Nakagawa Kasumi, *Gender-Based Violence during the Khmer Rouge Regime: Stories of Survivors from the Democratic Kampuchea (1975–1979)* (Phnom Penh: Cambodia Defenders Project, 2008).

21. Tallyn Gray, "Justice and Transition in Cambodia 1979–2014: Process, Meaning and Narrative" (Ph.D. dissertation, University of Westminster, 2014), 9.

22. Ibid., 20

23. Narrator #2, interview by author, January 26, 2012, Cambodian Women's Oral History Project. Twenty life-story oral histories were collected by the author between January 2012 and July 2014 from female survivors in 16 provinces throughout Cambodia. Interviews were conducted in Khmer through a translator. To mitigate risks to narrators, all had spoken publicly

about their experiences under the Khmer Rouge regime. Many narrators had participated in the public truth-seeking venue of a series of women's hearings convened by local human rights organization Cambodian Defenders Project, and others were formally attached as civil parties to the ECCC through victim-witness statements. All were supported directly or indirectly through Transcultural Psychosocial Organization Cambodia, which served as an intermediary for the project. The collection of oral histories will be deposited for public access in March 2016 at Tuol Sleng Genocide Museum. Excerpts included in this chapter were translated from Khmer to English by You Sotheary and Thorn Sina.

24. Ofer and Weitzman, *Women in the Holocaust*, 2.

25. William Shawcross, *Sideshow: Kissinger, Nixon and the Destruction of Cambodia* (New York: Simon & Schuster, 1979), 15. Between 1965 and 1973, the United States dropped a greater tonnage of bombs on the Cambodian-Vietnam border than had been dropped by the entire Allied forces during World War II.

26. For more discussion on how the controlling tenets of *Chpab Srey* have influenced women's status in Cambodia throughout history until today, see Katherine Bricknell, "'We Don't Forget the Old Rice Pot When We Get the New One': Discourses on the Ideal and Practices of Women in Contemporary Cambodia," *Signs: Journal of Women in Culture and Society* 36, no. 2 (2011): 437–462.

27. Katherine Bricknell, "'Plates in a Basket Will Rattle': Marital Dissolution and Home 'Unmaking' in Contemporary Cambodia," *Geoforum* 51 (2014): 265–268.

28. Concluding Observations on the Combined Fourth and Fifth Periodic Reports of Cambodia, CEDAW Comm., 56th Session, UN Doc. CEDAW/C/KHM/CO/4-5 at 3-4 (2013). Indeed, in 2013, the Committee on the Convention on the Elimination of All Forms of Discrimination Against Women (CEDAW) called on the Royal Government of Cambodia to reform restrictive cultural traditions—naming *Chpab Srey* specifically—that result in women's exploitation and abuse, and prevent women from realizing their full human rights.

29. Jan Ayako, "Toward an Effective Strategy for Women's Empowerment: Experiences of the Women in Livelihood Improvement Projects, Takeo Province, Cambodia" (master's thesis, Ritsumeikan Asia Pacific University, 2008), 41.

30. Judith Ledgerwood, "Changing Khmer Conceptions of Gender: Women, Stories and Social Order" (dissertation, Cornell University, 1990), 24. Ledgerwood stresses that it is virtually impossible to over-emphasize the "extreme importance" that Khmers place on the "virginity of girls at marriage" to signify the honour and status of the family. See also Katrina Natale, "'I Could Feel My Soul Flying Away from My Body': A Study on Gender-Based Violence During Democratic Kampuchea in Battambang and Svay Rieng Provinces" (Phnom Penh: Cambodia Defenders Project, 2011), 19. Natale says of *Chpab Srey*: "sexual encounters outside of marriage, consensual or otherwise, would have devastated a bride's chances for marriage and family life."

31. In 1970, U.S. backed Lon Nol unseated King Sihanouk as prime minister by military coup, marking the beginning of the civil war, which lasted until the Paris Peace Agreement of 1993.

32. Traditional Khmer houses are raised on stilts to prevent damage during the monsoon-season flooding.

33. The sister's name has been changed to protect identity and privacy.

34. For an overview of existing and emerging research, see Theresa de Langis, Judith Strasser, Thida Kim, and Taing Sopheap, "'Like Ghost Changes Body': The Impact of Forced Marriage under the Khmer Rouge Regime" (Phnom Penh: Transcultural Psychosocial Association, 2014). The research covers instances in which husbands raped wives under the excuse of the policy; where wives and husbands mutually agreed to have sex to save their lives; and where wives and husbands agreed to simulate sexual activity in order to survive.

35. Beini Ye, "Forced Marriages as Mirrors of Cambodian Conflict Transformation," *Peace Review* 23, no. 4 (2011): 470.

36. Theresa de Langis et al., "Like Ghost Changes Body."

37. This is not to suggest that men were not also victims of sexual violence, including rape. Yet, from the research on hand, the reported victims are overwhelmingly women and the perpetrators are overwhelmingly men. See Natale, "I Could Feel My Soul," 2, 27, 41–45.

38. The forced marriage did not get Sok Samith out of working in a mobile unit, and she did not live with her mother and sister.

39. Henri Locard, *Pol Pot's Little Red Book: The Sayings of Angkar* (Chiang Mai: Silkworm Books, 2005), 489: "Marriage signified a dramatic change in status, especially for the bride." See also Trudy Jacobsen, *Lost Goddesses: The*

Denial of Female Power in Cambodian History (Copenhagen: Nordic Institute of Asian Studies, 2008), 97: "Marriage gave women status and legal protections."

40. See Bricknell, "'Plates in a Basket Will Rattle'"; and Ledgerwood, "Changing Khmer Conceptions of Gender."

41. May Ebihara, "Svay, a Khmer Village in Cambodia" (dissertation: Columbia University, 1968), 315–316; Ledgerwood, "Changing Khmer Conceptions of Gender," 177; Patrick Heuveline and Bunnak Poch, "Do Marriages Forget Their Past? Marital Stability in Post-Khmer Rouge Cambodia," *Demography* 43, no. 1 (2006): 101.

42. For a full background on traditionally arranged marriages, see Ebihara, "Svay, a Khmer Village," 112–117, 474–475.

43. Peg LeVine, *Love and Dread in Cambodia: Weddings, Births, and Ritual Harm under the Khmer Rouge* (Singapore: National University of Singapore Press, 2010), 25. LeVine argues that Cambodians experienced "cultural genocide" under the Khmer Rouge regime.

44. Indeed, one of the four senior living leaders accused by the ECCC in Case 002 is a woman: Ieng Thirith, Minister of Social Affairs. She is the sister-in-law to Pol Pot, and was deemed unfit to stand trial due to dementia in 2012. See www.eccc.gov.kh/en/indicted-person/ieng-thirith.

45. Youk Chhang, "Letter from the Director," *Searching for the Truth* 15 (2001): 2. DC-Cam serves at the central repository of records of the Khmer Rouge era. See www.d.dccam.org.

46. For example, "immoral offences" are defined as "secret love affairs" in Sokhym Em, "Criticism and Self-Criticism," *Searching for the Truth* 31 (2002): 18. Compare, for example, Katrina Anderson, "Turning Reconciliation on Its Head," *Seattle Journal of Social Justice* 3, no. 2 (2005): 790: "[I]n contrast to other regimes, the Khmer Rouge was widely known to have espoused a policy strictly forbidding rape."

47. Natale, "'I Could Feel My Soul Flying'" 3.

48. In 1977, the Khmer Rouge began purging "internal" enemies to the regime's ideology. Vietnamese in Cambodia faced mass expulsion and execution— crimes that are now part of the genocide proceedings of the ECCC. See Kiernan, *The Pol Pot Regime.*

CHAPTER 6

Genocide in Central America:
Testimonies of Survivors in Guatemala

Martha C. Galvan-Mandujano

Introduction

During the 1970s and 1980s many Central American countries experienced internal armed conflicts—Guatemala was no exception. Between 1960 and 1996, the country suffered a 36-year civil war whose death toll claimed the lives of more than 200,000 persons, displaced more than one and a half million, and created more than 100,000 refugees who fled to Mexico.[1] Throughout the civil war, the years with the highest number of killings were between 1981 and 1983—the genocidal period known as *La Violencia*. During this period, the Guatemalan military and their paramilitary proxies massacred entire Mayan communities. The most affected areas experiencing widespread killings, torture, and rape were in the department of Quiché, and particularly in the mountainous Ixil and the Ixcán regions. According to a report of the Historical Clarification Commission (CEH), of the total 626 villages where massacres occurred, 344 were in the Quiché region alone. The CEH reported that the National Army of Guatemala was responsible for 93 percent of the atrocities and massacres committed against indigenous Mayan victims.

This chapter examines how these genocidal acts during *La Violencia* affected Mayan women. I examine the testimonies of women from the CEH, along with personal interviews I conducted in 2000 and 2002 during fieldwork in one of the Communities of Population in Resistance (CPR) in Nebaj in the highlands of El Quiché region, testimonies from female Mayan survivors from Guatemala City, and other testimonies from various media resources. In exploring these testimonies, I utilized the framework identified by Dalia Ofer and Lenore J. Weitzman to answer the following questions regarding the experiences of Mayan women: How did the genocidal period affect Mayan women culturally and in the overall civil war? What were women's anticipatory reactions during *La Violencia*? Were Mayan women treated differently than men because of their gender? What were the reactions and processes of women to the physical and emotional circumstances they experienced in the genocide? As a prelude, I provide a brief historical overview of the Guatemalan internal conflict in the late 1970s and early 1980s that led to the genocidal period of *La Violencia*.

Historical Overview: Guatemalan Internal Armed Conflict, 1970s and 1980s

Guatemalans suffered violent massacres in the late 1970s and early 1980s under the presidencies of Fernando Romero Lucas García and José Efraín Ríos Montt. During the time of Lucas Garcia's presidency, human rights violations included the "disappearances" of peasants, religious leaders, scholars, and many Mayan individuals. The main goal of state terrorism between 1978 and 1980 was to destroy the mass movement that arose in the 1970s.[2] This revolutionary movement had its beginnings primarily in the rural areas. State-sponsored terrorism focused on quashing any dissent, and was renewed from time to time, as was deemed necessary. Beginning in 1980 the focus changed, and state terrorism began to target insurgent organizations. By the late 1970s and early 1980s the two primary groups fighting were the Ejército de Guatemalteco (Guatemalan army) and the guerrilla forces, which were composed mainly of leftist rebel groups. One of the most important guerrilla groups was the Guerrilla Army of the Poor

(EGP). Another important guerrilla group was known as the Committee for Peasant Unity (CUC).

The EGP was based in the department of El Quiché. For this reason, the army classified El Quiché as one of the main enemy zones in the highlands of Guatemala. Carlos Figueroa noted that, "unlike the previous period of state terrorism, this time the emphasis was no longer on the mass organizations but was basically aimed against the insurgent organizations. From late 1979, repression was unleashed against the mass bases of the Guerrilla Army of the Poor (EGP) in the department of El Quiché."[3] The EGP became a targeted enemy because it was gaining sympathizers in the highlands. The EGP's success at gaining recruits was demonstrated when EGP-orchestrated protests broke out in each of the Ixil towns between October 1979 and March 1980. In Cotzal, "a large crowd of men, women and children marched from the plaza to the army garrison, demanding that soldiers return their kidnapped relatives and leave."[4] Alarmed at the EGP's success in gaining sympathizers for its cause, the government began killing individuals, and later graduated to entire communities. Indigenous Mayans were caught in the middle of this war. As one witness stated, "both the army and the guerrillas were killing us. We were trapped between two cannons. One cannon here and another there. We had nowhere to go."[5] David Stoll describes this situation when he notes that the Ixil *municipios* bore the most suffering, especially because these areas were believed—rightly or wrongly—to be bastions of the EGP. The government security forces initially targeted those individuals who were presumed to be members of the EGP's underground network; in particular men (and less often, women) who had been betrayed by former EGP members, denounced by someone for personal gain, or who had been named by a victim of a torture session.[6] Following the first public meeting of the EGP, in January 1979, the military occupied Nebaj and then began implementing "random homicides." This began a chain of massacres against not only the men, but also women and children.

Other leftist organizations began to unite, attempting to stop the violent attacks by the army. The EGP and the CUC, in conjunction with the Robin García Student Front (FERG), occupied the Spanish embassy on January 31, 1980. The occupation resulted in substantial tragedy, with

36 people killed, including former Vice President Eduardo Cáceres Lenhoff, as well as former Minister of Foreign Affairs Adolfo Molina Orantes, former Spanish Consul Jaime Ruiz del Árbol, and Mayan activist Vicente Menchú, father of the well-known Nobel Peace Prize winner Rigoberta Menchú. In response to the occupation, the army became even more violent against the guerillas and anyone else suspected of sympathizing with the guerillas.

The government's goal to eliminate the guerilla groups was aided in large part by the use of the patrol systems (PACs), or *patrullas de autodefensa*. President Lucas García's brother, Army Chief of Staff Benedicto, initially created the PACs to spy on the indigenous residents and create instability within the communities:

> The army, in its attempts to extend its reach into the rural hamlets of Guatemala, forcibly conscripted thousands of indigenous men to form civil patrols (patrullas de auto defense), PACs.... The civil patrol system was integral to the army's counterinsurgency campaign, providing a means of controlling and terrorizing the population, while simultaneously creating distrust and division within whole communities.[7]

The army began to militarily and politically support gangs in other areas of Guatemala to instill the same fears of "instability, division, and mistrust within the community."[8] The PACs were an important tool for the army in gaining control over these Mayan communities. Testimonies reveal that the formation of the civil patrols basically had the effect of turning the Ixils' war against the government into a civil war among the Ixils themselves. An officer told the first patrollers of Nebaj, "now we're all going to get our hands dirty."[9] In the beginning, many civilians joined the PACs because they were afraid they would be killed if they refused to take orders from the army. Stoll cites the case of a massacre that occurred in Ixil on February 13, 1982, in which the army "ordered Cotzaleños under its control to punish the aldea of Chisis, located in the mountains above Cotzal." The patrollers assassinated more than two hundred men, women, and children when the civil patrol at the aldea of Santa Avelina refused to comply with orders from the army. Sometime later, the skulls in the river were said to look like "the smooth stones in the river at Sacapulas."[10] Enduing the PACs to aid the military in exercises of organized massacres allowed the military to better control regions. Although the formation of the PACs is generally associated with Ríos Montt's government, his administration simply took the system that had already been created by his predecessor, Lucas García, and expanded it to include the western highlands.

Beginning in 1982, as President Lucas García began to lose his grip on power, there was a high level of distrust among members of the military over many of his actions. Lucas García's presidency (1978–1982) is characterized by death squads terrorizing dissidents, massacres of villagers, corruption of government funds, and electoral fraud. By March 1982 Lucas García had effectively angered both the left and right sides of the political spectrum when he endorsed his defence minister, Ángel Aníbal Guevara, as the next president. This resulted in a coup d'état by the General of the Guatemalan Army, José Ríos Montt, on March 23, 1982. Under the presidency of Ríos Montt, the army began the period of greatest violence and murder in the 1980s, and the genocide against the indigenous Maya population came to full force. According to Susanne Jonas, the main goal was "to 'drain the sea' in which the guerrilla movement operated and to eradicate its civilian support base in the Maya highlands."[11]

The atrocities that occurred during in the 17-month presidency of Ríos Montt are considered the bloodiest period of the entire 36-year civil war. Montt's scorched-earth policies between 1982 and 1983 meant that the military literally burned and destroyed buildings, crops, or other resources, destroying anything that the guerillas could use to restock or that would possibly aid them in their fight. Jennifer Schirmer notes that not only were guerillas targeted in this scorched-earth strategy, but there was also complete destruction of non-combatant civilians in the enemy zones. The goal of the government forces was to destroy any bases or networks the guerillas could use to recruit new members. According to Schirmer,

On the drawing boards of the Army General Staff and in garrison headquarters, villages were assigned a color pin. Those villages in the "red zones" were in the enemy territory: no distinction was made between guerrilleros and their peasant supporters. Both were to be attacked and obliterated. All villages in the Ixil were considered "red".... Those villages in the "pink" zones were to be attacked but left standing, and those in "white zones" (with green pins) were "safe villages" to be left alone.[12]

Ríos Montt's agenda against the guerrillas changed drastically as the army increased the number of massacres. In this particular phase of the genocidal period, Ríos Montt continued to fight the guerrillas primarily in the highlands, increasing military attacks in these areas, which were now classified as enemy zones. These highland communities had become systematically directed targets of the army. Jonas points out that "the goal of the 'genocide' and the scorched-earth policies went beyond elimination of the insurgents' support base and the material base of local economy. The deeper objective was to fracture the very bases of the communal structures and of the ethnic unity destroying factors of reproduction of culture."[13] Thus violence against women during this period was particularly brutal, since they were the ones who not only bore the Mayan children, but also transferred cultural identity to the young. This was a threat to the goals of the government. During the army's campaign of terror, in addition to many innocent Mayan people being murdered, women were sexually abused; many became widows, while other women were left psychologically traumatized. A large number of women also became internally displaced during this same period.

Culturally Defined Roles of Mayan Women

The role of women throughout the conflict changed in several distinct ways; among these were the domestic role of women, their traditional way of dress, and the women's economic role within their family. Before the conflict, Mayan indigenous women were culturally expected to take charge of raising the children and complete all the housework-related tasks, while their men worked in the fields.[14] Women were also commonly engaged in weaving, and they often contributed economically to the household by selling some of their weavings. Culturally, women kept up many Mayan traditions without outside influence, largely because they stayed in the home and normally spoke only their native language. Women were in charge of weaving their own family's clothing, and these family weavings served a very important function within their culture. Mayan women in rural areas wore traditional dress as a symbolic marker of their identity within a family group and village. This, however, changed out of necessity during the civil war. Mayan textiles are specific to villages based on colour, weave, and various patterns and motifs. Women would establish their own unique weaving design, but only within the larger village weaving identity, all of whose members were distinguished by their clothing. The traditional women's garment—the *huipil*—is the primary symbol of a woman's Mayan identity. Out of necessity as a survival tactic, women abandoned their traditional dress because it could readily identify them to the marauding army as a member of a particular Mayan group.[15] Wearing village-specific clothing was especially dangerous if they were from one of the zones classified as "red enemy zones," which could identify them as targets for violence or assassination. Post-conflict, this important cultural custom could sometimes take years to return. Some women were able to immediately resume wearing their traditional dress "as a symbol of ethnic pride, solidarity and survival, and to weave to help support their families."[16] Yet many other women who remained in their villages were fearful and reluctant to once again readily identify their family and village through the use of their traditional patterns of weaving.

The role of women also changed when they became widowed and were forced to move from their traditional role of homemaker to that of head of their household. Many women migrated to the larger cities in order to support their families. Others fled to Mexico—first as refugees fleeing for their lives during the height of the genocide, but later because natural resources were exploited in their own communities, and farmland had become extremely scarce. For those Mayan women who stayed in Guatemala, land scarcity changed their traditional roles as homemakers. Many women found their lives disrupted economically. Additionally, some Mayan communities were subsequently forced into seasonal migration to the coast, where entire families worked on plantations. For those families, even women, who traditionally would not work in the fields, were hired as agricultural labourers.[17] While conducting post-conflict fieldwork as a translator in one of the CPRs in Nebaj, I spoke with many Mayan women. They frequently spoke to me of how the conflict had changed their traditional roles. During one interview, I asked a woman from the CPRs about the whereabouts of the parents of three Mayan children I observed playing nearby. The woman responded that "They are working in other fields, they will come back later, the land here is not fertile anymore."[18] In another interview, a Mayan woman who had relocated to Guatemala City told me that economic considerations had forced her to move from her family village to the city for better financial opportunities.[19] This was a common theme among Mayan women. Antonella Fabri explains that it became a constant characteristic for Mayan women living in the capital to work in the *maquila* factory, and that these women were willing to work for next to nothing just to have a job.[20]

In many of the interviews I conducted with Mayan women who had moved to Guatemala City, I found that they were often reluctant to discuss what had actually happened to them during the civil war—even years later, they still seemed afraid to talk about their experiences. Women not only lost their husband but sometimes their entire families, as well as their property. Even if some family members survived, life changed dramatically for many of these women. Within the larger cities these Mayan women relocated to, they found a quasi–caste system in effect, in which they were generally viewed as less than human because they were recognized as indigenous. As a consequence, some relocated Mayan women decided to move back to the highlands, where they had already experienced so much loss. Those who remained in the city typically sought work as domestic help, in keeping with their traditional cultural roles. Women now stuggled to escape from poverty, just as they had earlier tried to escape the violence of the Guatemalan army during *La Violencia*.

Women's Anticipatory Reactions

At the beginning of the conflict, many women did not anticipate the unmitigated violence of the army and the PACs. It simply did not occur to either them or their families that the soldiers and their collaborators would kill women or children; rather, the women anticipated that they would not be subjected to direct violence *because* they were women. Men were the presumed main targets in communities because so many of them were leaders and sympathizers of the guerrillas. Women were aware that they could be raped, so many of them took refuge in the highlands during times of perceived danger. Still other women chose to remain behind in the villages, because they did not want be accused of being enemies of the state, fearing that running would make them appear guilty. One survivor explained why she chose to stay within her village when other women fled to the highlands: "They said we are trying to run away, we said, why would we run away, we have done nothing wrong. We said we are free people and asked why they were threatening us. I was trembling with my kids."[21] But one of the main tactics of the government forces during *La Violencia* was to rape and kill women, and the women who chose to stand their ground, rather than hide, often became their victims.

Mayan women are known to be traditionally submissive, and Mayan communities before *La Violencia* had a very patriarchal way of looking at rapes when the perpetrators were their own husbands or members of their community. Often, women would not report the rapes because they were ashamed, and because their silence was expected. This silence was the result of social pressures from the local community, as well as internalized cultural ideologies and traditions.[22] Mayan culture is considered *machista*, or strongly masculine, whereby many women who are victims of rape are not considered, even by their own husbands, to have been "really raped." For unmarried women, if the abuser was a man from the same community, there was the option of marriage, which in the eyes of the community effectively resolved the problem of rape. Julie Hastings's research in one Mayan community found that women typically did not report many of the rapes that occurred in the Mayan town of San José. In many cases within this particular community, rape was not considered an act of aggression. According to Hastings, "Among Joseños, unmarried females are considered to have been raped only when marriage does not follow, and the criterion for determining rape in such instances depends not on the consent of the woman but on the intent of the man."[23]

Therefore, sexual aggression prior to marriage was not considered rape in Joseño sexual ideology. However, if the San José women were raped by outsiders or non-Joseños, then the act would be classified as "real rape." This *machista* view of rape was not particular to Joseños, but was common in many Mayan communities.

During *La Violencia*, the Guatemalan government clearly targeted women in a state-sponsored rape policy, and many Mayan women, including those from San José, became victims of brutal rapes perpetrated by the army. According to Joseños' testimonies, Guatemalan soldiers raped girls and women of all ages and marital status: "unmarried girls as young as nine years old, older married women, women who were pregnant, and elderly widows were all victims of rape. Regardless of how closely they fit Joseño notions of the 'ideal victim,' these women generally did not make their rapes part of public testimonies of the state sanctioned violence."[24]

As mentioned earlier, Mayan women who remained in their communities during *La Violencia* believed that perpetrators would consider them innocent because they did not leave, and so subsequently would be viewed as having nothing to hide. Hastings's interview with a female survivor named Micaela speaks of this predicament:

> What we see here is that when speaking about women, Micaela does not hesitate to admit that they fled from soldiers. However, the acts of fleeing the house and hiding are represented very differently than when Micaela referred to men's flight. Earlier in the interview, when Micaela had spoken of the violence directed at her father and other men, she emphasized that staying at home represented political innocence. When soldiers entered her town, Micaela had said, "We knew we hadn't committed any crimes so we were at home." The men (collectivized into a "we" that included her) believed that soldiers would not punish them for something they had not done. But Micaela, and all the women who were able, fled their houses because they "didn't want to be raped by the soldiers." The women's innocence of guerrilla subversion was irrelevant. It would not have protected them from being raped.[25]

Hastings concludes that even if the women were innocent, this did not save them from rape. The army was trained to rape in order to create a stigmatization and shame within the female survivors—it was part and parcel of the process of war. Because women played such an important role in the Mayan culture—as transmitters of the traditions to their families, they became attractive targets for sexualized violence and murder. Women became an "easy target" for the government and its brutal actions against the Mayans. The state-sponsored violence toward women was made that much easier because the army understood the gendered social values of Mayan women, which assured their silence about the rapes. One survivor named Teresa illustrates how difficult it was to differentiate—let alone recognize—the reasons behind the rapes.

> Teresa: "A lot of women were raped and little girls were raped by the soldiers because they were left alone by their husbands. Most of the husbands were coming to the United States to work and bring them to the United States. And they were left alone and when they were left alone, the army got in and raped them."
>
> Interviewer: "Why did they do that to the women? Did they think the women were guerrillas?"
>
> Teresa: "I don't know the reason why they get the women. I guess they just wanted them."[26]

Many women, like Teresa, did not recognize themselves as systematic victims of a state-sponsored rape policy; nor would they describe in detail the acts of sexual violence that were directly perpetrated against them. Conversely, when male survivors were interviewed, they described in graphic detail the atrocities committed by the army.

Women had no choice but to take control of their home and family after the men of the family were killed, putting the women in the position of making the decision to either flee or stay in the community. On one of my visits to Guatemala City in 2000, one female speaker at an NGO stated, "We had to escape from our communities because we were afraid to die, my father and my brothers were tortured and finally assassinated by the Army."[27] Again, the women initially had not anticipated that they would be killed or become victims of violence—primarily because they were women—and historically, women were protected somewhat from the violence.

Difference in Treatment of Women and Men

The severity of the government's treatment of men and women varied by location during the Mayan genocide. In the zones of conflict that consisted of the departments of El Quiché, El Petén, Alta Verapaz, San Marcos, and Huehuetenango, men and women experienced government repression equally. Within those zones, the government defined both men and women as enemies of the state, all of whom allegedly were involved with the guerrillas. Throughout the civil war, and specifically during the scorched-earth counterinsurgency, the government destroyed the Mayans' ability to engage in subsistence agriculture, through the destruction of their villages. When indigenous men began to assert land rights and formed unions in an effort to advance those rights, the government labelled them as subversives. These men then became targets of the army and the death squads as a result of their organizing. If the women and children did not cooperate when interrogated as to the whereabouts of their male relatives, they were tortured, raped, and often killed. In some communities, women, prior to *La Violencia*, did not experience the fear that other women faced, primarily because the army was initially targeting the men. But during *La Violencia*, women came to understand that they had also become the intended targets of the army and its collaborators.

The women, at this point, began to comprehend that the destruction of their culture necessitated their own destruction, since women were the cultural bearers of the group. And so women, in addition to men, became victims of the government's repression and violent acts. Victoria Sanford's seminal study, *From Genocide to Feminicide: Impunity and Human Rights in Twenty-First Century Guatemala*, explains that women and girls were primary targets of the genocide, owing to their reproductive capacity.[28] In mid-1982, only three months into Ríos Montt's dictatorship, the proportion of women and girls killed increased, and 42 percent of the total victims during that time were female.[29] A priest interviewed by Amnesty International as an eyewitness to a massacre in Huehuetenango described that the treatment of men and women was the same, with the only difference being that some of the women still carried their live babies on their backs when "they were stacked for burning."[30]

In 2008, at the Guatemala Genocide trial in the Spanish National Court, women began to speak about their experiences during the Ríos Montt presidency. Two protected female witnesses and two male witnesses stated that women had been raped. The witnesses concurred in their descriptions of the Guatemalan soldiers' and civil patrol members' use of rape in order to abuse and humiliate the Mayan women of Rabinal. One female witness described how the army camped "in front of her neighbor's house for three days and [then] raped her in front of her children."[31] Another witness described the killing of her neighbour: "I saw the soldiers enter the house of my neighbor, María Modesta, who lived with her children. They were shooting them." The female witness said she herself had been able to survive the violent attack on their village because she "took her baby and ran into the mountains" with her sister-in-law, where they spent a miserable night under a tree in the cold and rain. They "could hear the women and children screaming below. Later there was a huge plume of smoke from the village and a strong smell."[32]

The Ixil triangle was one of the most affected regions during *La Violencia*. The government perpetrated various types of violence against women as part of its scorched-earth policy. Women were sexually abused and assassinated, and many of the villages in this region were completely destroyed. Some scholars will argue that if a community was in the "red zone," all community members were slated for death, and that the military was not specifically targeting women. In those cases, the entire community was considered enemies of the state—male and female alike. In contrast, there are also scholars who state that, as a means to create instability within the community, women had to be eliminated or raped. Because women had the responsibility to hand down traditions to their children and were the physical bearers of the culture through reproduction, they were targeted specifically. According to Alison Crosby, when a group's identity becomes intensified, "women are elevated to the status of symbol of the community, becoming iconic representations responsible for the reproduction of the groups."[33] The army practised root and branch genocide through the assassination of women to eliminate reproduction, thereby eradicating the "seed." One of the testimonies collected by the Recuperación de la Memoria Histórica (REMHI) portrays the highly sexualized nature of the killing of some Mayan women: "There are women hanging, with a stick inside their private parts, the stick comes out in their mouths, like a serpent."[34]

In a testimony in *Memoria, Verdad y Esperanza*, interviewee 0803 confirms that, in their view, the women were particularly targeted for sexualized forms of violence: "I believe that there was intentionality when treating women, through sexual violence, a policy directed to affect women and communities: the sexual massive violations, insertion of stakes, the treatment towards pregnant women, were also captured."[35]

These testimonies are illustrative of a systematic pattern to not only violate, but also to eliminate women. According to one witness to this violence, "the PACs and the Army rape[d] children and women, they killed them by shooting and hang[ed] them by the neck, and kick[ed] them in the stomach."[36] During the massacres in the Ixil triangle, many government soldiers committed brutal attacks on pregnant women. Some scholars, such as Greg Grandin, claim that the objective was not to specifically kill women, children, and men, but that they became collateral damage in the course of the war; thus the violence against them was rather counterinsurgent and not genocidal.[37] However, in a 2013 North American Congress on Latin America (NACLA) report that disputes this argument, author Jo-Marie Burt reveals that the courts have found that the rapes and killings of women were systematic. Burt writes,

> The court also found that women were raped not only as the "spoils of war," but as part of the systematic and intentional plan to destroy the Ixil population. Women reproduce life as well as culture, thus the exercise of violence on women's bodies destroys the social fabric and helps ensure the group's destruction. Judge Barrios made reference to the testimony of one woman who narrated her rape

by more than 20 soldiers while she was held prisoner in a military base. The tribunal noted that many of the women still suffer pain and anguish as a result of the sexual violence they experienced.[38]

In another NACLA report, Kate Doyle examines survivor descriptions of the rape of women, and recounts one woman's witnessed account of her rape and the killing of her family. The woman describes her rape by soldiers in Rabinal, the forcible disappearance of her husband, and the brutal murder of her mother, who was burned alive inside her house. She further describes the rape of her aunt and sister-in-law, and how she herself was held at an army base for 15 days, naked, bound, and raped repeatedly by soldiers until she was finally rescued by her uncle. She told the judge, "I wanted to die," following her ordeal.[39]

Many women who survived the massacres endured countless hardships, including repeated rape, torture, and the disappearance of loved ones. When women were separated from men, it was often for gang rape or additional torture. One survivor stated, "They raped me, around 30 soldiers, people was in line, why I did not die."[40] While the woman survived the mass rape, she became pregnant and subsequently bore a child with special needs. During *La Violencia*, repeated rape was a commonplace act; one out of every six massacres investigated for the REMHI report specified that the rape of the village women by the soldiers and the PACs was part of their modus operandi.[41] Many women were left with emotional scars and severe trauma after either experiencing or witnessing the atrocities that were part of the government's treatment of the Mayan communities.

Reaction of Mayan Women to Their Experiences During the Genocide

Women's reactions—as women—to the physical and emotional circumstances of their experiences during the Guatemalan genocide have been difficult to ascertain, because of a silencing blanket of shame or guilt that has been placed on the women in many cases. Many of the women I interviewed in 2000 would not talk openly about their rape in the beginning. Many felt ashamed, and the experience was still too raw and temporal for the female survivors. In many cases, women were also killed after being raped. Witnesses who could give testimony to these brutal acts of murder—like the female survivors of rape—were left traumatized by their experiences, and had an understandable reluctance to bring back the flood of memories by relating it to others. Many women who had survived rape held the belief that they could not marry afterward, because their rape had brought shame not only to themselves, but also to any potential husband. Still, there were others who managed to get past the trauma to the extent that they could marry or remarry and start new families.

Many widows who managed to survive the violence found that they had no choice but to take control of their families. After the violence subsided, some of the widows, realizing that it would take a cooperative effort in order to get the help so many of the female survivors needed, created organizations such as the Guatemalan group CONAVIGUA (Coordinadora Nacional de Viudas de Guatemala), which was created in 1988 by a group of widows. In 2000, I visited with the women of CONAVIGUA, and found that through the cooperative sale of their weavings, they were helping each other survive. The women banded together to overcome their economic vulnerability and also to heal their psychological scars of familial loss. Over time, some of these widowed survivors began sharing their testimonies and experiences.

Many families were left traumatized, and this trauma was evident in their private as well as their community lives. A visit to a resettled Communities of Population in Resistance community in Nebaj in 2002 required more than six months of communication in order for me to arrange admittance. Many people I spoke with believed that the civil war was still ongoing—at the psychological rather than physical level—and there was still an atmosphere of deep distrust and fear. As I was escorted to this community by two Mayan men, I inquired about the fallen trees used as a barricade for the road, several kilometres from their community. They replied that it was for security purposes, so that they "were prepared in case that the Army could come back and attack us again."[42] My conversation with the two men took place a full six years after the peace accords were signed, yet the survivors were still struggling to overcome their fears. Memories of what they had experienced or witnessed clearly still haunted not only those men, but also the women and children of these Mayan communities.

During my interviews with some of these still-grieving families, they told me that soldiers had raped women and then assassinated them in front of their husbands. Some of the women talked of how they had become physically ill—sometimes as a direct result of the violence applied toward them, and sometimes because of the stress or trauma of witnessing such horrific events. According to one survivor, many people died as consequence of the weather because it was very cold in the highlands where they had escaped and they were exposed to the raw elements of nature.[43] Additionally, a common theme among the people interviewed was their hunger during *La Violencia* because of food scarcity. If they fled to safer ground, they could carry very little in the way of supplies with them; and if they remained in the village, the scorched-earth policy of the military left little in the way of food sources for the villagers.

Mayans in the vicinity of El Petén fled across the border to Mexico as refugees. Many died due to the cold temperatures during the perilous journey, and some were left behind on the trail as the others sought to keep the journey moving toward Mexico at all costs. Many of these survivors remember the atrocities in Guatemala that they were trying to escape, as well as their harrowing journey away from Guatemala. Yet once out of Guatemala, they became, in many cases, unwanted refugees with limited economic potential; some had also been forced to leave loved ones laying unburied along their escape route.

Conclusion

Mayan women continue to struggle for survival, even many years after the genocide. Many of them continue to ask for justice and beg to simply know where their loved ones were buried. Many women were left widowed and traumatized psychologically because they witnessed the murder of their family members. Other women suffered mass rape. Still other women were able to escape, but often suffered from guilt at having left their families behind. Women who made the decision to remain in their villages continue to struggle economically, while those who migrated to the cities or to other countries often receive low salaries as domestic employees. Although the civil war officially ended with the peace accords in 1996, the Mayan women from Guatemala still live in a state of psychological terror.

To the female survivors, the scars of the government's violence against some of its own people remain vivid and unhealed. In most cases, the women suffer in silence. In 2013, José Efraín Ríos Montt was put on trial, and in May 2013 he was found guilty by a three-panel tribunal on charges of genocide and crimes against humanity. Within two weeks of this verdict, however, the Constitutional Court in Guatemala overturned his conviction and confined him to house arrest. While many of the survivors and their advocates were left disappointed that Ríos Montt would not serve time in prison, his initial conviction did provide a symbolic victory for the historical record—it established the fact that a genocide had occurred in Guatemala during the period of *La Violencia*.

Questions

1. The genocide that occurred in Guatemala during the early 1980s has been understudied, and is sometimes called a "silent" genocide. Why do you think it has only recently become more known, with more researchers taking an interest in what happened in Guatemala during *La Violencia*?

2. Humiliation of the victims has worked as a central factor in many genocidal events. Why do you think this is? Can you give examples of the ways men, women, and children were humiliated during the Guatemalan genocide?

3. How did the role of Mayan women change during the genocide and post-genocide periods in relation to their family and community, and as citizens of the state of Guatemala?

Notes

1. Victoria Sanford, "From Genocide to Feminicide: Impunity and Human Rights in Twenty-First Century Guatemala," *Journal of Human Rights* 7, no. 2 (2008): 106.

2. Carlos I. Figueroa, "Genocide and State Terrorism in Guatemala, 1954–1996: An Interpretation. Bulletin of Latin American Research," *Journal of the Society for Latin American Studies* 32 (2013): 151–73.

3. Ibid., 167.

4. David Stoll, *Between Two Armies in the Ixil Towns of Guatemala* (New York: Columbia University Press, 1993), 79.

5. "Restoring Lives," January 18, 2011, www.youtube.com/watch?v=tFj18tCCENA &t=164s&list=PLXhuzKSXJ9OSv5oWcdLtMKt8e8SIpuRlI&index=3.

6. Stoll, *Between Two Armies*, 96.

7. Nina Kanakarajavelu, "Legacy of Repression: Violence against Women in Post-Conflict Guatemala" (dissertation, University of Oklahoma, 2010), 28, hdl.handle.net.ezproxy.lib.ou.edu/10192/23865.

8. Robert S. Carlsen, *The War for the Heart and Soul of a Highland Maya Town* (Austin: University of Texas Press, 1997), 146.

9. Stoll, *Between Two Armies*, 115.

10. Ibid., 116.

11. Susanne Jonas, "Guatemala: Acts of Genocide and Scorched-Earth Counterinsurgency War," in *Centuries of Genocide: Essays and Eyewitness Accounts*, ed. Samuel Totten and William S. Parsons (New York: Routledge, 2013), 317.

12. Jennifer Schirmer, *The Guatemalan Military Project: A Violence Called Democracy* (Philadelphia: University of Pennsylvania Press, 1998), 48.

13. Jonas, "Guatemala: Acts of Genocide," 317.

14. Gabriele Kohpahl, *Voices of Guatemalan Women in Los Angeles: Understanding Their Immigration* (New York: Routledge, 1998), 41.

15. Deborah A. Deacon and Paula Calvin, *War Imagery in Women's Textiles: An International Study of Weaving, Knitting, Sewing, Quilting, Rug Making and Other Fabric Arts* (Jefferson, NC: McFarland Company, 2014).

16. Ibid., 105.

17. Kohpahl, *Voices of Guatemalan Women*, 41.

18. Interviewee A, interview by Martha C. Galvan-Mandujano, June 2002, Nebaj, Guatemala.

19. Interviewee B, interview by Martha C. Galvan-Mandujano, June 2002, Nebaj, Guatemala.

20. Antonella Fabri, "Silence, Invisibility, and Isolation: Mayan Women's Strategies for Defense and Survival in Guatemala," in *Women and War in the Twentieth Century: Enlisted with or without Consent*, ed. Nicole Ann Dombrowski (New York: Garland Publishing, 1999), 292.

21. "Bringing Ríos Montt to Justice—Guatemala," March 20, 2013, www.youtube.com/watch?v=Pe1yM1uxOd4&list=PLXhuzKSXJ9OSv5oWcdL tMKt8e8SIpuRlI&index=2&t=34s.

22. Julie A. Hastings, "Silencing State-Sponsored Rape: In and Beyond a Transitional Guatemalan Community," *Violence Against Women* 8 (2002): 1153–1181.

23. Ibid., 1161.

24. Ibid., 1162.

25. Ibid., 1172.

26. Interviewee C, interview by Martha C. Galvan-Mandujano, May 2000, Guatemala City, Guatemala.

27. Hastings, *Violence Against Women*, 1175

28. Sanford, "From Genocide to Feminicide," 104–122.

29. Ibid., 107.

30. Amnesty International, "Guatemala—No Protection, No Justice: Killings of Women in Guatemala" (London: Amnesty International, International Secretariat, 2005), 63.

31. Kate Doyle, "Guatemala's Genocide: Survivors Speak," *NACLA Report on the 3Americas* 41, no. 3 (May/June, 2008), nacla.org/node/4626/termsofuse.

32. Jo-Marie Burt, "Historic Verdict in Guatemala's Genocide Case Overturned by Forces of Impunity," *NACLA Report on the Americas* 46, no. 2 (Summer 2013): 1–3, nacla.org/news/2013/6/17/historic-verdict-guatemala%E2%80%99s-genocide-case-overturned-forces-impunity-0.

33. Alison Crosby, "To Whom Shall the Nation Belong? The Gender and Ethnic Dimension of Refugee Return and the Struggle for Peace in Guatemala," in *Journeys of Fear: Refugee Return and National Transformation in Guatemala*, ed. Lisa L. North and Alan B. Simmons (Montreal: McGill-Queen's University Press, 1999), 181.

34. REMHI, *Guatemala, Nunca Más: Impactos de la Violencia* (Guatemala City: ODHAG, 1998), 215.

35. REMHI, *Memoria, Verdad y Esperanza: Versión Popularizada del Informe REMHI, Guatemala, Nunca Más* (Guatemala City: ODHAG, 2000).

36. REMHI, *Guatemala, Nunca Más*, 212.

37. Greg Grandin, "History, Motive, Law, Intent: Combining Historical and Legal Methods in Understanding Guatemala's 1981–1983 Genocide," in *The Specter of Genocide: Mass Murder in Historical Perspective*, ed. Robert Gellately and Ben Kiernan (New York: Cambridge University Press, 2003), 347.

38. Burt, "Historic Verdict."

39. Kate Doyle, *The Guatemalan Genocide Case Chronicles: Day 3*, February 28, 2008, nacla.org/node/4479.

40. Guatemala: Mujer, Violencia y Silencio 2, Periodismo humano, March 2, 2014, www.youtube.com/watch?v=rHJESXf9nNw.

41. REMHI, *Guatemala, Nunca Más*, 210.

42. Interviewees D and E, interviews by Martha C. Galvan-Mandujano, June 2002, Nebaj, Guatemala.

43. Interviewee F, interview Martha C. Galvan-Mandujano, June 2002, Nebaj, Guatemala.

CHAPTER 7

Survival and Rescue:
Women During the Rwandan Genocide

Sara E. Brown

Introduction

When the genocide reached Elana's village in the eastern province of Rwanda, she was largely unaffected.[1] As a Hutu, she was safe from the murderous Interahamwe militias who were hunting down and massacring the Tutsis who lived in her village. As a woman, she was left to her own devices, ignored by the predominantly male gangs of perpetrators who made their rounds every morning, recruiting able-bodied sons and husbands to participate in the killings. Elana could have spent the duration of the genocide at home and on her farm, tending to her family and her crops, essentially removed from, but not heedless of, the genocide taking place outside of her compound. Instead, Elana decided to venture to a neighbouring hill and check on her friend, a Tutsi woman named Amanda. Upon arrival, Elana found Amanda and her five children inside the house, huddled around her badly beaten husband. As she stood in the doorway and assessed the situation, two Interahamwe militiamen ran up the hill. They forced their way past Elana into the home and dragged Amanda's husband out to the garden to interrogate him. Realizing that once the killers had finished with the husband, they might come for Amanda and her children, Elana sprang into action, pleading with them to follow her down the hill to her home. But Amanda was in shock and refused to leave her husband's side, even when Elana grabbed the children and fled. Amanda eventually made her way to Elana's home but only after she confirmed that her husband had been murdered. Together, the women devised a plan to rescue Amanda and her children. By the time Elana's husband returned home to find the household doubled in size, Elana was resolved that "We are going to stay the way we are, we are not going to give them out. They are going to stay with us and if they decide to kill them, then they'll kill all of us altogether."[2] After several harrowing months, a group of armed Tutsi rebels known as the Rwandan Patriotic Front liberated their village. Due to their bravery and tenacity, Elana and Amanda survived the genocide.

This chapter explores and analyzes the role of female rescuers and survivors who exercised agency during the genocide against the Tutsi.[3] Women who chose to rescue during the genocide did so at great risk and in instances of tremendously limited options, while female survivors often faced sex-specific violence and navigated constrictive gender norms in their struggle to survive. Current literature does not scrutinize women who rescued during the genocide. It remains an as yet unexplored chapter in the history of the genocide in Rwanda. This is partly due to the fact that during war, genocide, and ethnic cleansing, women are traditionally cast as victims, and little literary real estate remains in which to address female rescuers, perpetrators, or active bystanders. In Rwanda, many women did suffer horrific abuses at the hands of perpetrators, and their experiences are addressed in this chapter. However, society's interpretation of conflict focuses upon the role of women as *passive* victims, a stereotype that extends into existing scholarship. While a large body of work addresses the victimization of women during the Rwandan genocide, it rarely examines the agency they exercised. But victims are rarely passive, instead exercising agency in instances of tremendously limited options. Just like Elana and Amanda, many Rwandan women devised strategies in the midst of the genocide, due to their victimization and in order to ensure their survival, often manipulating their subordinate status in 1994 Rwanda to their advantage.

This chapter revisits the narrative of women's passivity and will address J. Ann Tickner's observation that "too often women's experiences have been deemed trivial, or important only in so far as they relate to the experiences of men."[4] Agreeing with Erin Baines's assertion that "Life stories are a particularly useful method to shed insight into the social positions of oppressed groups within a given institution and historical setting," it utilizes oral testimonies in order to shed light on women's agency, impressions, feelings, and actions during the Rwandan genocide.[5] Relying upon analysis of first-hand oral testimonies and archival sources,[6] this chapter applies the four-point comparative framework developed by Dalia Ofer and Lenore J. Weitzman to examine women as rescuers and survivors during the Rwandan genocide.[7]

History

Rwanda is a small country, roughly the size of the state of Maryland in the United States, and located in the Great Lakes region of Central Africa. Formerly an established kingdom with a hierarchical monarchy and recognized borders, it was ruled by Germany and later Belgium during colonialism. Rwanda gained independence in 1962 during a period marred by ethnic polarization and violence. The Tutsis, an ethnic minority in Rwanda, were initially favoured by their colonial rulers, but were abandoned in the late 1950s by the Belgians in favour of the Hutus, the ethnic majority. As part of the newly dubbed "Hutu Revolution," pro-Hutu political leaders exacerbated ethnic tensions and encouraged violence against Tutsis. Over the following decade, approximately 20,000 Tutsis were murdered and more than 300,000 were forced into exile in Uganda and abroad.[8] In the end, despite the belated and half-hearted attempts of the Belgian colonialists, Rwanda did not transition to democracy, instead being ruled by two dictators, Grégoire Kayibanda (1962–1973) and Juvénal Habyarimana (1973–1994), prior to the genocide.

In October 1990, after decades of exile, a band of Tutsis formed a rebel group known as the Rwandan Patriotic Front (RPF) and invaded Rwanda from Uganda. They demanded, among other things, the right to return home, and a role in Rwanda's government. Their initial advance was swift and alarmed President Habyarimana, who sought the intervention of French military forces, longtime allies of the president. French troops drove back the RPF fighters. A resulting stalemate catalyzed uneasy peace negotiations that eventually led to a peace agreement known as the Arusha Accords. Signed in 1993, the Arusha Accords were widely unpopular among the Hutu elite who resisted any challenge to their power. The contentious negotiations tarnished President Habyarimana's popularity and coincided with international pressure for Rwanda to transition to a multiparty democracy, further weakening the president's dictatorship. A number of political parties formed, including several extremist parties who championed Hutu nationalism and advocated for violence against Tutsis. The political parties clashed, as skirmishes, mob violence, and assassinations increased in frequency. Under cover of war and political instability in the country, Rwanda's national army, the Forces armées rwandaises (FAR), began training young men under the pretense of defending neighbourhoods and tracking down infiltrators; these same men would later compose the core of the Interahamwe killing militias.[9]

On the evening of April 6, 1994, a private jet carrying President Habyarimana began its descent into Kigali, Rwanda. As the plane approached Kigali's international airport, it was shot out of the sky and crashed into the presidential compound, killing all of the passengers on board, including a number of Rwandan officials, the president of Burundi, and Rwanda's president. Immediately, the FAR and Interahamwe militia groups sprang into action, setting up road blocks, distributing lists of influential Rwandans marked for murder, and conducting home raids. Rwanda's Radio Télévision Libre des Mille Collines, the popular mouthpiece for Hutu extremists and a key component of the anti-Tutsi propaganda machine, quickly assigned blame for Habyarimana's assassination to the RPF and Tutsi fifth columnists and launched a heated campaign of genocide incitement. It is clear that the assassination of President Habyarimana triggered a pre-arranged series of actions that culminated in genocide. By the morning of April 7, the genocide was well underway in Kigali, and spread throughout the country soon thereafter.

Local leaders who accepted the genocidal ideology rallied their constituents to participate in the "work" of eradicating all Tutsis in their area, promising looted resources and land as their reward. Able-bodied Hutu boys and men who resisted participating were rarely ignored; they were often coerced into joining the Interahamwe, threatened if they refused, and occasionally murdered—especially if they were caught aiding Tutsis. Over the course of the next 100 days, and under the cover of war with the RPF, at least 800,000 Tutsis and Hutu moderates were systematically hunted, tortured, raped, and murdered as part of an orchestrated genocide in Rwanda. Viewing the genocide of the Tutsi population in Rwanda and subsequent attacks against their forces as an effective end to the previously negotiated ceasefire, the RPF renewed their campaign against the FAR and militia forces. Despite the presence of United Nations (UN) peacekeeping forces stationed in Kigali, the genocide continued unabated and without international interference; in the end, the genocide was only stopped by the RPF, who took control over the country and began a lengthy reconstruction and rehabilitation process that continues to this day.

The Impact of Culturally Defined Roles of Rwandan Women

Before the genocide, Rwandan women, regardless of ethnicity or class, were impacted by culturally prescribed "norms" that limited their autonomy and mirrored the reality faced by Jewish women in Europe in the period before the Holocaust and World War II. In 1994, Rwanda's public and political spheres were spaces restricted primarily to men, while women were consigned to the home.[10] A popular proverb in Kinyarwanda, the primary language spoken in Rwanda, illustrates women's relegation to the private sphere: *umugore niwe 'mutima urugo, or the woman is the heart of the home.* While this proverb has since been reclaimed by Rwandan feminists to show the importance of women as the cornerstone of the home and therefore in need of equal rights and protection from gender-based violence, at the time, it was used to emphasize the primacy of a woman's place within the four walls of her compound. Similarly, while Ofer and Weitzman are quick to highlight the differences between Eastern and Western European gender norms, they note that "in most Jewish families, as in most non-Jewish families, married men were responsible for the economic support of their families, while women, even if they had learned a trade or were helping in the family business, were responsible for the home and the children."[11]

Even though Rwandan cultural norms restricted women to the domestic private sphere, they were often marginalized within their homes, unable to challenge the decisions of their husbands. One scholar observed that in pre-genocide Rwanda, "Whatever men could do, a woman should and must obey. And then there is a saying in Rwanda that there is no mistake for men. Even beating a woman, even wasting money, even doing whatever he wants, there is no mistake for a man."[12] In a culture that demanded obedience and subordination to men, Rwanda's women were hard pressed for a space wherein they could exercise agency. In terms of ethnic identity—a decisive factor for success and acceptance in pre-genocide Rwandan society—women were not accorded a determining role in the identity of their children. While they were responsible for the rearing of children, ethnic identity was determined by a child's paternal lineage, regardless of the identity of the mother.

An elaborate legal framework ensured that women remained economically and politically marginalized in Rwandan society. Men were legally recognized as the heads of Rwandan households according to the Family Code of 1992. In 1994, Rwandan women were prohibited by law from inheriting property, opening a bank account without the consent of their husband, and, representing just 5 percent of the executive branch of Hutu-controlled Mouvement républicain national pour la démocratie et le développement (MRND) government, were not in a political position to advocate for change.[13] There was just one female minister, Pauline Nyiramasuhuko, who was in charge of Family and Women's Development, a ministry that addressed women and the home—areas considered appropriate for a woman to manage. During the period leading up to the genocide, Rwanda had its first and only female prime minister, Agathe Uwilingiyimana. While this was a significant achievement, Prime Minister Uwingiliyimana was repeatedly sidelined by Habyarimana's government and, as a voice for moderate Hutus, was one of the first politicians murdered on April 7, 1994. As a result of these deeply entrenched patriarchal systems that regulated women in Rwanda and the pre-existing cultural norms of passivity that constrained their agency, women had little latitude for autonomous action.

The Rwandan genocide proved a catalyst for the dissolution of many of the socially prescribed and perpetuated gender roles that dictated the behaviour of Rwandan women. For Jewish women during the Third Reich, the increasingly repressive measures instituted by the Nazis meant that women experienced a shift in gender roles rather than their dissolution. Mass violence upends the rule of law and compromises the functionality of state institutions; additionally, it tears at the social fabric of a community and results in the suspension of some, but not all, gendered behaviours. In Europe in the 1930s and early 1940s, Jewish women experienced a marked increase in their workload. While they remained the primary caregivers at home, responsible for the emotional and psychological well-being of their perceptibly distressed family, many were also forced to find work in order to survive. In Rwanda, the violence created a temporary space for the inclusion of women, by force or by choice, in previously restricted public spheres and capacities. As a result, it was not unusual to find women working alongside the Interahamwe killing militias, exposing Tutsis in hiding, looting homes and bodies, and in some instances, committing murder.[14]

At the same time, gendered perceptions of women's passivity and weakness inadvertently enabled other women to participate in acts of rescue. One female rescuer, Ruth, was able to save a newborn infant she rescued from an open mass grave, as a result of Interahamwe militia members' underestimation of her strength. When the Interahamwe learned of her act of rescue from a neighbour, they marched to her home to punish her and kill the child. Upon arrival, they found Ruth seated outside, breastfeeding the newborn alongside her own several-month-old infant. She recalled that "when they saw that, they were like 'Ah, just leave them, they will die very soon anyway.'"[15] The Interahamwe left, convinced that Ruth, a slight woman with a meek disposition, lacked the strength to maintain the newborn. When I asked Ruth what became of the baby girl, she smiled. She is now a full-time high school student.

Culture continues to be significant in modern Rwandan society. In 1994, it played a determining role in the experiences of women during the genocide and their individual and collective capacities to react to the genocide, facilitate their survival and the survival of others, and provide for their post-genocide reconstruction and rehabilitation. Today, Rwanda's post-genocide trajectory reflects a positive shift away from traditional gender-based marginalization of women, and toward empowerment and inclusion of women in public and political spheres.

Women's Anticipatory Reactions

Based on prior experiences of violence during the pre-independence period, early independence, upheaval in 1973, and the early 1990s, many Rwandans assumed (correctly, at first) that men would be the primary targets for violence during the genocide. Women and children, as had been the tendency in the past, would hide with neighbours, at home, or at religious sites and be more or less safe from the violence. While this held true at the outset of the genocide, a shift occurred as a result of deliberate incitement by the media, local leaders, and Interahamwe. Eventually, as the killings continued and spread unevenly throughout the country, women and children were also targeted for murder without distinction. For many women who were now on their own, having been separated from the men who headed the household, survival required unilateral decision making and a level of agency previously discouraged by Rwandan cultural norms. From never chairing a meeting in the family to suddenly making life-or-death decisions on one's own, survival often required a combination of luck and action.[16] A number of women recounted to me how the prospect of death or the death of their loved ones catalyzed them. When Jane's mother was first visited by members of the Interahamwe in search of her brothers, she and her children were left unharmed. When the leader of the group asked his men what they found in the house, they replied, "We only find little kids and an old woman in there. Those cockroaches are not there." Because the genocide had just begun, the men ignored her and her small children, focusing instead on the men. This echoes Ofer and Weitzman's observation that "Most Jews believed—at least in the beginning—that the Germans were 'civilized' and would honor traditional gender norms and would not harm women and children. Because the Jews believed that only men were in real danger, they responded with gender-specific plans to protect and save their men."[17] In both instances, the assumption that gender norms would not be suspended and women and children would be overlooked resulted in a short-lived sense of false security. Somehow, Jane knew this reprieve would be ephemeral and told her children, "If a second group is coming here and they find us here, maybe they are not going to have mercy for me. They are going to kill us." Jane gathered her children and fled to the St. Famille Church since it had been a place of sanctuary during prior periods of conflict.[18] In many instances, despite the aforementioned difficulties and marginalization they experienced experienced, women strategized ways to survive the genocide, conscious of this shift against them.

As the genocide ravaged the western region of Rwanda, Beth, a Tutsi woman married to a Hutu man, aided her husband in hiding their friends and family members within the family compound. The Interahamwe quickly found out and captured her and her husband, their five children, and her sister. The Interahamwe marched them to a building near the town market, imprisoned Beth and her children, killed her sister, and took her husband to another location, where he was also killed. After Beth was informed of her husband's death, the Interahamwe militia who were guarding her asked, "Where are you going now?" Now alone, Beth considered her options:

> I was thinking of hiding with the kids, there was a farm close by and I was like, "I can't hide with these kids—they are very young." Because I gave birth every year, they were still very young. I thought of killing myself first, I was like, "That's not possible. Should I first kill the kids? Throw ourselves in [Lake] Kivu?" It wouldn't be something—I just didn't know what to do at that moment. So I told the two guys, "Ok, just escort me to this friend of ours."[19]

Beth had weighed her options—some of which were horrific—with respect to the existing situation and realized that their best chance of survival was to reach out to an influential Hutu man who had been a friend of her late husband. Due to confusion as to Beth's ethnic identity, they escorted her to the home of this family friend who agreed to hide her. This was a surprisingly common occurrence; Tutsi women recount hiding— often as a known secret among the neighbours and community—with

Hutu men who shared a familial relationship, a personal connection, or as a result of the man's nefarious motivations. Beth managed to survive the genocide with her children, in part by surveying each situation, weighing her options, and deciding accordingly.

All the while, it is difficult to determine women's awareness of the dynamic and nuanced social and political underpinnings of the genocide. A national level of awareness was not apparent in my interviews, despite extensive knowledge on the local level with respect to individual actors and occurrences in women's immediate community and their impact. Still, this local knowledge and anticipation assisted many survivors who had to strategize to ensure their survival, as well as female rescuers who had to act in order to save the people they were protecting. Josephine Dusabimana, a well-known rescuer from Kibuye who was honoured by the United States Department of State in 2011, gave multiple examples of times she outmanoeuvred the perpetrators of the genocide as well as her own family in an effort to rescue those targeted for murder. In one instance, when negotiating transport for two Tutsis in hiding across Lake Kivu to the Democratic Republic of the Congo (DRC), she noted the following:

> All of a sudden, something hit me and I was like "The way this person accepted to help me when they are taking them across the lake—will they merely throw them in the lake?" I got one of them [a Tutsi in hiding] who was called Paul and told him "Let's go outside." So when I took Paul outside to talk to him, I told him "Now, you are going to go. But how will I know that you reached where you are supposed to go?"[20]

In the end, Josephine and Paul agreed that he would hand the marble he carried in his pocket over to the man navigating the boat, Josephine's own cousin, upon arrival in the DRC, with instructions to deliver the marble to Josephine. When Josephine received the marble the next day, she knew they had arrived safely. In another instance, realizing that her husband's patience was growing thin with the number of people she was hiding in their home, Josephine devised a plan to steal the boat of Kanyenzi, a local businessman and prominent Interahamwe member. She brought her two boys to serve as a distraction while she cut through the lock securing the boat. Josephine calculated that a mother and two children bathing at the lake would not arouse the suspicions of the Interahamwe or nearby guards and encouraged her children to swim and make a commotion while she worked. In the end, she was correct in her assumption; the guards over-looked their prolonged stay and ignored their activities. As their splashes and shouts masked the sound of the bolt cutters, Josephine freed the boat, later using it to transport more Tutsis across the lake to the DRC.[21]

Other women knowingly chose to endanger themselves in order to stand alongside their families. At Murambi in southwestern Rwanda, Margaret was faced with a choice: as the genocide spread throughout their region, her husband encouraged her to flee and save herself. She was a Hutu, and therefore exempt from the murderous intentions of the gathering Interahamwe. Considered Tutsi as a result of the aforementioned primacy of paternal ethnic identity, Margaret knew she would have been safe if she had left her Tutsi husband and their three children. But she refused, explaining that "because I had a little baby, I had given birth in the month of March, I saw I couldn't leave my kids behind and my husband, so I decided to stay."[22] Margaret instead sought refuge with them at a technical school that held tens of thousands of Tutsis. Late at night, she huddled in the corner of a small room with her family as the killers threw stones and spears at them. After being pushed from the room by her husband in an attempt to save her life, Margaret was surrounded by members of the murderous Interahamwe militia and threatened with death if she would not put down the infant tied to her back. Margaret refused to let go of her child, kneeled before their raised machetes, and, realizing she was about to die, began to pray. Just before the machetes fell, Margaret was rescued by a man in the crowd who intervened and stopped the killers. Today, Margaret and her daughter are 2 of the 14 (at the time of publication) known survivors of that massacre. Her husband and two sons perished. Margaret stood by her family even as they were targeted for annihilation, in spite of the knowledge that doing so would likely result in her death.[23]

In each of these instances, the women who took action were aware that their lives were at risk, albeit with varied degrees of understanding of the complexity and breadth of the conflict, and nevertheless acted with the intent to save themselves, their family members, and in Josephine's case, the people who they were rescuing.

Difference in Treatment of Women and Men

During the genocide, women's experiences differed significantly compared to those of men. For Tutsi women, this meant that they were often subjected to sex-specific torture and abuse during the genocide. Rene Lemarchand found that "Tutsi women ... were a favorite target of Hutu cartoonists in search of pornographic effect,"[24] while Catherine MacKinnon noted that "vicious sexualization and denigrating sexual stereotyping of Tutsi women was a staple on the radio and in newspapers preceding and throughout the atrocities."[25] Utilizing fear as a powerful catalyst, the sexualization of Tutsi women by the government was part of a deliberate strategy to mobilize Hutus against Tutsi women, specifically as a double threat due to their ethnicity and their sex. Publications like the "Hutu Ten Commandments," radio programming from the extremist radio station Radio Télévision Libre des Mille Collines, and cartoons and articles published in the periodical *Kangura* demonized and sexualized Tutsi women and resulted in horrific instances of sexual torture endured by Tutsi women before they were murdered.[26]

Examples abound. In the town of Nyamata, a genocide memorial that was once a Catholic Church houses the corpse of a young woman who was killed by impalement; the sharp stick that was inserted into her vagina and exited her skull still remains. Pauline Nyiramasuhuko, the former minister of Family and Women's Development, was instrumental in the perpetration of genocide in the southwestern region of Rwanda. In 2011, she was the first and only woman found guilty of genocide and rape as a crime against humanity by the International Criminal Tribunal for Rwanda (ICTR). Dubbed the "minister of rape" by journalist Peter Landesman, witnesses at the ICTR testified that Nyiramasuhuko "shouted at the Interahamwe to 'choose the young girls and the women that are still useful.'[27] She ordered that the women be raped because they refused to marry Hutus and then to be loaded onto the [Toyota] Hilux to be killed."[28] Adalbert, one of ten convicted perpetrators of the genocide interviewed by

Jean Hatzfeld, noted that "There were two kinds of rapists. Some took the girls and used them as wives until the end.... Others caught them just to fool around with, for having sex and drinking; they raped for a little while and then handed them over to be killed right afterward."[29]

At the same time, "studies show that rape is not an aggressive manifestation of sexuality, but rather a sexual manifestation of aggression," that aggression is not restricted to women alone.[30] Janvier Forongo, executive secretary (at the time of my interview) of IBUKA, an umbrella group for genocide survivor organizations throughout Rwanda, asserts that there is overwhelming evidence of woman-perpetrated rape and sexual assault during the Rwandan genocide—particularly against Tutsi boys and young men.[31] These acts of sexual violence were intended to dishonour the victims as well as the community, further tearing at the social fabric that bound them together. While one victim, Charles, agreed to describe his experience to me, recounting his harrowing experience of being bound, drugged, and gang-raped by four women, many victims are reticent to discuss their victimization.[32] This silence is a result of gendered perceptions of masculinity that maintain that male victims of sexual violence are no longer masculine and thus ostracized by the community. Charles alluded to this ostracization, describing his feelings of shame, disbelief, and emasculation. Additionally, the meta-narrative of the Rwandan genocide labels women as the exclusive victims of sexual violence, with little space left in popular discourse to explore men who experienced such crimes. As such, it must be noted that this section of the chapter's analysis is an illustration and perpetuation of the shortfalls of scholarship that, through an unintentionally gendered lens, explores sexual violence as being exclusively experienced by women.

For some female rescuers, the fact that they were women played a significant role in their success. The Interahamwe killing militias regularly recruited "ordinary men" to perpetrate genocide. As explained by Scott Straus, these men were representative of the "demographic profile of adult Hutu men at the time of the genocide ... with average levels of education and who had no prior history of violence." Driven by coercion, social pressure, fear, and the promise of economic incentives, those men reticent to join the Interahamwe complied.[33] While some women were recruited, the majority were exempt from this genocidal extension of *umuganda*, a state-instituted practice of compulsory community works that existed well before the genocide of 1994. This had a manifold effect on Rwandan women, especially those living apart from or without a husband in the home.[34] First, it meant that her home was exempt from the sometimes daily visits from the Interahamwe in search of recruits or those who were hiding to avoid participation.[35] Second, she did not have to struggle with the daily ideological indoctrination promulgated by the Interahamwe that pitted Hutus against Tutsis. Third, in some instances, it meant that the Interahamwe were less inclined to suspect women of hiding anyone in their homes. One rescuer, Denise, relied on this strategy multiple times, expecting that the Interahamwe would underestimate her as a woman and refrain from searching her home. While this worked on most days, in one instance the Interahamwe insisted that they enter her home and search for Tutsis. Denise bluffed, brazenly inviting them in. "So when I told them 'please search the house,' they became scared of entering the house. They could see I was only a woman and they decided not to bother going into the house."[36] By forwardly inviting them in and causing them embarrassment, she avoided further interrogation. Other women hid people in areas of the house traditionally restricted to women. Martha, another rescuer, knowingly hid a woman and her child in her kitchen, explaining that "because the men, they rarely went to the kitchen, they thought the kitchen was for babies, so they never checked most of the time the kitchen."[37] Relying on this gendered demarcation of the home, Martha hid the mother and child for several days before the RPF liberated her village.

As survivors and as rescuers, women experienced the genocide in Rwanda in a manner unique to them *as women*. Women who were victimized by the perpetrators were subject to sexual abuse that targeted them as women and as Tutsis. And while the majority of Tutsi men did not experience this sex-specific torture, those boys and men who did experience sexual violence during the genocide have suffered as a result of both the gendered narrative that excludes male victims of sexual torture, and the existing stigmas that liken men who experience sexual violence to women, emasculated by existing cultural norms in Rwanda. Female rescuers were able to utilize gender norms that emphasized women's passivity and meekness to their advantage, often avoiding suspicion or participation in the genocide as a result. For female survivors and rescuers alike, their experiences during the genocide differed significantly from those of men.

The Reactions and Processes of Rwandan Women

Women suffered greatly as a result of the genocide in Rwanda. Many women were widowed or separated from their husbands, lost their family network, and were impoverished by the scorched-earth policies of the Interahamwe killing militias and government forces. This section will address some specific challenges faced by women following the genocide, forgoing a comprehensive overview of the subsequent myriad of experiences of both Tutsi and Hutu women due to the limited space and the focus of this overall chapter.

Following the genocide, Odette Kayirere inventoried her life. She was a widow, her husband a victim of murder during the genocide, but she had survived. She had lost her home but her daughters were still alive and became the reason to rebuild her life. After a period of mourning, she realized that many other women were suffering all around her and explained that "From there, I took a commitment, really, and I found a response from there, my life, that I survived, to encourage others."[38] Odette began gathering other female survivors to share their experiences, to mourn collectively, and to find meaning in their survival. She later went on to become an influential leader in Association des Veuves du Génocide (AVEGA Agahozo), one of the largest and most active survivor organizations in Rwanda.

According to a 1996 report drafted by the United Nations Special Rapporteur of the Commission on Human Rights, between 250,000 and 500,000 Rwandan women experienced widespread systematic genocidal rape during the genocide in Rwanda.[39] The women who survived genocidal rape continue to experience physical trauma as a result of their victimization, which many of them continue to live with today (including, for example, HIV/AIDS), as well as psychological, spiritual, and emotional trauma. Recognizing that something must be done and that "enough is enough," as one woman put it, widows of the genocide joined together and formed AVEGA Agahozo in 1995.[40] These women participated in a unique form of rescue—after the violence, they ensured that female survivors of the genocide would endure, heal, and prosper. Now the executive secretary of AVEGA Agahozo, Odette pointed out that many survivors "couldn't overcome from trauma ... because of what they experienced. Having been raped or seeing their children killed in front of their eyes ... it's really really sad and very hard to understand and really to accept.... So AVEGA started this program to help them, to help members to understand what happened, to reconcile their life and their past experiences."[41]

Combining a holistic approach that includes medical aid, counselling, job training, legal representation, and other forms of assistance, AVEGA Agahozo reached out to women around the country, documented the experiences of women, and fought to reverse a negative stigma that shamed and isolated female survivors of genocidal rape, thereby increasing their vulnerability. AVEGA Agahozo lobbied the government to address issues—including laws of succession—that were limiting the likelihood of women-headed households to prosper, and funded research on violence against women during the genocide to raise awareness and inform policy makers of the specific needs of women following the genocide. As a result of these initiatives, many women overcame their initial reticence to speak openly about their experiences and joined counselling groups wherein they could communicate with fellow survivors about their trauma and the challenges they faced moving forward. Today, AVEGA Agahozo continues to offer medical, psychological, and legal services, and also provides job training and economic development opportunities for thousands of survivors every year, including male survivors of genocidal rape. [42]

Those who rescued during the genocide, displaying courage and a tenacity against societal pressures and constructs that sanctioned violence, have often faced considerable issues following the genocide—sometimes as a result of their bravery, but also due to their sex. Many female rescuers remain impoverished as a result of their heroism. When a member of the Interahamwe approached Allison's home outside of Butare and demanded that she hand over the young girl she was hiding, she refused and instead resorted to bribery to save the girl's life. She explained that "I would sometimes give him money or sometimes I would give him maybe a goat or anything that I had so that he would go."[43] Eventually, Allison ran out of money and livestock to hand over in exchange for the girl's life and resorted to lying to the Interahamwe, claiming that the girl was no longer in her home. When I met Allison 20 years later, she suffered from persistent poverty, unable to recuperate or make up for the lost wealth. For other women, the stigma of rescue meant that neighbours no longer shared basic food items and water with them or boycotted their businesses, thereby causing continued economic harm post-genocide.[44] While the government has made considerable efforts to ensure that women are provided equal access to economic opportunities, land, and inheritance, the cooperation and interreliance of neighbours is vital to the rural communities. In instances where an individual or family is ostracized by the community, they are exponentially more vulnerable, and therefore cannot rely on their neighbours to support them in instances of crop failure, business failure, illness, or unexpected emergencies.

Another issue faced by female rescuers—particularly those who headed their households—is insecurity, especially in more remote areas of Rwanda where law enforcement is stretched over broad tracts of land with few access roads. During the genocide, Martha and her husband rescued six people, five women and one child. In the midst of the killings, her husband disappeared; Martha suspects that he was a victim of murder, based on comments and taunts from her neighbours regarding the fate of her husband. When the RPF arrived in her area, she brought out the six people she was hiding, shocking her neighbours, and travelled with them to an internally displaced person camp that was guarded by the RPF. Several months later, when she returned home with her four children, her neighbours seized the opportunity to attack her as punishment for her acts of rescue, with her own godson beating her about the head. Three months later, after Martha recovered from the injuries she had sustained, she changed churches and moved to another town. She continues to live in fear, refusing to share her testimony publicly and hiding her past from her new neighbours. My interview with her was her first, apart from her participation in the Gacaca courts, a hybrid court that was established to try crimes perpetrated during the genocide. Martha felt she was vulnerable to attack because she did not have a man in her home protecting her. As she put it, "I was tried so much when especially my husband died.... Actually they were surprised to see them [survivors] come out of my house. And after that, that's why they came after me, they were very angry for what I did and they attacked me, they hit me on my head, and all my friends became my enemies—all people have become like animals to me.... I'm always scared now."[45] The association between security and the existence or absence of a man in the household was a recurring theme in my interviews with feamale rescuers. Some expressed relief that they were not alone. Denise confided that "Right now I feel safe and most especially because my husband came back and he was with me and I felt more safe. But if I was still alone, I don't think I would be safe here."[46] Others rejected this association out of hand, and insisted that they were secure despite being the head of the household. Still, Josephine was the only female rescuer I interviewed who requested that her real name be used "so that people learn from it"; the rest preferred anonymity.[47]

Lastly, non-recognition, another challenge faced by female rescuers, is subject to debate. Some studies exist, including one by IBUKA, an umbrella organization that supports survivors throughout Rwanda, but it covers just 14 percent of Rwanda's sectors.[48] Other organizations have worked to identify the "righteous" in Rwanda but have not managed to make significant gains.[49] In their anonymity, female rescuers may be shielded from further insecurity, as discussed above. On the other hand, while these women must be protected, their stories must be recorded for several important reasons. First, these stories must be documented so as to change the culture of silence and fear that accompanies female rescuers. Their stories must become mainstream, accepted, and cause for celebration—measures that would shift the paradigm of rescuers and make it unacceptable to target them for discrimination or violence. Second, their stories further develop the comprehensive narrative of the Rwandan genocide that is still being compiled. This is an untold chapter of great importance to academics, policy makers, and the Rwandan people. Additionally, identifying more rescuers who could serve as peace brokers benefits Rwanda's efforts to unify the country. Naphtal Ahishakiye, the current executive secretary of IBUKA, noted that rescuers often play a significant role in Rwanda's post-genocide reconciliation initiatives.[50] They often serve as a bridge between survivors and perpetrators, as both sides are more inclined to trust former rescuers than they are each other. Finally, these stories will serve our future generations. Investigation and recognition of female rescuers provides an opportunity to celebrate and emulate the women who rejected the culture of genocide and took a stand against the murderers. They are embodiments of the United States' Ambassador to the United Nations Samantha Power's "upstanders," and should be held up as role models for the youth in Rwanda. Rwanda's prisons are filled with genocide perpetrators who serve as cautionary tales for the youth—now is the time to provide that generation with positive examples of who they could become.

Conclusion

Western literature and media emphasize the role of women as victims of the genocide with the occasional, almost offhand, mention of women who participated in the genocide. This limited monolithic narrative overlooks a more complicated, and in some instances, uncomfortable analysis of women during genocide. There is a limited amount of literary real estate allotted to women during genocide—they are given a finite amount of space in the narrative and so their stories are simplified and amalgamated into the category of "victimhood," because anything more nuanced would (1) take space, time, and effort; and (2) make many uncomfortable, since it challenges the perception of the essentialized woman, according to local and loaded gender norms.

At the same time, the complicated story is necessary—not only to accurately document, learn from, and prevent mass violence, but also, and at the risk of overgeneralization, to return to women their identities, their personhood, and their narratives. Utilizing Ofer and Weitzman's four-point framework designed to elucidate the history of women during the Holocaust, genocide scholars can begin to piece together the experiences of women during other instances of mass atrocities. In the case of Rwanda, examining the impact of culturally defined roles, women's anticipatory reactions, how women were treated differently from men, and the reactions and processes of women following the 1994 genocide illustrates the history of women during the fastest genocide of the 20th century, and their impact on Rwanda today. By examining the roles and experiences of women, an often overlooked but essential component of the whole and complicated story of genocide is brought to light.[51]

Questions

1. What can we extrapolate from the strategies employed by female rescuers during the 1994 genocide in Rwanda?
2. Some may express skepticism about a woman's ability to participate in genocide. Why do we assume that women would not participate in genocide?
3. What are the advantages of utilizing oral histories to analyze the 1994 genocide in Rwanda? What are the disadvantages?

Notes

1. All the names of rescuers and survivors have been changed with the exception of Josephine Dusabimana, at her request.
2. Interviewee R 10 Elana, interview by Sara E. Brown, March 18, 2014, Rwamagana, Rwanda.
3. Also referred to as the genocide in Rwanda, the Rwandan genocide, and the genocide throughout this chapter.
4. J. Ann Tickner, "Feminism Meets International Relations: Some Methodological Issues," in *Feminist Methodologies for International Relations*, ed. Brooke A. Ackerly, Maria Stern, and Jacqui True (New York: Cambridge University Press, 2006), 25.
5. Erin Baines, "Gender, Responsibility, and the Grey Zone: Considerations for Transitional Justice," *Journal of Human Rights* 10, no. 4 (2011): 482.
6. Including 10 oral testimonies gathered and published by the Genocide Archive Rwanda, 15 oral testimonies provided by Association des Veuves du Genocide (AVEGA), and other archival materials. In addition, the author collected and analyzed 51 interviews and meetings with individuals living in Rwanda who could speak about female rescuers and survivors during the Rwandan genocide. Interview participants included community and government stakeholders, survivors of the genocide, and individuals who rescued others during the genocide. In-country research was conducted over the course of five trips, in 2010, 2011, 2012, and two in 2014. Whenever

possible, testimonies were triangulated with archival sources, corroborating testimony and documents from government and community stakeholders.

7. Dalia Ofer and Lenore J. Weitzman, eds., *Women in the Holocaust* (New Haven: Yale University Press, 1998).

8. Allison Des Forges, *Leave None to Tell the Story: Genocide in Rwanda* (New York: Human Rights Watch, 1999), 40.

9. Ibid., 140.

10. Lisa Sharlach, "Gender and Genocide in Rwanda: Women as Agents and Objects of Genocide," *Journal of Genocide Research* 1, no. 3 (1999): 391.

11. Fatuma Ndangiza, interview by Sara E. Brown, August 1, 2014, Kigali, Rwanda; Dalia Ofer and Lenore J. Weitzman, "The Role of Gender in the Holocaust," in *Women in the Holocaust*, ed. Dalia Ofer and Lenore J. Weitzman (New Haven: Yale University Press, 1998), 3.

12. D. E., interview by Sara E. Brown, June 25, 2011, Kigali, Rwanda.

13. Sharlach, "Gender and Genocide in Rwanda," 391.

14. Ofer and Weitzman, "The Role of Gender in the Holocaust," 9; Odette Kayirere and Sabine Uwase, interview by Sara E. Brown, June 15, 2011, Kigali, Rwanda; Rwanda Government, "Summary of the Report Presented at the Closing of Gacaca Courts Activities," (Kigali: Rwanda Government, 2012).

15. Interviewee R 7 Ruth, interview by Sara E. Brown, February 22, 2014, Kibuye, Rwanda.

16. Fatuma Ndangiza, interview by Sara E. Brown, August 1, 2014, Kigali, Rwanda.

17. Ofer and Weitzman, "The Role of Gender in the Holocaust," 5.

18. Interviewee S 9 Jane, interview by Sara E. Brown, March 30, 2014, Kigali, Rwanda.

19. Interviewee S 6 Beth, interview by Sara E. Brown, February 22, 2014, Kibuye, Rwanda.

20. Josephine Dusabimana, interview by Sara E. Brown, February 22, 2014, Kibuye, Rwanda.

21. Ibid.

22. Interviewee S 1 Margaret, interview by Sara E. Brown, June 28, 2011, Murambi, Rwanda.

23. Ibid.

24. Rene Lemarchand, *The Dynamics of Violence in Central Africa* (Philadelphia: University of Pennsylvania Press, 2009), 63.

25. Catherine MacKinnon, *Are Women Human? And Other International Dialogues* (Cambridge: Belknap Press of Harvard University Press, 2006), 226.

26. For examples, visit the collection of *Kangura* publications made available online by the Genocide Archive of Rwanda, including the "Hutu Ten Commandments," *Kangura* no. 06 (December 1990), www.genocide-archiverwanda.org.rw/index.php/Kangura_Issue_06; Lemarchand, *The Dynamics of Violence in Central Africa*, 62.

27. Peter Landesman, "The Minister of Rape," *Toronto Star*, September 21, 2002.

28. International Criminal Tribunal for Rwanda, "Judgment and Sentence," June 24, 2011, 555.

29. Jean Hatzfeld, *Machete Season: The Killers in Rwanda Speak* (New York: Farrar, Straus and Giroux, 2003), 97.

30. Ruth Seifert, "War and Rape: A Preliminary Analysis," in *Mass Rape: The War Against Women in Bosnia Herzegovina*, ed. Alexandra Stiglmayer (Lincoln: University of Nebraska Press, 1994), 55.

31. Janvier Forongo, interview by Sara E. Brown, June 14, 2011, Kigali, Rwanda.

32. Interviewee S 2 Charles, interview by Sara E. Brown, June 29, 2011, Kigali, Rwanda.

33. Scott Straus, *The Order of Genocide: Race, Power, and War in Rwanda* (Ithaca: Cornell University Press, 2006), 96–110.

34. Just over 50 percent of 21 female rescuers (16 interviewed by the author, 5 interviewed by staff at the Genocide Archive Rwanda) were widowed, divorced, or apart from their husbands during the genocide. None of the rescuers referenced a son old enough to join the Interahamwe ranks.

35. For more on the coercive element of participation in the genocide, see the chapter titled "Punishment" in Hatzfeld's *Machete Season*.

36. Interviewee R 9 Denise, interview by Sara E. Brown, March 18, 2014, Rwamagana, Rwanda.

37. Interviewee R 12 Martha, interview by Sara E. Brown, April 24, 2014, Gasabo, Rwanda.

38. Odette Kayirere, interview by Sara E. Brown, July 30, 2014, Kigali, Rwanda.

39. United Nations Commission on Human Rights, "Report on the Situation of Human Rights in Rwanda Submitted by Mr. René Degni-Ségui, Special Rapporteur of the Commission on Human Rights," January 29, 1996.

40. This sentiment was repeated to me in multiple interviews by members of parliament, ministers, and humanitarian workers who stressed how fed up women were with genocidal violence as well as their marginalization in society.

41. Odette Kayirere, interview by Sara E. Brown, July 30, 2014, Kigali, Rwanda.

42. Odette Kayirere and Sabine Uwase, interview by Sara E. Brown, June 15, 2011, Kigali, Rwanda; Odette Kayirere, interview by Sara E. Brown, July 30, 2014, Kigali, Rwanda.

43. Interviewee R 4 Allison, interview by Sara E. Brown, February 20, 2014, Kigali, Rwanda.

44. Interviewee R 7 Ruth, interview by Sara E. Brown, February 22, 2014, Kibuye, Rwanda; this was documented by PROOF: Media for Social Justice's "The Rescuers" project, which was viewed while on display in Sarajevo, Bosnia-Herzegovina, July 2011.

45. Interviewee R 12 Martha, interview by Sara E. Brown, April 24, 2014, Gasabo, Rwanda.

46. Interviewee R 9 Denise, interview by Sara E. Brown, March 18, 2014, Rwamagana, Rwanda.

47. Josephine Dusabimana, interview by Sara E. Brown, February 22, 2014, Kibuye, Rwanda.

48. Naphtal Ahishakiye, interview by Sara. E. Brown, January 14, 2014, Inyanza, Rwanda.

49. Examples include MEMOS, an organization that selected 15 rescuers from the IBUKA list to receive gifts; the Kigali Genocide Memorial's collection and publication of female rescuer testimonies in their Genocide Archive of Rwanda; and the US Department of State's "60th Anniversary of the Refugee" convention event.

50. Naphtal Ahishakiye, interview by Sara. E. Brown, January 14, 2014, Inyanza, Rwanda.

51. I am grateful to the Stern Family, NSEP Boren Fellowship, and Aegis Trust Genocide Research and Reconciliation Programme for their generous support of this research. Two interviews were conducted in July/August 2014 as part of research for "Women Spoilers and Peace Builders in Rwanda 1994–2014," developed and submitted to the International Institute for Democracy and Electoral Assistance in 2014. Special thanks to Susan Mbabazi, Yannick Tona, and Sharon Batamuriza for their research and translation assistance and to the Genocide Archive Rwanda and AVEGA Agahozo for allowing me access to their testimonies. I am indebted to Debórah Dwork for her advice. Many thanks to Barbara Brown, Elliott Nahmias, JoAnn DiGeorgio Lutz, and Donna Gosbee for their comments on earlier drafts of this chapter. Lastly, warm thanks to the individuals who agreed to participate in this study.

CHAPTER 8

Breaking the Protracted Silence about Genocidal Rape in Kosova

Shirley Cloyes DioGuardi

Introduction

In their groundbreaking work *Women in the Holocaust,* Dalia Ofer and Lenore J. Weitzman express their conviction that we arrive at a "more complex and complete account" of Jewish life before and during the Holocaust "by bringing together the experiences particular to women and those relevant to all Jewish survivors."[1] Consequently, they decided to make the voices of the female survivors the essential starting point for their analysis of the Nazi extermination of European Jewry in World War II.[2] The same must be said about the decade-long Serbian occupation, culminating in the 1998–1999 war in Kosova.[3] Not enough attention has been paid to the gender-specific dimensions of Serbia's genocidal war against Kosova's Albanian majority. For this reason, the recognition and healing of Kosova's female survivors is incomplete, along with the integration of women's voices in the narratives of the war and the post-conflict peace process.

This chapter merges traditional scholarship with oral history, including the personal testimonies of female survivors of the Kosova war and the experiences and analyses of three highly educated, professional Kosovar women of different ages—Nora Ahmetaj, Linda

Gusia, and Hana Marku—all committed to a "more complex and complete account" of women's roles before, during, and after the war, and to the pursuit of a more equitable and sustainable future. Using the theoretical framework set forth by Ofer and Weitzman in their study of women in the Holocaust, I explore the lives of Kosovar Albanian women before, during, and after the war, and analyze the way that their experiences and social and political awareness were shaped by Serbian efforts to expel or exterminate Albanians. The application of this framework reveals how forms of victimization in genocide are often gender-specific and that, in the case of the war in Kosova, rape was used as an instrument of genocide. Until recently, the reality of mass rape during Serbia's genocidal war has been concealed, and as a result it has not been integrated into the collective narrative about the war and its roots in anti-Albanian racism. By examining the experiences particular to Kosovar women, we arrive at a more nuanced understanding of what happened to Kosova's Albanian majority population during the Serbian occupation and the war. In addition, we also arrive at an understanding of how predominant pre-war sexism in both Serbian and Albanian societies converged to shape a Serbian policy of rape during the war, and a rejection of female survivors of rape after the war by the majority of Albanian men steeped in patriarchal tradition.

Historical Overview: The Path to War

In 1981, Albanian students, both male and female, went into the streets to demand Republic status for Kosova, then an autonomous province within Yugoslavia's eight equal juridical units. The Serbian police admitted killing at least 300 students and arresting thousands, some of whom were jailed for a decade. From 1981 onward, a systematic dismantling of Kosova's autonomy continued unabated. By the end of 1987, more than 600,000 Kosovar Albanians, about one-third of the population, had been arrested by Serbian police and passed through the "legal" system.[4]

In 1989, Kosovar Albanians of all ages held massive demonstrations again, this time in opposition to Serbian dictator Slobodan Milosevic's preparation to invade Kosova. By the summer of 1990, Serbian forces had disbanded Kosova's legally elected assembly, amended the constitution to revoke Kosova's autonomy, dismissed all Albanian doctors and nurses from their positions, fired hundreds of thousands of Albanians in other professions and in the public sector, closed all Albanian schools, taken over all Albanian radio and TV stations, banned the display of the Albanian flag, and replaced the Albanian language with Serbian. Arbitrary arrests and police brutality became routine, and 350,000 Kosovar Albanians, thrust into poverty and peril, fled the country.[5]

From September 26 to 30, 1991, Kosova's leaders in exile held a referendum, in which Kosovars exercised their right of self-determination and overwhelmingly voted for independence from Serbia.[6] By then, the breakup of the former Yugoslavia was well underway, with the populations of Slovenia, Croatia, and Bosnia-Herzegovina all declaring their independence from the Socialist Federal Republic of Yugoslavia. Milosevic would wage wars in Croatia and Bosnia-Herzegovina, killing more than 200,000 Bosnian Muslims and displacing four million men, women, and children before the United States and the European Union intervened.[7]

The Dayton Peace Accords were signed on December 21, 1995. As part of a deal made with the late U.S. Balkan Envoy Richard Holbrooke and Slobodan Milosevic, Albanians were not invited to Dayton, Ohio, and Kosova was kept off the table.[8] This meant that the hot war would continue—moving from Bosnia back to Kosova. As conditions under the Serbian occupation worsened, the Kosova Liberation Army (KLA) emerged in 1996. As events would bear out, Milosevic's original target was not, in his words, the "terrorist, separatist" KLA, but the entire civilian population of ethnic Albanians.

In February 1998, the KLA came to the defence of Kosovar Albanians when the Serbian paramilitary and military troops attacked the town of Drenica, pillaging and plundering their way across Kosova. Ten years of brutal occupation had now culminated in genocidal warfare. The United States and Western Europe sat on the sidelines until it became clear that Kosova was about to turn into another Bosnia. Following failed peace talks in Rambouillet, France, NATO launched air strikes against Serbia on March 24, 1999. Seventy-eight days later, Milosevic would capitulate. At war's end, in June 1999, the international community reported that more than 12,000 Kosovar Albanians had been killed, thousands more arrested and tortured (including the mass rape of women), and more than a million driven from their homes to refugee camps in Albania and Macedonia by Milosevic's paramilitary and military forces.[9] Two years later, on June 28, 2001, Milosevic was extradited to the International War Crimes Tribunal in The Hague and charged with war crimes and genocide in Bosnia, Croatia, and Kosova.

While NATO's intervention in Kosova brought an end to Milosevic's decade-long genocidal march across Europe, more than 13,000 Kosovars had disappeared or been murdered, more than half of the population had been impacted by the conflict, and many survivors were experiencing trauma. The intervention did not bring an end to regional turmoil, and it did not heal all of the wounds of war—certainly not the pain of Kosovar women who had suffered rape, other forms of violence, and the deaths of their family members and communities.[10]

Kosovar Women: The Rural/Urban Divide in Culturally Defined Roles of Women

Sixty percent of Kosova's population resides in rural areas. Sociologist Linda Gusia of the University of Prishtina and Nora Ahmetaj, the Executive Director of the Center for Research Documentation and Publication, a think tank researching transitional justice issues, concur that the differences in how rural and urban women were perceived and treated by Albanian society before the occupation and the war cannot be empirically determined because the data does not exist. Nevertheless, they agree that the divide between urban and rural communities is genuine and that it deepened when Kosova was part of the Yugoslav system because Yugoslavia "invested more economically, educationally, and ideologically in the cities." As a result, women in the rural areas—with less access to education and employment, poorer, and with an inadequate infrastructure—were far less able to prepare for and cope with the realities of the Serbian occupation and the war.[11]

Anthropologist Janet Reineck is one of the few social scientists who explored the lives of rural Kosovar women before the Serbian invasion.

In the 1980s, she found that masses of rural Albanians were "still steeped in a rhetoric of honor and shame" derived from the past, and that the embrace of this patriarchal historical tradition rose in response to mounting Serbian oppression.[12] She documented Albanian allegiance to that tradition, characterized by "observance of age and gender stratification, submission to the will of the collective, the restriction of women's movement outside the home, arranged marriages, inflated bride-wealth and wedding rituals, and in some rural districts, the denial of secondary education to women."[13] Reineck acknowledged that there was a difference in the degree to which rural people living in extended families and the urban elite abided by historic tradition and conformed to it out of fear of collective rejection.[14]

Nora Ahmetaj was quick to point out, in one of my discussions with her, that adherence to traditional gender patterns was a matter of degree, not of kind, and that domestic violence (which Reineck did not address) was a reality for both rural and urban women, with its roots in the very patriarchal tradition that Reineck wrote about. Ahmetaj told me about growing up in an enlightened family that educated all four daughters and one son, including study and travel abroad:

We thought everyone treated daughters the way that we were treated. Later in life I came to realize that the concept of the paterfamilias works not only through the husband, but through the grandfather, the father, and the father-in-law. There is a vicious cycle. Men do not know how to stay in power, and so the only power they can use or misuse is through their spouse. The fathers do not educate the sons. They do not say that you do not need to go through the same vicious cycle as your father and your grandfather. You do not need to mistreat your wife; you need to treat her better. The paterfamilias is so dominant because it is the legacy of Kosova's past, in which there is a lack of a strong state, strong communities, and strong institutions. This leads people to gather around the family in search of strength and security. But in this form it is a fake security, because the family can interfere in your life, the way that you think and the way that you live. And when this happens, the family becomes a horror, not a source of strength.[15]

A 2005 case study produced by the United Nations Population Fund on "Gender-Based Violence in Kosova," showed that domestic violence was "persistent and pervasive" especially following the 1998–1999 war, when a quarter of the women interviewed had been subjected to such violence. The same study documented that in the year before the war a total of 36 percent of all women with partners reported at least one incident of violence at the hands of their partners.[16]

After the war, the realities of rural and urban Kosovar women would converge in two ways: their experience of domestic violence and wartime rape at the hands of Serbian paramilitary and military forces, coupled with an Albanian patriarchal effort to silence knowledge and public discussion of both. Male allegiance to a culture of honour would lead to the silencing of the discussion of genocidal rape during the Kosova war for more than 13 years.

Anticipatory Reactions of Women to Genocide: The Changing Roles of Women in the Face of Serbian Oppression

The seeds of current efforts to break the protracted silence about wartime rape were sewn during the occupation because the occupation disrupted traditional gender roles. A critical mass of women became more confident, empowered, and outspoken as activists in the resistance movement. During the decade of Serbian occupation that preceded the Kosova war of 1998–1999, all Kosovar Albanians, who make up 92 percent of Kosova's population, were needed in the struggle for liberation, regardless of gender. A shared mobilization for survival under Serbian oppression momentarily suspended the strictures of a strong patriarchal tradition, which also concealed the reality of domestic violence. The common struggle enabled women—rural and urban, young and old—to play bigger roles.[17] Gender issues were put aside during the occupation while the entire Kosovar Albanian society lived under threat of violence. The national movement for liberation opened up new opportunities for women to "enter the public space."[18]

A system of parallel structures was created to provide humanitarian services, education in private homes, and health care, supported by a government-in-exile that levied, on a voluntary basis, a 3 percent income tax on Kosovars in the diaspora. As journalist Hana Marku has observed, women were "the lynchpins" of the parallel state, working primarily as doctors, teachers, and activists "in what would eventually become a surrogate public sector, funded heavily by remittances from the diaspora."[19]

During the occupation, Kosovar Albanians lacked access to state health-care services. Following the ousting of Albanian doctors and nurses from public health clinics, Kosovars funded their own health care services, albeit limited, that were operated for a decade by the Mother Teresa Society. Women made up at least half of the 2,000 doctors, nurses, and volunteers, often operating at great personal risk. A gynecologist who was a field doctor for the Mother Teresa Society recounts that women were "distributing medical supplies and endangering ourselves, while under the constant surveillance of the Serbian police. I expected to be arrested any time," she said.[20]

Motrat Qirazi, one of the first women's organizations in Kosova, played a major role during the occupation in providing education and health care for women and girls in rural areas. It also integrated gender awareness, women's rights, and women's education into the fabric of the national cause in a society where women were second-class citizens. Even so, most women's organizations worked within the framework of defending human rights. Women's rights were seen as equivalent to human rights. While both were perceived to challenge existing patriarchal norms, they simultaneously de-emphasized redefining social roles.[21] Once the war began, national resistance and the struggle to free Kosova from Serbian domination overshadowed women's efforts to explore new gender models.[22] As human rights lawyer and American University professor Julie Mertus observed in "Women in Kosovo," nationalism "was becoming a powerful legitimizing force for organizing women, giving a legitimacy needed by women as much as men."[23] Some women believed that national liberation could not happen without the simultaneous liberation of women, but many more placed the national cause above women's emancipation. Nevertheless, as conditions grew worse for Kosovar Albanians under Milosevic, it became clear, according to Mertus, that women "had not negotiated well the relationship between gender and nation."[24] Nora Ahmetaj agrees with this assessment:

> Because of the struggle to survive economically during the occupation, every other issue was thrust aside as less important. I came to regret it then, and now I regret it even more that we made domestic violence, for example, an issue less important than the national cause. We should have raised our voices in support of both. Most of the feminist organizations that got established during the occupation and other NGOs focused on changing the political situation, fighting against the Serbian regime, and left other, seemingly women's issues for later.[25]

Regret about postponing discussion of domestic violence and championing equal rights for women would intensify during the war because of a new dimension that Kosovar women, young and old, rural and urban, were not prepared for: genocidal rape.

The War: The Unforeseen Reality of Mass Rape

In his examination of the history of genocide, Roger W. Smith observes that "genocide almost always includes rape as a means of victimization"; that victimization in genocide is gender-specific; and that our understanding of rape as a policy "deliberately chosen [at the highest levels] to humiliate, intimidate, and demoralize a victim group, making resistance to genocide more difficult" is only very recent.[26] In exploring rape as an instrument of genocide, Smith focused on the Bosnian war in the early 1990s to demonstrate that repeated incidents of mass rape were part of an official policy of the Serbian leadership. The Serbian policy was designed to terrorize Bosnian Muslims into fleeing Bosnia-Herzegovina, to undermine the population's ability to resist, and to break the biological connection by killing the men and forcing pregnancy on women—all in the service of a racially driven quest for Greater Serbia. Smith also stressed that an important goal of genocidal rape is the infliction of continuing pain, humiliation, and shame on girls and women. The Serbian policy of genocidal rape in Bosnia aimed to inflict lasting consequences in the form of ruining the prospect of marriage for young women, and ensuring the rejection of raped girls and women by their own families in a society where rape is a cultural stigma.[27]

So, too, the mass rape of Kosovar women by Serb paramilitary and military forces was an instrument of genocide. Rape was a primary instrument of the Serbian effort to destroy the Albanian family through violence against women and to drive the entire population of Kosovars out of their homeland. As Human Rights Watch reported in 2000, "rapes and sexual assaults served as a weapon in the systematic campaign of 'ethnic cleansing' in Kosovo."[28] Almost all of the sexual assaults documented by Human Rights Watch in refugee camps in Albania and Bosnia had been gang rapes, often in front of relatives and neighbours, and the organization would later call on the International Criminal Tribunal for the Former Yugoslavia (ICTY) to indict both the perpetrators of rape and their commanding officers.[29]

Difference in Treatment of Women and Men

The genocidal process in Kosova was gender-based, involving the separation of men and boys from women and girls. The men and boys were murdered, and the women and girls were raped and driven from their land. This process began during the Serbian summer offensive in 1998, a year before the Kosova war was officially declared by the international community. The rural areas were the hardest hit, and the women—who had had more freedom of movement than men during the occupation because the latter were more frequently picked up by the police (true also in the cities), but who lacked adequate information about unfolding events—thought that only men were in real danger. Kosovar women did not anticipate a Serbian onslaught that would rape them, kill 3,000 Albanians, drive 400,000 from their homes, burn their farms, and destroy their livestock in the course of three months.[30]

In 2014 Amra Zejneli interviewed a woman from the rural Drenica Valley who, like so many others, had believed that the Serbian soldiers "wouldn't harm defenseless women and children" and whose traditional patriarchy scorned the victim of rape instead of the rapist. In September 1998, her husband and eldest son left with all of the men in the village to hide from approaching Serbian troops who had been fighting Kosova Liberation Army soldiers in the area for eight months. Many mothers and their children fled as well. But Jeta (not her real name) and others decided to stay. She told Zejneli the following:

> They [Serbian soliders] jumped out of the tank into our yard. There were five armed men. They came in the house, one after another. And I remember them putting black masks over their faces immediately. I told my daughters to come stand close to me. We gathered together, and they ordered us to go into the basement of the house. And that's where the tragedy took place. My youngest was thirteen.

Jeta and her three daughters were then beaten and brutally raped for hours. When the soldiers left at nightfall, a male relative returned to the house. Learning what happened, he "ordered them to 'bury' the experience, saying that the rapes were 'a bigger tragedy than being murdered.'" Jeta, who Zejneli said has been "psychologically traumatized ever since," remained silent for 15 years. She never told her husband. He actually told her that "rape would dishonor the family and that he would abandon her if she were ever 'touched' by a Serb." Three of her daughters left Kosova. One got married, but was then rejected by her husband when he found out about the rape. Jeta is one of a very small group of women who have spoken to the press about their rapes during the war. She did not even seek help with the Kosova Rehabilitation Centre for Torture Victims in Prishtina until 2013. Most rape victims have not done so. The Centre told Zejneli that only 100 rape victims have sought help from them, and out of those, 80 percent will never tell their husbands, out of fear of abandonment or abuse.[31]

Reports about rape in Kosova and the cultural stigma attached to it began trickling out in 1999. Carol Williams of the *Los Angeles Times* was able to capture the consequences of rape for Kosovar girls two months into the war (which was officially declared once NATO dropped bombs on

Serbia on March 24, 1999), when she interviewed the parents of 13-year-old Pranvera Lokaj. Pranvera's parents explained to Williams that in April 1999, while the men of the village of Bileg were in the hills with KLA fighters, Serbian police and paramilitary entered the town and forced Pranvera and at least 20 other girls into the cellar of an empty house and gang-raped them for four nights. Their mothers and brothers who were held at gunpoint on the floor above them could hear their screams. After four days, the girls, covered with blood, were handed over to their terrified mothers. All of them were pushed into tractor-driven carts that would take them into exile.

By the time that Williams interviewed Haxhi Lokaj, he and his wife were in a refugee camp in Albania. Haxhi told Williams that he had sent Pranvera into the mountains to fight with the Kosova Liberation Army. "I have given her to the KLA, so she can do to the Serbs what they have done to us.... She will probably be killed, but that would be for the best. She would have no future anyway after what they did to her."[32]

While Haxhi Lokaj represents the prevailing patriarchal views of rural Kosovars who perceive rape as an attack on the victim's entire family, Williams interviewed more sophisticated urban women who admitted that they "would rather die than bear the humiliating brand of a rape victim—a view that had compounded the efficacy of the Serbian forces' war crimes by driving survivors to suicide and depleting the ethnic Albanian population of women of childbearing age."[33]

As upwards of one million Kosovars fled across the border in the spring of 1999, they brought with them stories of massacres, torture, and rape. Dominique Serrano-Fitamant, a French psychologist specializing in sexual violence and trauma counselling, was asked by the United Nations Population Fund (UNFPA) office in Geneva to undertake an assessment of sexual violence in Kosova by conducting interviews with women in refugee camps in Albania and Macedonia.[34] In her May 1999 report to the UNFPA, Serrano-Fitamant noted that alarming accounts of sexual violence and abduction had been circulating since April, but the international community had failed to respond to them because it was focused on arriving at an agreement between Belgrade and Prishtina in the peace talks at Rambouillet, France.

After Milosevic refused to sign an agreement and continued to amass his troops and tanks on the Kosova border, the negotiations broke down. When the NATO bombing of Serbia followed in March, Serrano-Fitamant stated that there was a "significant upsurge" in rape and other forms of torture and the forced expulsion of families from their homes on a moment's notice before they were burned to the ground.[35] Her report represented the first attempt by a UN organization to verify the accounts and nature of the sexual violence among female Kosovar refugees and of mass expulsion.[36] Regarding women and girls, Serrano-Fitamant wrote that rape was "the primary act of taboo used by the Serbian military and paramilitary. It is primarily the young women who are rounded up in villages and small cities," she said. "The soldiers take groups of 5 to 30 women to unknown places in trucks, or they are locked up in houses where the soldiers live. Any resistance is met with threats of being burned alive."[37]

Serrano-Fitamant produced a groundbreaking, sensitive, and nuanced report about sexual violence against Kosovar women, because she spoke on behalf of the survivors of wartime rape, whom she said should be provided with immediate assistance and have their dignity protected. She specified the need for a coordinated approach in response to Kosovar women—devoted especially to women who had been raped and were now pregnant, to children born of rape, and to the reintegration of victims into their families and communities.[38]

A Turning Point at Krusha e Vogel

A turning point in the international community's understanding of the Serbian genocidal response to Kosovar Albanian men and women occurred when one of the most horrific massacres of Albanians during the Kosova war took place in the village of Krusha e Vogel on March 26, 1999. Occurring just two days after NATO began its bombing of Serbia, Krusha e Vogel was part of "the significant upsurge" in torture, rape, and mass expulsion that Dominique Serrano-Fitamant had documented for the UNFPA. Seventy percent of the men were separated from their families and massacred by their own Serb neighbours. Rape and torture of women and girls took place before the Serb neighbours and Serbian paramilitary troops set fire to this farming village of 800 and drove the women out on foot, telling them that it was their last chance to look at their sons and husbands, and ordering them to cross the Drini River, to either "drown themselves or walk to Albania."[39]

The men and boys 13 years and older were herded into a barn and gunned down with automatic weapons before the building was torched and then blown up. That day 113 men and boys were killed (only six survived), and 86 of the bodies have still not been found. Based on strong evidence found by ICTY forensic teams, it is assumed that many were either burned beyond recognition or dumped into the Drini River by government forces attempting to conceal the murders.[40] Today, Krusha e Vogel is a village without men, with 82 widows and 150 orphans. Their story after the war paints a common portrait of the lives of rural women. International organizations have helped to rebuild homes, a day care center, a women's meeting room, a primary school, and a small factory that produces powder from locally grown peppers. But the women were left to cope with their grief, to take on new roles such as learning to drive and plant crops, and to work hard to rebuild their lives and their children's without any governmental support.[41]

As far back as 2003, female survivors had given testimonies to the UN Mission in Kosovo (UNMIK), but no investigation was launched. It would take 13 years before the European Union Rule of Law Mission in Kosovo (EULEX Kosovo) launched an official investigation into the massacre at Krusha e Vogel. In June 2012, EULEX announced that "So far, the prosecution has identified 56 potential defendants who would be facing charges of war crimes against the civilian population—including the killing of 113 villagers, deportation of the whole women and infant population from the village, and pillage and destruction of property."[42] On March 3, 2014, the bodies of 27 victims of the massacre were handed over to their families at a ceremony in Prishtina and then reburied in Krusha e Vogel on March 26, the 15th anniversary of the massacre.[43]

Redefining Rape under the Law

Because of the media's revelations of the widespread use of rape and forced impregnation as instruments of ethnic cleansing and genocide in Bosnia-Herzegovina, the international community was for the first time challenged to redefine war crimes, crimes against humanity, and genocide to include sexual violence.[44] Wartime rape would no longer be perceived as the act of individuals and an unfortunate by-product of war.[45] In 1994, attorneys and international human rights law specialists Kathleen Pratt and Laurel Fletcher asserted that the historical invisibility of the rights violations of women and the misrepresentation of rape as "an unavoidable dark side of conflict" had finally come to an end in the context of the Bosnian war of the 1990s. They said that this was "largely because of international press attention to the mass rapes and because of the actions of local, non-governmental, international, and women's organizations['] investigation of these violations."[46] Wartime rape would now be punishable. Pratt and Fletcher called on the international community "to ensure recognition of and accountability for the atrocities committed against women in the former Yugoslavia."[47]

The UN Security Council responded by giving the first judicial support for rape as an instrument of genocide since it passed the Convention on the Prevention and Punishment of the Crime of Genocide in 1948. In its 1994 Final Report on whether there had been violations of international humanitarian law in the former Yugoslavia, a Commission of Experts, which had been established in October 1992 pursuant to Security Council Resolution 780, concluded that "Under the Genocide Convention, sexual assault and rape were to be included within the meaning of Article II of the Convention provided that 'the prohibitive conduct is committed with intent to destroy in whole or in part, a national ethnical, racial or religious group.'"[48] Years later, in 2008, the Security Council would adopt Resolution 1820 on Women, Peace, and Security, in which it would affirm that "rape and other forms of sexual violence can constitute a war crime, a crime against humanity, or a constitutive act with respect to genocide."[49]

From 1998 to 1999, international and local journalists reported on continual rape by Serbian paramilitary and military forces in Kosova who had previously served in Bosnia.[50] According to Michelle Hynes and Barbara Lopes Cardozo, between 23,200 and 45,600 Kosovar Albanian women were raped in those years.[51] Twenty thousand is the number typically cited in Kosova, based on a January 2000 World Health Organization report that evaluated data from local NGOs, but the number has yet to be verified.[52] The number notwithstanding, by the year 2000, owing to the reality of mass rape, local and international NGOs were demanding that the Serbian paramilitary and military troops who had committed rape in Kosova be brought to justice. Regan Ralph, Executive Director of the Women's Rights Division at Human Rights Watch, argued in "Serb Gang-Rapes in Kosovo Exposed" that since rape was used as an instrument of war in Kosova, it should be punished as such. She said that "The men who committed these terrible crimes must be brought to justice.... Women in Kosovo are waiting for justice, and so far none of the Kosovo indictments have included sex crimes. The sooner there are investigations and prosecutions, the sooner these women can begin to rebuild their lives."[53]

Even though the international legal framework had been established for recognizing wartime rape as an act of genocide and prosecuting the perpetrators, it would take 12 more years before genocidal rape would even become part of public discussion in Kosova and the subject of local law. Primarily, but not exclusively, educated urban women who had become empowered during the occupation and the war spearheaded the call to end the cultural silence about the rape of Kosovar women during the war, to recognize Kosovar victims of wartime rape, to give them reparations, and to bring the Serbian military and paramilitary troops to justice.

Reactions of Kosovar Women to Their Experiences During the Genocide

After the war ended in June 1999, four factors impacted the lives of women in postwar Kosova, including the victims of wartime rape; resisters during the occupation and the war; and educators, activists, and politicians (as of September 2015, the president, two ministers, and 39 parliamentarians are female) seeking to participate in shaping and directing Kosova's future. The first factor was the stigma of rape.

In Kosova all men, women, and children were targeted by the Serbs for either death or expulsion, but sexual exploitation was specific to women.[54] The postwar attempt to erase genocidal rape in Kosova as part of the collective narrative about the war is directly connected to the status of rape in Kosovar Albanian society. Part of the reason for the protracted silence about genocidal rape in Kosova was women's unwillingness to tell their stories in a society where rape had been stigmatized for centuries. Most, but not all, of Kosova's raped women, especially those living in tradition-bound rural villages, concealed their suffering to shield themselves from reprisals, including abandonment, by men in their families and to protect themselves and their men from public shame.[55] Their fear fed into the fabric of collective denial.

Nora Ahmetaj, the Executive Director of the Centre for Research, Documentation, and Publication, was one of the senior investigators of war crimes during the wars in the former Yugoslavia for the Humanitarian Law Centre. In my interview with her in September 2014, I asked her how she responded to the persistence of the stigma and its destructive impact on Kosovar women who had been raped by Serb forces. Her response follows:

I was introduced to raped women in the refugee camps in 1999 in northern Albania, when Elisabeth Bumiller of *The New York Times* asked if I could help her find raped women. We contacted the ICTY, Amnesty International, and Human Rights Watch to determine in which camp we could locate raped women and which parts of Kosova they were coming from. There were at least three regions where women had been massively raped, not individually, but in groups. We started in Suhareka. I remember that the media and researchers were coming in large numbers, and everyone in the community was in a completely defensive position. The raped women were escaping from us. It must have been extremely difficult for these women to survive. I will never forget their faces, never ever. None of the women wanted to talk because they were afraid, since they were also stigmatized by the community. This was my first experience as a war crimes investigator with raped women, and I told Elisabeth that this is something that I can do mechanically, but I cannot handle it emotionally. It is not the women, but the community, the stigma, and the blaming that I cannot handle—as if it were the fault of the women that they were raped.[56]

Ahmetaj said that two local NGOs—Medica Kosova, based in Gjakova and devoted only to women, and the Kosova Rehabilitation Centre for Torture Victims, based in Prishtina—had been working to counsel and treat the physical and psychological wounds of female survivors since the war ended. Meanwhile, no Kosovar politicians had allocated funding for rape victims, given public recognition to them, or denounced their torturers.

When I asked Linda Gusia if there were rape victims willing to talk, she replied that there were in fact some women "who have never stopped talking, but the majority of women will always be silent." Like Ahmetaj, she confirmed that stigmatization and isolation made it very difficult for women to talk. She said that especially in rural Kosova, girls and young women who had been raped by Serbian forces, often in front of their families and neighbours, have never married, and some never even leave their houses because everyone knows about the rape. "There is a huge pressure and shame," she said.[57]

In the summer of 2014, when I asked journalist Hana Marku if she thought that there were victims of wartime rape who would be willing to go public with their experience, she was skeptical of survivors coming forward in the near future because of the unresolved reality of domestic violence against women in Kosova.

> As long as violence against women is normalized within Kosovo's society, it will be very difficult for a wartime victim of rape to come forward. There is no culture of support for women who experience sexual violence within their own homes and communities, and I think being a victim of wartime rape just compounds the stigma of being raped. I think that this stigma is very much consistent with "traditional" Albanian values, in which ... a woman who has been raped is "sullied," beyond redemption; hence their silence. Traditional Albanian masculinity is the problem, and until this changes, the culture will not change.[58]

The depth of the problem was well illustrated in October 2014, when a retired law professor, Vesel Latifi, published a textbook entitled

Kriminalistika (Criminology), in which he referred to rape victims as "females who are easily fooled, careless, thoughtless, and immoral, and put themselves in surroundings that are accompanied by a victimizing situation (their attack)." The outcry from civil society, especially from women's groups, pushed the University of Prishtina to remove the textbook from the law school's curricula.[59]

The second factor impacting women in postwar Kosova is the unwillingness of the Kosovar male elite to recognize the contributions of women, both rural and urban, during the occupation and the war. While the massacre at Krusha e Vogel revealed the extent of the Serbian effort to destroy Kosovar Albanian society, it also contained within it an example of the courage and ingenuity of Kosovar women during the war. Marta Prekpalaj, a teacher whose role at Krusha e Vogel has been ably documented by Hana Marku, observed the Serbian attack from a distance and drove a tractor for the first time to assist the women who were forced to flee on foot to safety on the other side of the Drini River. Aided by her uncle and brother, Prekpalaj forded the river and rescued hundreds of women and girls.[60]

When Marku interviewed Marta Prekpalaj in a café in 2013, she already knew that women were "the unsung heroes of the fight for Kosova." Marku reported that Prekpalaj had high standing for her role during the massacre, demonstrated by local men repeatedly interrupting the women's conversation upon recognizing her. Nevertheless, Prekpalaj lamented to Marku that women were "appreciated at home, but not in public." She told Marku that she was part of a group of rural women who had believed that national liberation and women's liberation had to be pursued simultaneously. She never thought that once the war ended "we would still have so much work left. I thought that we had reached a degree of emancipation through our efforts in the 1990s." As Marku has concluded, the state that emerged after the war "has not repaid the faith of all who struggled for it."[61]

The failure to recognize women's activism during the occupation and the war, often equal to that of men, is directly connected to the third factor: the elevation of the Kosova Liberation Army (KLA) in postwar Kosova. In my 30 trips to Kosova between the end of the war and the declaration of independence in 2008, I came to know women who had played major leadership roles during the occupation; urban and rural women whose husbands had been killed by Serbian military and paramilitary forces; female fighters in the KLA; and female MPs elected to the first Kosova Assembly in 2001. Most were revered by the Albanian majority, but many were marginalized when the postwar power vacuum was filled by men who were members of the KLA or who claimed to be freedom fighters.[62] There was no effort on the part of Kosova's male leaders to recognize the considerable contributions of women to the war effort, or to include them in the commemoration of the struggle to free Kosova, or in the process of state building. As Iliriana Hasaj, a field doctor in the KLA, has said, "No one wants to talk about what women did during the war. We have the respect of our former brothers-in-arms, but not the people who achieved office through our efforts."[63]

Linda Gusia, who was in the field daily during the war, working as an interpreter and translator for *The Washington Post*, explained to me that after the war "everything got twisted by the male elite into glorifying the war and winning power and prestige." While most of the 12,000 Kosovar Albanians who died during the war and the 1,700 still missing were civilians, she explained that the postwar construction of remembrance focuses heavily on male freedom fighters and especially the male leaders of the KLA. As a result, Gusia said that it is not only women's experiences of the war that have been marginalized, "but the entire civilian side of the story has been completely silenced and left out of the discourse."[64]

A large number of women were student protestors in 1981 and 1989 and activists during the occupation. Thousands more would become central to the war effort. And yet women still remain largely invisible in the history of the war, the postwar commemoration, and the struggle for independence.[65] Hundreds of war monuments have been dedicated to KLA fighters since war's end, but only one to a woman, out of the more than 600 who served: Xheve Lladrovci fought with her husband, Fehmi Lladrovci, and was killed by the Serbian military. Only because of the efforts of her husband's family has she been kept alive in the public consciousness.[66] No memorials or street names have been given to a single female doctor, teacher, or civilian who participated in the struggle.

The fourth factor to impact the lives of women in postwar Kosova is the impact of the international administration, which, on the one hand, has worked to document the rape of Kosovar women and to institute the concept of gender mainstreaming in postwar Kosova, but, on the other, has participated in the erasure of women's activism in the resistance of the 1990s and the war. Soon after the war ended, the UN Mission in Kosova (UNMIK) was established under UN Resolution 1244 with the mandate to govern Kosova, which was technically under Serbian control until its final political status could be decided. Because of Kosova's statelessness, UNMIK, the United States, and the European Union limited the decision-making power of all Kosovar Albanians, male and female, in order to suppress their call for independence. In the end, UNMIK would hand the reins of power to men who fought in the war and who would comply with their mandates.[67]

Kosovar women lamented the fact that they were largely excluded from postwar negotiations, so that both their contributions in the resistance to Serbian aggression and their experiences of rape were not taken into account. In 2006, female activists and politicians thought that UN Security Council Resolution 1325 on Women, Peace, and Security in Kosovo, "which called for strengthening women's role in shaping conflict prevention and peace process, but also generally in governance,"[68] would offer the legal basis for giving women a key role in the status talks and state-building outlined in the Ahtisaari plan. Authored by UN Envoy Martti Ahtisaari, the plan was the final document in a U.S. and EU–led state-building process meant to create a path for the recognition of Kosova's independence. But, in the end, women were excluded from the talks between Belgrade and Prishtina led by Ahtisaari, and gender issues were not addressed. On March 8, 2006, women-focused NGOs and other civil society took to the streets to protest their exclusion under the banner of "No More Flowers; We Want Power."[69]

Veprore Shehu, then executive director of Medica Kosova, the NGO that aids women traumatized by domestic violence and wartime rape, quoted an ambassador who said that "Albanian traditionalism was an obstacle to including women in the Ahtisaari discussion. We do not want to break with tradition."[70]

Postwar Justice: Kosovar Women Break the Silence about Genocidal Rape

Beginning in 2010, the issue of rape, the subject of silence since war's end 11 years earlier, became the linchpin for Kosovar women's efforts to achieve equality. "In 1999 and 2000, rape was still a forbidden issue; we talked, but we didn't talk publicly," says Nora Ahmetaj, whose Centre for Research, Documentation, and Publication was one of the women's organizations leading the drive to achieve public recognition of wartime sexual violence, legal status including reparation for survivors of wartime rape, and gender equality. That would change in 2010, when, she reports, "women in effect said 'Enough is enough. We want recognition. We want reparation.' This was when my NGO, the Kosova Women's Network, Medica Kosova, and the Kosova Rehabilitation Centre for Torture Victims (KRCT) began working with victims and their families and with some of Kosova's MPs pressuring for legislation."[71]

Once these groups (some of whom had been working since the start of the Serbian occupation and others who had begun aiding female survivors even before the war ended) sought legal recognition and reparation for wartime victims of rape, women's wartime experiences were finally brought into the public arena of reflection and debate. With this, the process of destigmatizing rape had begun.

In 2013, there was a breakthrough in the recognition of victims of wartime rape, when an amendment was proposed for addition to the 2012 Law on the Status and the Rights of Heroes, Invalids, Veterans, Members of the Kosova Liberation Army, Civilian Victims of War, and Their Families that would for the first time categorize female survivors of rape as victims of war, and therefore worthy of reparation and rehabilitation services under the law. Its passage did not come without fierce opposition. Several male members of parliament argued against it, with one MP, Gezim Kelmendi, suggesting that raped women would have to be medically examined if they wanted to receive governmental support.[72] On March 20, shortly after the parliamentary debate, Nazlie Bala, the head of the Women's Secretariat of the political party Vetevendosje, which had introduced the law in support of the request from the women's organizations that had been advocating for it, returned home from work to find an anonymous letter. It said, "Do not protect the shame. Otherwise we will kill you."

A week later, Bala was beaten outside of her apartment by two unknown assailants, was hospitalized for her injuries, and was then put under police custody for months. Outraged, Amnesty International issued a public statement worldwide, expressing shock at the incident and deploring the fact that, in the words of John Dalhuisen, Europe and Central Asia Programme Director, "More than a decade after the war, hundreds of women continue to live with the effects of rape and other forms of torture, without proper access to the medical, psychological and financial assistance they need to rebuild their shattered lives. Meanwhile, most of those suspected of criminal responsibility are not being investigated."[73] Amnesty International then called on Kosovar President Atifete Jahjaga, Prime Minister Hashim Thaçi, and other members of the Kosova government to denounce the attack on Bala and to implement the amendment to the law, guaranteeing the rights of women who had suffered sexual violence during the war. In addition, and most importantly, Amnesty International celebrated the law for challenging the "notion of shame" that "for so long has prevented women from publicly acknowledging the violations they suffered and from coming forward to provide testimony for criminal prosecutions, for fear that it would bring shame to their family or community."[74]

The law recognizing wartime rape victims was finally passed in 2014. Nora Ahmetaj called its passage "the only slight victory that I and a few other NGOs and some good MPs have achieved since war's end. We were threatened; we received messages not to do this. For more than two years, we worked hard. We worked with some MPs on a daily basis, and trust me there are some good MPs, who understood how important it was to amend the law. Ultimately we succeeded and saw how our intervention through legislation could change lives."[75]

The year 2014 marked another turning point, with authorities in Kosova and human rights activists launching a national petition to pressure the United Nations to investigate rapes committed during the war and to produce a report about it. By the end of July, 120,000 individuals in Kosova had signed the petition. In part, the petition drive was the result of

Kosovar President Jahjaga participating in the June 10–13 Global Summit to End Sexual Violence in Conflict, held in London and co-chaired by William Hague, then–UK Foreign Secretary, and Angelina Jolie, Special Envoy of the UN High Commissioner for Refugees. Returning from the conference, Jahjaga called for "engaging with and giving comprehensive answers to the needs of sexual violence victims during the war."[76]

The amendment to the law, in particular, and the petition demonstrate significant progress. But at the same time, the petition is the subject of debate among female activists, academics, and politicians. As journalists Hana Marku and Lura Limani have observed, the petition amounts to "a kind of camouflage for the absence of action and support for rape victims by Kosovo institutions since the end of the war.... In order to have real justice, Kosovo and Serbia should have an extradition agreement. If most of the rapists are assumed to be Serbian soldiers and paramilitaries, it will be impossible to see justice done unless they appear in court, be it in a Kosovo court or an international one."[77]

Marku and Limani have questioned why the UN, which did not investigate rape and other war crimes when it had executive power from 1999 to 2008, should now be asked to investigate rapes committed during the war in Kosova. They argue that a report on the location and scale of wartime rapes does not need to be outsourced to the UN, when Kosova has state mechanisms that should be called on to produce a document, such as the War Crimes Institute (which has yet to publish any research on crimes committed during the war since its founding in 2011) and the European Union Rule of Law Mission in Kosovo (EULEX).[78] In addition, Marku told me that both Medica Kosova and the Centre for the Rehabilitation of Torture Victims have been gathering testimonies of rape victims since the end of the war, and so local archives of documented cases are already available.

Above all, Marku and Limani insist that wartime rape victims should not be cast as victims, but as "activists fighting for their rights, without shame, in the public sphere."[79] Along with female leaders in civil society, they are concerned that neither the amendment to the law nor the petition serves to open up public recognition of women's contributions during the occupation and the war, because both keep the focus on women as victims of sexual violence. Sociologist Linda Gusia told me that she has interviewed many strong female survivors, and she is concerned that the discourse has the potential of silencing them once again:

> By focusing only on rape, these women are being sexualized. There is no interest in really giving voice to them or empowering them. There is also no attempt to humanize raped women or tell their stories. Only powerful women like the president speak of them and on behalf of them. My position as a feminist is that there are women ready to speak and we should give them a voice. But we have to be careful about how this happens. They don't want to be overexposed and stigmatized. I think that this whole petition drive removed their humanity, because they are spoken of as an object. We don't know their stories; we don't hear their stories.[80]

Although Gusia applauds the breaking of the political and public silence in Kosova about wartime rape, she shares my belief that a vital next step in destigmatizing wartime sexual violence and deepening the understanding of rape as a weapon of genocide is providing ways for women to articulate their experiences. The importance of personal testimony for female survivors has been well articulated by oral historian Selma Leydesdorff, who, in *Surviving the Bosnian Genocide: The Women of Srebrenica Speak*, states that "a person who manages to tell about her suffering and explain how it has affected her life might also succeed in rediscovering her place in the world."[81] So, too, the renowned psychiatrist and oral historian Dori Laub has concluded over decades of work with Holocaust survivors that "repossessing one's life story through giving testimony is itself a form of action, of change, which one has to actually pass through in order to continue and complete the process of survival after liberation."[82]

Conclusion

Just as Ofer and Weitzman have demonstrated that the exploration of Jewish women's distinct experience during the Holocaust fills a previously unseen gap in the Holocaust literature and in our understanding of the Nazi genocide, it is essential to examine Kosovar women's gender-specific experience to understand the Serbian genocidal war against Albanians in the late 1990s. Even though, for the first time in history, wartime rape was declared under international law a punishable war crime, a crime against humanity, and an act of genocide during the Bosnian war, the reality of mass rape in Kosova did not become the focus of local and international discussion until 2013. This was largely because of the centuries-old stigma of rape in male-dominated Albanian society and the role of Western governments in suppressing dialogue about wartime history in order to stymie the Kosovar Albanian call for independence in a short-sighted pursuit of its strategic interest in the region. The breaking of the protracted silence about genocidal rape in Kosova reveals the importance of using gender as a framework for the analysis of genocide. Far from making the attempt by the Serbian government of Slobodan Milosevic to expel or exterminate all Albanians in Kosova secondary to the wartime experience of Kosovar women, the exploration of women's gender-specific victimization during the Kosova war has revealed rape as a central instrument of Serbia's genocidal strategy. Meanwhile, the Serbian military and paramilitary troops who subjected Kosovar Albanian women to rape and other forms of torture have yet to be brought to justice.

Questions

1. Dominque Serrano-Fitamant, on behalf of the UN Population Fund in 1999, and Human Rights Watch in 2000, reported that rapes and sexual assaults were used by Serbia as a weapon of war in Kosova. Why, then, did the United Nations (which had executive power in Kosova from 1999 to 2008) and the EU Rule of Law Mission in Kosova (which still has executive power in Kosova) fail to investigate and document cases of wartime rape? And why did the International Criminal Tribunal for the Former Yugoslavia fail to indict both the perpetrators of rape and their commanding officers?

2. Why did Bosnia more quickly and effectively than Kosova reveal Serbia's widespread use of rape as a weapon of war, resulting in the UN Security Council giving the first judicial support for rape as an instrument of genocide? Does the 14-year silencing of

wartime genocidal rape in Kosova mean that Kosova is more patriarchal than Bosnia?

3. What new steps can be taken in Kosova, and in other societies in which patriarchal concepts of shame and honour exist, to break the fabric of collective denial and stigmatization of rape victims and to raise the understanding of rape as torture and an act of violence against women?

Notes

1. Dalia Ofer and Lenore J. Weitzman, eds., *Women in the Holocaust* (New Haven: Yale University Press, 1998), 1–3.

2. Ibid., 2.

3. *Kosova*, the Albanian spelling, is used throughout the text to reflect the preference of the survivors, except in the citation of official documents, books, and articles that use the Serbian spelling, *Kosovo*.

4. Joseph DioGuardi, *The Agony of Kosova: A Resource Book on the Albanians of Kosova* (New York: Albanian American Civic League, 1992), 12.

5. Noel Malcolm, *Kosovo: A Short History* (New York: Harper Perennial, 1999), 349.

6. Ibid., 37; Shirley Cloyes DioGuardi, "Unfinished Business in Southeast Europe: Debunking the Myths that Underlie US and EU Foreign Policy in Kosovo," in *The EU, Security and Transatlantic Relations*, ed. Finn Laursen (Brussels: P. I. E. Peter Lang, 2012), 188–189.

7. Cloyes DioGuardi, "Unfinished Business."

8. Shirley Cloyes DioGuardi, *Presiding over Genocide: The Shame of the West* (New York: Illyria, 1998), 7. See also Noel Malcolm, *Kosovo: A Short History*.

9. Samantha Power, *A Problem from Hell: America and the Age of Genocide* (New York: Basic Books, 2002), 450; Cloyes DioGuardi, "Unfinished Business," 190.

10. Center for Research, Documentation, and Publication (CRDP), "Missing Links: How Kosovo's Institutions and Society Are Failing Civilian War Families in Mitrovica" (Prishtina, Kosova: CRDP, 2014), 4.

11. Linda Gusia and Nora Ahmetaj, interview by author, September 2014.

12. Janet Reineck, "Seizing the Past, Forging the Present: Changing Visions of Self and Nation among the Kosova Albanians," *Anthropology of East Europe Review* 11, nos. 1/2 (Autumn 1993): 103, scholarworks.iu.edu/journals/index.php/aeer/article/view/593/695.

13. Ibid., 104.

14. Ibid., 104.

15. Nora Ahmetaj, interview by author, September 2014.

16. United Nations Population Fund (UNFPA), "Gender-Based Violence in Kosovo: A Case Study," Women Peace, and Security Initiative, Technical Support Division, 2005, 7, www.unfpa.org/women/docs/gbv_kosovo.pdf.

17. Hana Marku, interview by author, August 2014. For an exploration of the changing role of women during the occupation, see Howard Clark, *Civil Resistance in Kosovo* (London: Pluto Press, 2000).

18. Nita Luci and Linda Gusia, "Our Men Will Not Have Amnesia: Civic Engagement, Emancipation, and Transformations of the Gendered Public in Kosova," in *Civic and Uncivic Values in Kosovo: Transformation, Education, and Media*, ed. Sabrina P. Ramet, Albert Simkus, and Ola Listhaug (Budapest: Central European University Press, 2014), 4.

19. Hana Marku, "No Rewards for Kosovo's Women of War," *Balkan Insight* (Pristina: BIRN, December 18, 2013), www.balkaninsight.com/en/article/no-rewards-for-kosovo-s-women-of-war.

20. Ibid., 3.

21. Luci and Gusia, "Our Men Will Not Have Amnesia," 10.

22. Arta Ante, *State Building and Development: Two Sides of the Same Coin? Exploring the Case of Kosovo* (Hamburg: disserta Verlag, 2010), 296–297.

23. Julie Mertus, "Women in Kosovo: Contested Terrains," in *Gender Based Politics in the Western Balkans*, ed. Sabrina P. Ramet (Philadelphia: Pennsylvania State University Press, 1999), 177.

24. Ibid., 176.

25. Nora Ahmetaj, interview by author, September 2014.

26. Roger W. Smith, "Genocide and the Politics of Rape: Historical and Psychological Perspectives," in *Genocide Matters: Ongoing Issues and Emerging Perspectives*, ed. Joyce Apsel and Ernesto Verjeja (London: Routledge, 2013), 83–85.

27. Ibid., 88–90.

28. "Kosovo: Rape as a Weapon of 'Ethnic Cleansing,'" Human Rights Watch, Chapter 5, March 1, 2000, www.hrw.org/legacy/reports/2000/fry/index.htm#TopOfPage.

29. Regan Ralph, "Serb Gang-Rapes in Kosovo Exposed," report to Human Rights Watch, March 20, 2000, www.hrw.org/news/2000/03/20/serb-gang-rapes-kosovo-exposed.

30. Power, *A Problem from Hell*, 445.

31. Amra Zejneli, "How Long Can You Keep a Secret? For Kosovo's Wartime Rape Victims, the Answer Is: Maybe Forever," Radio Free Europe/Radio Liberty, May 29, 2014, www.rferl.org/content/kosovo-wartime-rape-victims-kept-secret/25403115.html.

32. Carol J. Williams, "In Kosovo, Rape Seen as Awful as Death," *Los Angeles Times*, May 27, 1999, articles.latimes.com/print/1999/may/27/news/mn-41524.

33. Ibid.

34. Kosova Women's Network, *1325: Facts & Fables* (Prishtina, Kosova: 2011), 81–82.

35. Dominique Serrano-Fitamant, "Assessment Report on Sexual Violence in Kosovo, for the United Nations Population Fund," May 28, 1999, reliefweb.int/report/serbia/assessment-report-sexual-violence-kosovo.

36. As reported in Judy Aita, "UN Agency Reports on Rape and Abduction of Kosova Refugees," May 1999, www.alb-net.com/pipermail/kcc-news/1999-May/000079.html.

37. Serrano-Fitamant, "Assessment Report on Sexual Violence," 4.

38. Ibid., 6.

39. See Kosova Women's Network, *1325: Facts & Fables*, 2.

40. See Human Rights Watch, "The Prizren-Djakovica Road," in *Under Orders: War Crimes in Kosovo* (Human Rights Watch, 2001), 358, www.hrw.org/reports/2001/kosovo.

41. Richard Mertens, "Kosovo: Learning to Cope in Krushe e Vogel," BCR 359 (August 2002), iwpr.net/global-voices/kosovo-learning-cope-krushe-e-vogel.

42. Fatmir Aliu, "Kosovo: Krusha e Vogel Massacre to be Investigated," *Balkan Insight*, June 18, 2012, www.balkaninsight.com/en/article/krusha-e-vogel-massacre-to-be-investigated/1452/6/12.

43. Edona Peci, "Kosovo Returns War Victims' Remains to Families," news release, *Balkan Insight*, March 24, 2014, www.balkaninsight.com/en/article/kosovo-missing-persons-remains-to-be-buried.

44. Frances T. Pilch, "Sexual Violence and the Crisis in Kosovo," *Refuge* 18, no. 3 (August 1999): 30, pi.library.yorku.ca/ojs/index.php/refuge/article/viewFile/22021/20690. See also Smith, "Genocide and the Politics of Rape," 103, citing Roy Gutman's August 23, 1992, article, "Mass Rape: Muslims Recall Serb Attacks," in *New York Newsday*, based on interviews with 20 rape victims in the former Yugoslavia, which catapulted genocidal rape into public awareness.

45. See Rhonda Copelon, "Gendered War Crimes: Reconceptualizing Rape in Times of War," in *Women's Rights Human Rights: International Feminist Perspectives*, ed. Julia Peters and Andrea Wolper (New York: Routledge, 1995). Copelon was on the ground floor of reconceptualizing rape as a war crime. See also Roger W. Smith's argument in "Genocide and the Politics of Rape."

46. Kathleen M. Pratt and Laurel E. Fletcher, "Time for Justice: The Case for International Prosecution of Rape and Gender Based Violence in the Former Yugoslavia," *Berkeley Journal of Gender, Law & Justice* 9, no. 1 (September 2013): 78, 81. scholarship.law.berkeley.edu/cgi/viewcontent. cgi?article=1080&context=bglj.

47. Ibid., 102.

48. United Nations Security Council, "Final Report," on evidence of grave breaches of the Geneva Conventions in the former Yugoslavia, tasked by its Resolution 780 (1992) S/1994/674, May 27, 1994, www.icty.org/x/file/ About/OTP/un_commission_of_experts_report1994_en.pdf.

49. United Nations Security Council Resolution 1820, D/Res/1820, June 19, 2008, www.securitycouncilreport.org/atf/cf/%7B65BFCF9B-6D27-4E9C-8CD3-CF6E4FF96FF9%7D/CAC%20S%20RES%201820.pdf.

50. Human Rights Watch, "March–June 1999: An Overview," *Under Orders: War Crimes in Kosovo* (Human Rights Watch, 2001), www.hrw.org/ reports/2001/kosovo.

51. Michelle Hynes and Barbara Lopes Cardozo, "Sexual Violence against Women in Refugee Settings," *Journal of Women's Health and Gender-Based Medicine* 9, no. 8 (2000), as reported in "Exploratory Research on the Extent of Gender-Based Violence in Kosova and Its Impact on Women's Reproductive Health" (Prishtina: Kosova Women's Network, 2008), 14, www.womensnetwork.org/documents/20130120165614663.pdf.

52. Hana Marku and Lura Limani, "The Problem with the Kosovo War Rape Petition," *Balkan Insight*, July 23, 2014, www.balkaninsight.com/en/article/ the-problem-with-the-kosovo-war-rape-petition.

53. Ralph, "Serb Gang-Rapes in Kosovo Exposed," 2.

54. Joan Ringelheim makes the same observation about the connection between gender and genocide during the Holocaust in "The Split between Gender and the Holocaust," in *Women in the Holocaust*, ed. Dalia Ofer and Lenore J. Weitzman (New Haven: Yale University Press, 1998), 344.

55. Maria Olujic, "Embodiment of Terror: Gendered Violence in Peacetime and Wartime in Croatia and Bosnia-Herzogivna," *Medical Anthropology Quarterly* 12, no. 1 (1998): 38.

56. Nora Ahmetaj, interview by author, September 2014. Elisabeth Bumiller would publish "Crisis in the Balkans: Crimes; Deny Rape or Be Hated: Kosovo Victims' Choice," in *The New York Times*, June 22, 1999, www.nytimes.com/1999/06/22/world/crisis-in-the-balkans-crimes- deny-rape-or-be-hated-kosovo-victims-choice.html.

57. Linda Gusia, interview by author, September 2014.

58. Personal interview with Hana Marku, August 18, 2014. See also Rhonda Copelon, "Gendered War Crimes," 67, for a discussion about the need to make the connection between wartime rape and domestic violence.

59. Nektar Zogjani, "Sexist Textbook Angers Kosovo Women's Groups," *Balkan Insight*, October 10, 2014, www.balkaninsight.com/en/article/sexist-textbook-spurs-calls-for-reform-at-university.

60. Hana Marku, "No Rewards for Kosovo's Women of War," 1.

61. Ibid., 1–2.

62. Hana Marku also made this point in an interview with me in August 2014. Linda Gusia discusses this issue at length in "Silence versus Recognition of Survivors of Sexual Violence in Kosovo," a significant essay that she has translated into English, but which has been published thus far only in Albanian in *Njoha*, vol. 3 (Prishtina, Kosova: University of Prishtina, 2014).

63. Hana Marku, "No Rewards for Kosovo's Women of War," 4.

64. Linda Gusia, interview by author, September 2014; Gusia "Silence versus Recognition of Survivors of Sexual Violence in Kosovo," 1.

65. Selma Leydesdorff, *Surviving the Bosnian Genocide: The Women of Srebrenica Speak* (Bloomington: Indiana University Press, 2011), 2.

66. Dori Laub, MD, "Bearing Witness, or the Vicissitudes of Listening," in *Testimony: Crises of Witnessing in Literature, Psychoanalysis, and History*, ed. Shoshana Feldman and Dori Laub, MD (New York: Routledge, 1992), 85–86.

67. Linda Guomundsdottir, "Gender, Power, and Peacebuilding: The Struggle for Gender Equality in Post-War Kosovo" (master's thesis, University of Iceland, 2012), 83, skemman.is/en/item/view/1946/13017.

68. Kosova Women's Network, *1325: Facts & Fables*, 8.

69. Nita Luci, "Seeking Independence: Making Nation, Memory, and Manhood in Kosova" (dissertation, University of Michigan, 2014), 173–174, deepblue.lib.umich.edu/bitstream/handle/2027.42/107225/nluci_1.pdf?sequence=1.

70. Ibid., 175; Nicole Farnsworth, "The Pervasiveness of Gender-Based Violence in Kosova," in *Exploratory Research on the Extent of Gender-Based Violence in Kosova and Its Impact on Women's Reproductive Health Peace, and Security in Kosovo* (Prishtina, Kosova: Kosovo Women's Network, 2008), 47, www.womensnetwork.org/documents/20130120165614663.pdf.

71. Nora Ahmetaj, interview by author, September 2014.

72. Hana Marku, "Shame: Talking about Rape in Kosovo," *Kosovo 2.0*, March 29, 2013, 4, www.kosovotwopointzero.com/en/article/852/shame-talking-about-rape-in-kosovo.

73. Amnesty International, "Kosovo: Amnesty International Condemns Threats to Woman Human Rights Defender," public statement, March 22, 2013, www.amnesty.org/en/library/asset/EUR70/005/2013/en/8e5237bc-cf6e-4867-94fb-cde565111e5/eur700052-13en.html.

74. Ibid.

75. Nora Ahmetaj, interview by author, September 2014.

76. Edona Peci, "Kosovo President Urges Support for War Rape Victims," *Balkan Insight*, May 20, 2014, www.balkaninsight.com/en/article/kosovo-president-urges-increase-of-support-for-war-rape-victims.

77. Marku and Limani, "The Problem with the Kosovo War Rape Petition," 2.

78. Ibid.

79. Ibid.

80. Linda Gusia, interview by author, September 2014.

81. Leydesdorff, *Surviving the Bosnian Genocide*, 2.

82. Laub, "Bearing Witness," 85–86.

CHAPTER 9

"We Want Justice!" Women and the Gujarat Genocide

Dolores Chew

Introduction

The 2002 Gujarat genocide against Muslims was carried out by per-petrators committed to making India a Hindu nation (Hindutva). The official death toll was 2,000 but unofficially the numbers are higher, as many remain missing. As a result of the genocide, indi-viduals lost entire families, children became orphans, and often, women who survived found themselves widowed. In the aftermath, there has been little in terms of holistic rehabilitation. Additionally, genocidal conditions continue as Muslims are socio-economically and politically marginalized and continue to face violence or the threat of violence.[1]

In this chapter, the four structural sources regarding the role of gender identified by Dalia Ofer and Lenore J. Weitzman in regard to Jewish women before and during the Holocaust are compared to the experiences of Muslim women in Gujarat in 2002, in order to iden-tify similarities and differences for women within the two distinct events.[2] Looking at these genocidal events from a gendered perspec-tive does not mean that we ignore the experiences of men—it sim-ply gives us another way to view these genocides, and enhances our knowledge.

Historical Overview

Beginning on February 28, 2002, continuing into March (and sporadically until May), mass killings of the Muslim minority population occurred in the western Indian state of Gujarat.

The day preceding the start of the genocide, a train carrying Hindu religious volunteers burst into flames as it left Godhra station in Gujarat. Fifty-eight men, women, and children died in the inferno. Although unverified, Gujarati-language newspapers published as fact allegations blaming Muslims for the fire. To date, although forensic investigations have not conclusively determined the cause of the fire, they have established that the fire did not start from outside the train. The genocide that followed was widespread in the state, but was concentrated especially in the north and northeast.[3]

Communal violence[4] in India, especially between Hindus and Muslims, resulted in some of the worst atrocities during the partition violence of 1947.[5] However, since 1947, in Gujarat alone there were communal riots in 1969, 1982, 1985, and 1992.[6] But 2002 was not a riot; it was genocide. What made it qualitatively different were the scale, fury, and one-sidedness of the attacks, as well as the organization, planning, and intent. The Gujarat genocide was additionally marked by the mind-numbing brutality and glee with which murder, dismemberment, and torture were carried out. Also separating 2002 from earlier incidents of communal violence was the involvement of state agents and government partisanship. On the eve of the genocide, Chief Minister of Gujarat Narendra Modi called a meeting to instruct state officials not to intervene, and in the aftermath there was a striking absence of government relief efforts.[7] Instead, as people fled the violence, Muslim charitable organizations set up refugee camps, and only later did the government provide paltry sums of four or five rupees per person in the camp, less than the bare minimum required to sustain the refugees.[8]

Another departure from earlier incidents of violence was the complicity of the middle-classes, who joined in the looting, helping themselves to goods from vandalized Muslim shops and directing family and friends by cellphone to the best locations. But most horrifying was the deliberate way women and children were targeted and killed. Pamphlets circulated in Gujarat prior to the genocide demonstrated a combination of misogyny and communal hatred. What happened to Muslim women in Gujarat crossed every threshold of previous incidents of communal violence.

After the attacks, there were attempts to cover up the genocide. Members of Hindu nationalist organizations stood alongside doctors who examined corpses with bullet wounds, and pressured them to certify that victims had died of "natural causes."[9] Bodies were thrown into mass graves and the perpetrators made efforts to hasten decomposition to prevent identification. However, owing to documentation by numerous Indian and international groups, the details of what transpired as well as the buildup to the killing and its immediate aftermath are available.[10] Judicial proceedings against the accused have resulted in some convictions,[11] but there has also been witness intimidation, ongoing harassment of Muslims, economic hardship, and ghettoization.

Not everyone would define the events that transpired in 2002 as genocide. They are commonly referred to as "communal riots" by government officials and politicians obliged to investigate abuse of rights. *Riot* implies an element of spontaneity, and it fits within an official narrative of somewhat normative sporadic communal violence that erupts at indefinite intervals. However, the Gujarat event in 2002 is genocide as set out in Article 2 of the Convention on the Prevention and Punishment of the Crime of Genocide.[12] Additionally, the violence was not spontaneous. In the time leading up to the genocide, Muslims had been targeted by Hindutva organizations, such as the Rashtriya Swayamsevak Sangh (RSS), in hate campaigns in which they were classified as "others." Flyers were circulated with instructions on how to kill Muslims, or warning Hindu parents not to allow their daughters to associate with Muslim men because the men would "marry" them in order to sell them into sexual slavery in Saudi Arabia. History books were systematically rewritten to include narrow, biased, and factually inaccurate histories of oppression of Hindus by Muslim invaders. Hindutva activists visited businesses and ordered them not to hire Muslims, and to sack Muslim employees they may have had. If they disregarded these warnings, there were follow-up visits and threats of violence. The groundwork for genocide had been laid. The perpetrators built up arsenals. Emotions were inflamed, lists were prepared, and neighbourhoods divvied up by leaders. The train fire provided the excuse.

Culturally Defined Roles of Women

In most of India and South Asia, patriarchal constructs dictate that community and family identity are predicated on the sexual integrity of the women. Women have been forced to bear this burden for centuries, even as they have struggled to break free from such constraints. Women's lives are also implicated closely in ideological and psychological ways with the well-being of their families and communities. Gendered sexualized violence predicated on constructs of honour and shame becomes a weapon in situations where religious, ethnic, or caste groups, or the state seek to dominate or humiliate a particular group, or wrest compliance from them. As a consequence, women may be doubly oppressed as objects of attack, but also as survivors of sexualized violence, which might cause them to be rejected by society and their own families.[13] More recently, the term *love jihad*, coined and popularized by Hindu nationalists in parts of North India to insinuate threats of sexual danger to Hindu women from Muslim men, are reminiscent of rumours circulated prior to the 2002 massacres in Gujarat. These rumours helped create fear and distrust of the "other."

Muslims in Gujarat usually observe normative forms of female respectability with regard to public space, whereby men are generally the primary breadwinner, with women assigned to the domestic realm, depending on their socio-economic level. Not unlike women in other genocidal contexts, many of the women in this study were responsible for helping in the family business or outside the home, but they generally still retained responsibility for maintaining hearth and home. Many Muslim women of Gujarat also have sub-identities that impact their role within the family and community, such as religion—whether they are Shia or Sunni. Among Gujarati Shia Muslims there are further distinctions, such as Bohra or Khoja affiliations. The growth of religious organizations such as Tablighi Jamaat have also influenced religious practices and social norms. Other factors that could influence Gujarati women's world view and lifestyle include caste, class, being native Gujarati or out-of-state migrants, and whether they are rural or urban dwellers.

Some Muslims have Gujarati as their mother tongue, others Urdu. The linguistic differences indicate migration patterns. In urban Gujarat, the Muslim population includes migrants from other parts of India drawn there over the years by the state's relative prosperity. There are affluent Gujarati Muslims, but many of the families are made up of daily wage earners, and women in these households make valuable contributions to the family income. They might be employed in informal-sector work at home or in small-scale workshops outside the home, making things like paper kites or thread.[14] Still other women might work in family-based artisan production. Before 2002, some Muslim women also had small shops or food stalls. In rural areas, some owned land. Women in middle-class families are able to be housewives or professionals. The degree of women's autonomy and independence is a factor of their economic contribution to the household, as well as prevailing class norms. However, patriarchal constructs ensure that, nominally or practically, the man is the head of the household. Women are expected to marry, usually at a young age, and marriages are arranged within one's community, though some individuals do make their own choice, which may include selecting marriage partners outside the community.

During the genocide, a non-Muslim partner may have been spared. But the evidence suggests that when the Hindu partner was a woman, she was viciously attacked for betraying her community by marrying a Muslim. Depending on class, family traditions, and denominational affiliations, girls might be educated and even encouraged to complete their schooling and go on to post-secondary education.[15] But in poorer families, even boys might receive little or no education, since all who can contribute to the family income begin work as soon as they are able, to help provide for the family.

Anticipatory Reactions of Women

Prior to the genocide, Muslims had been labelled "other" and marginalized, but this was incremental. Moreover, intermittent communal violence had come to be seen as normative. There was no anticipation of anything on the scale of genocide and there were definitely no signals of impending violence in February 2002. There were no preparations or anticipatory measures taken prior to the genocide. No weapons were stockpiled and there were no arrangements made to protect neighbourhoods. Families did not flee to the relative safety of Muslim majority areas. On February 28, Muslims, like other Gujaratis, woke up and started going about their normal everyday activities. They had no inkling that very shortly their world would be turned upside down. Even when the violence began, some survivors say they did not think they personally would be affected, because they either lived in "safe" (majority Hindu) areas, or in Muslim housing estates in middle-class neighbourhoods, which, during past episodes of violence, had remained untouched. Additionally, some victims recount how their Hindu neighbours were their friends, and they thought these friends would protect them. Survivors also indicate that they believed the rumours of impending violence were without substance. When the mobs arrived, Muslim men and women appealed to their Hindu neighbours for assistance, and in some cases they were sheltered. However, in many cases, it was the neighbours themselves who became perpetrators. Terrified Muslim women turned to the police for assistance, but the police did not intervene on their behalf. If the police were present, they joined in, humiliating the women with lewd gestures, and either encouraged the perpetrators or attacked the women themselves.

As people tried to flee the attackers, escape became difficult or even impossible in places like Narod Patiya, with its narrow lanes that were easy for the mobs to block. It was in Narod Patiya where the brutal murder of Kausar Bano, who was nine months pregnant, became the iconic representation of the genocide and Muslim women. Kauser Bano's attackers raped her, slashed her body, and removed her fetus, which they burned along with her body. A survivor of Narod Patiya was Farzana Ayub Khan, who recounted the following:

> The police were present on the road near the Noorani mosque, but when the mob started attacking us in the morning they did not help. I ran with my two daughters, then seven and fifteen-years-old,

my mother, my sister-in-law and her one-year-old son and hid on the terrace of Gangotri housing society building nearby. But the mob reached there too.... Someone poured fuel over me. They broke my seven-year-old daughter Reshma's hands with rods, then they raped and stabbed my other daughter. My back was burning and my clothes melted. I tried to roll on the ground to douse the fire.[16]

In Ahmedabad, people flocked to a middle-class housing estate, Gulberg Society, hoping to find safety and relying on the political connections of Ehsan Jafri, a Muslim and former Member of Parliament (MP). In rural areas, families fled and tried to hide in fields. While many were on foot, others piled into overcrowded *tempos*.[17] Pregnant women ran on foot, often with young children in tow. In trying to escape the violence, one woman gave birth in a mosque, only to be killed, along with her newborn daughter, by the mobs.[18] One child reported that his mother gave him all the money she had with her, 60 rupees, and told him to run as fast as he could. He never saw his mother again, and he and one brother are the sole survivors of his family. A group fleeing in a rural area tried to disguise their Muslim identity by borrowing the clothes of local *adivasis*.[19] Bilqis Bano, who was pregnant at the time, incredibly survived the attack on her family, but remained unconscious for many hours, hidden from view under a pile of bodies. When she regained consciousness, she found the corpses of family and friends around her, including that of her young daughter:

They started molesting the girls and tore off their clothes.... Those men were using such foul language, I can't repeat it ever.... In front of me they killed my mother, sister and 12 other relatives. The way we kill animals, they slaughtered us.... When they were raping me I could not even tell them that I was five months pregnant because all the time their feet were on my mouth and neck ... when I opened my eyes I saw that my world had been destroyed. I could not even stand on my feet. But I was scared that people may see me and come back. A night and a day passed on top of the hillock. I was very hungry and thirsty. I could not bear it anymore. I thought I may die of thirst. So I started to come down from the hillock.... Five days after the rape and after taking a bath three times I finally went for a medical checkup. I have the medical certificate that proves rape.[20]

Those who managed to hide and escape detection provide harrowing accounts of being helpless to save family members as they watched the attacks and killings. Witnesses could not give away their hiding place and risk the lives of those in hiding with them. Parents witnessed the murder of their children, and vice versa. When the attackers found a girl or woman, they raped her, and age was of no consequence. Sexual violence endured by the victims included gang rape, mass rape, and assault with objects. The perpetrators followed this by slashing, mutilating, dousing with gasoline, and setting their victims' bodies on fire. As the killing unfolded, sexualized violence against Muslim girls and women became the norm.

Survivors fled, traumatized, confused, and bewildered. People slowly began to emerge from hiding after having gone days without food or water. Hindu neighbours who gave shelter did so only temporarily, possibly out of fear of reprisals or because they knew they would inevitably be detected. *Adivasis* also helped victims, although in some areas they were also perpetrators. At times those fleeing the violence were able to reach safety on their own. Eventually, many found their way to makeshift refugee camps set up by community organizations. Physically, psychologically, and emotionally traumatized, most survivors lived from day to day as they searched for their missing loved ones. The massacres continued unabated for almost two weeks, and in some areas the violence lasted well into May, and even June. While many survivors eventually left the relief camps, 10 years later there were still at least 16,000 who had not been settled anywhere.[21] Once people left the refugee camps, they rarely returned to where their homes had been, but instead moved to Muslim-majority areas for reasons of security. Families who did want to return to their villages were often prevented from doing so by the local Hindu population.

Since the spring and summer of 2002, there has been a continuation of the "genocidal project." Muslims in Gujarat have not recovered—psychologically or economically—from the violence and massacres. They still reel from the destruction of property and the loss of livelihood, the economic boycott of Muslim shops, and unemployment. Police continue to arrest Muslims—especially young males, and "encounter deaths" still occur.[22] Although the massacres have ended, the ongoing effects of the genocide persist.

Difference in Treatment of Women and Men

The Gujarat genocide stands out in the history of communal violence in the subcontinent because of the way perpetrators deliberately targeted girls and women, and also because of the high levels of sexualized violence they suffered. Boys and men were also killed, some tortured before their death. They were often stabbed repeatedly, had limbs hacked off, or were burned alive, but there are no accounts or records of sexualized violence against boys and men. The story regarding the attacks on girls and women was vastly different. Male Hindutva attackers forced sticks, bottles, and cricket balls into women's and girls' vaginas. Relief workers in one camp described how difficult it was to remove all the wooden splinters from one woman's vagina. Mothers told of how they pleaded for their daughters to be spared, only to have to watch helplessly as the girls were gang-raped and then killed, often burned alive. Numerous survivor testimonies describe how the police themselves attacked women. According to the survivors, they saw police beat women on their breasts and genitals. One witness recounts police telling the family of a young girl who was studying when they burst in, *Why do you want to educate her? She will become a prostitute anyway.* Police also joined gangs of men in opening their trousers, exposing their penises, and using crude language to humiliate the women, saying that the women *would enjoy sex with uncircumcised [non-Muslim] men.* In the period before the killing started, this type of sexual innuendo was also printed on flyers that were circulated.

Rape of girls and women was ubiquitous, as we can see in this testimony of child survivors who provided a unique definition of rape, based on what they had witnessed:

"Balatkaar" (rape)—they know this word. "Shall I tell you?" volunteers a nine-year-old. "Rape is when a woman is stripped naked and then burnt." ... For this is what happened again and again in Naroda Patia—women were stripped, raped and burnt. Burning has now become an essential part of the meaning of rape.... Hindus have done "bad things"—a euphemism for rape they tell us, as their eyes shift uneasily.[23]

Gender-based hatred was also visible in graffiti written on the walls of the charred houses: "Muslims Quit India—or we will f*** your mothers."[24]

Hindu women who had married Muslim men were seen as transgressors who had to be made examples of to dissuade others from intermarriage. They were stripped and attacked in public. One Hindu woman who was married to a Muslim was dragged from her house, stripped, and killed, her naked corpse left on the road. Another Hindu woman testified how she was publicly raped by nine men; they left her beaten and unconscious. The woman recalled the mob telling the men to "Cut her to pieces, don't leave her alive, we don't want her alive in the village."[25]

The gendered violence in Gujarat in 2002 happened in a changing globalized and economic reality. "Modernization" and "modernity" often come with a heavy price, especially for women, as patriarchal systems and forces of patriarchy adapt and find new and innovative ways to assert control. While violence and the threat of violence are always there, the forms may change. In India, economic liberalization and restructuring have also had an impact. There have been changes in attitude with respect to violence against women in India generally, in part due to the Indian population as a whole being increasingly exposed to media representations of women and violence against women.[26] Violence against women is used by state agents, within communities, at the individual level, or by one community or caste against the women of another. While Gujarat may be better off economically than some other states in India, its entrepreneurial and middle-classes have the dubious distinction of having some of the highest rates of female feticide and infanticide in the country.[27] At the time of the massacres, the sex ratio in urban Gujarat was 879 females per 1,000 males, the lowest in the last one hundred years,[28] and the areas with the most glaring discrepancies were also those that witnessed communal violence.[29] Misogyny, the burden of sexual integrity women bear, and high levels of Islamophobia came together with horrendous consequences for the Muslim women of Gujarat.

The ritualistic aspect to the ferocity of the murders and the fact that victims were often tortured before being killed suggests catharsis, the venting of deep-seated hatred that has been nurtured and fed. The intensity of the brutality and the deep desire to humiliate the other community caused one Hindu citizen of Gujarat to claim that the violence should send fear even into the hearts of the most Hindutva-identified Hindu man, for it manifested not just communal hatred, but deeply felt misogyny.[30]

While Muslims made up less than 10 percent of the population, anti-Muslim propaganda harped on Muslim men being allowed four wives, manipulating anxieties about Hindus being minoritized.[31] The nature of the sexualized violence inflicted on Muslim women—the mutilation of genitals, the tearing of fetuses from wombs—suggests the success of this propaganda.

Analyzing the highly communalized and influential history *Hindutva*, which was authored by the Hindutva activist and writer V. D. Savarkar (1883–1966), Purshottam Agarwal writes, "Muslims, both men and women, were defiling the chastity of Hindu women by design and the perversely virtuous Hindus have not paid them back in the same coin."[32] In Gujarat in 2002, violating the sexuality of a Muslim woman and torturing her in such brutal fashion, allowed an exorcision, revenge, and retaliation for imagined historic wrongs. A fabricated and revisionist history, implanted and popularized for many years, of Muslim invaders attacking Hindustan in the medieval period, destroying temples, sexually humiliating Hindu women, and degrading and weakening Hindu society, culminated in genocide and femicide.

Women's Reactions to the Physical and Emotional Circumstances

Women, along with their families and communities, experienced deep fear as the violence erupted and continued. As caregivers and nurturers, they naturally feared for their children and their families. Yet, prior to the genocide, these Muslim women were not overly worried about sexualized violence; there was the belief that Hindu men would refrain from doing to Muslim women what they would not want to happen to their own women. But as the violence began to unfold, horror and disbelief soon mounted as it became evident that this had been a miscalculation on the part of the Muslim women. As mentioned previously, police did not respond to, or in some cases were actually complicit in, the violence. Some neighbours and friends helped, others did not. For some of the Hindu neighbours, the lack of response resulted from their agreement that the violence was a justified response to the fire in the train, the deaths of 58 people, and the mutilation of Hindu women. The Gujarati media fanned the flames of communal hatred by unjustly placing the blame for the train tragedy on the Muslims. Gujarati media also printed erroneous accounts of the molestation of Hindu women, as well as making false claims of Hindu women having their breasts cut off. Any expectations of female solidarity between Hindu and Muslim women went unfulfilled; Muslim women began to realize that there was no safety for them.

In the aftermath of the genocide, those women who had survived the violence attempted to put together a semblance of familial life in the relief camps, trying to protect their children and provide for what portion of their family had survived. Muslim women—despite the traumas they had endured during the genocidal activity—now seemed to be more adept at carrying on to help their family. This was, in some situations, in contrast to Muslim men, who, having been unable to perform their expected duty of protecting their family, perceived a diminishment of their masculine identity.

When I visited Gujarat in July 2003, I found that when locals were asked "what could be done to help?", the unanimous response was that they wanted justice. During my time in Gujarat, I met women from many different walks of life—professionals, housewives, activists, social workers, legal workers, and cultural activists. I also met women who were left widowed and utterly destitute by the genocide. I saw visible physical scars and also met survivors with emotional scars, which can be more difficult to treat, and can also take much longer to heal. Women showed me vivid scars where they had been slashed with swords. A Hindu woman, whose husband was a Muslim, had her face terribly disfigured by fire.

I met Naseem in Godhra, the place where the train fire marked the beginning of genocide.[33] She had lost 26 members of her family in what she called the *toofan* (storm). Only Naseem and her son, who was being treated at a hospital at the time, had survived the genocidal violence. Today Naseem works with a group called Aman (hope). For Naseem, the only way to go forward is to live with hope and to create hope for others. Naseem took me on a tour of the villages around Godhra, and as we drove she showed me photographs of her family in happier times, when they were all alive. I found it difficult to comprehend, with what she has suffered, how this woman was able to do what she was doing. She pointed out a car that sped by, "There's Ashok Patel, and he was responsible for the killing in this village." The absence of justice in many instances means that the survivors live alongside their attackers. A little later we passed some fields and women who were riding with us in the vehicle pointed to where women of their family were raped. We visited sites where their family homes had once been, but where now stood only rubble. The former neighbours of these brave women coldly stared at us without any sign of recognition or welcome. The widows told me that every time they come to their former homes they see that villagers have taken something else from whatever had been left standing.

The women lived with constant reminders of what had happened, and also lived among the perpetrators of the violence that had destroyed not only their homes, but their families. An outspoken female Muslim lawyer from Gujarat told me with controlled fury of how difficult simply carrying on can be, when the perpetrators still walk among the victims. Since the genocide, this professional woman has carried an identification card with a Hindu name, in case she becomes stranded in a Hindu neighbourhood during another outbreak of violence. She also described how, on university campuses prior to the killing, leaflets were distributed telling Hindu families not to allow their daughters to mix with Muslim boys and not to watch films with Muslim actors.[34]

Many of these women survivors found their lives changing in unexpected ways, and in some cases, they found a strength and purpose that gave them more agency than they could have possibly had before the genocide. "A social change is happening in the community. It took a tragedy to trigger this."[35] As we have seen throughout history, ruptures, flux, and change—whether positive or negative—often result in women adapting either voluntarily or involuntarily to the situation, and in the process their lives change. Lifestyles they could not have imagined earlier become the norm as they step into new roles and take on new responsibilities and agencies.

Noorjehan Abdul Hamid Dewan was just 28 years old during the genocide. She had been married for 10 years, and both her natal family and her marital family were religious and traditional. Noorjehan's role prior to the violence of 2002 was to stay home and care for her husband and her family. When she went outside, she always had on her burka, the outer garment some Muslim women wear, which covers them from head to toe. Noorjehan and her family, as well as their home, survived the violence of the 2002 genocide. Afterward, she decided to visit a refugee camp that had opened up in her neighbourhood. What she saw there shocked her into action to help the displaced and impoverished Muslim refugees. Though her husband forbade it, Noorjehan refused to stay away, going to the camp each day to help, and sometimes taking her six-month-old daughter with her. Despite her husband's disapproval, Noorjehan joined a local NGO helping the local refugee camp. Her husband beat her, stopped talking to her, and threatened divorce, all to no avail. Noorjehan persisted, left her children with relatives, and worked in the camp—nursing, dispensing medicines, helping victims file police reports, and conducting surveys. She also made the calculated decision to stop wearing her burka because it made her a target for harassment by the non-Muslim population. Over time her husband changed his attitude. Now, Noorjehan says, "He helps me, supports me, understands me. I now live to get help, get justice."[36]

Many women found themselves in dire economic circumstances as a result of loss of home, property, family, and livelihood; however, in most cases, they found ways to adapt. Noorjehan has school-age sons who now work in call centres in order to help support their family. Another woman, Niaz Apa, had owned a house and the land it was on until the violence in 2002. Her home was burned down by her neighbours, who she says "had grown up in front of my eyes."[37] She sold her land even though she had to let it go for well below its market value. When talking about her situation, Niaz is very matter-of-fact about her diminished material position. For reasons of safety, like many other Muslims, she and her husband moved to the Muslim-majority area Juhapura, in Ahmedabad.[38] Niaz and her husband now live in a 100-square-foot, two-room apartment that was built by a local NGO for refugees of the 2002 violence.

In Ahmedabad—already fairly segregated—ghettoization has become a post-genocidal reality. From 250,000 before the genocide, Juhapura's population has almost doubled, and it now bears the dubious distinction of being the largest Muslim ghetto in Asia, with all that the term *ghetto* entails.[39] Being away from the Hindu mainstream often also means a lack of basic amenities such as water, electricity, sanitation, and garbage removal. As well, many women have said they miss the vibrant pluralism of living in mixed communities and participating in each other's festivals—proof that Hindu-Muslim tension is not primordial. Apart from religious homogeneity, areas like Juhapura have become more crowded, with haphazard construction going up in many places.[40] Wealthier Muslims also moved to Juhapura for security reasons, which caused real estate prices to skyrocket. Justice, for women like Niaz Apa, living in her tiny, cramped apartment, seems elusive. She sought legal remedies against the men who destroyed her home, but the judge told her to compromise with the perpetrators. Since 2002 she has worked with survivors and the community, going to police stations, courts, and food shops on their behalf.[41] Niaz asserts, "It's all about securing justice by raising my voice. When the owners of the cheap food shops cheat us [Muslims], I take up the cudgels. If the police station refuses to register a case, I raise my voice."[42]

Latifabano Mohammad Yusuf Getali had lived, until the violence of 2002, as a cloistered homemaker. The genocide transformed her from a woman hidden at home to an influential and outspoken activist. She began working with and advocating for victims, trained to open schools, and also trained to start an NGO that provides a range of activities and services to empower women and help them and their families in the wake of the dire economic crisis the Muslim community has faced since 2002. In 2005, Latifabano was nominated as one of 1,000 PeaceWomen Across the Globe, a global initiative nominating women for the Nobel Peace Prize. The citation notes:

> From the uneventful life of a Muslim housewife to a relief and peace activist, she has walked a long mile.... Braving the wrath of her conservative community, Latifabano has helped hundreds of Muslim women in the state gain access to relief and legal assistance.... Latifabano's organisation was the first Muslim women's organisation in Godhra, so she faced the considerable wrath of the conservative Muslim community. But she continued undeterred.[43]

Suhanaben, who already lived in Juhapura before the genocide, found a different way in which to help her Muslim brethren who had survived the violence and relocated to Juhapura. Suhanaben had already embarked on a life of more visible religious practice prior to the genocide, but later got involved in the construction business, supervising construction sites as well as selling and renting real estate. While this work took her outside her home, she saw it as "service" to the community, facilitating the movement of Muslims from insecure areas into Juhapura.[44] In this way she felt she was not transgressing gender boundaries, but merely extending her private sphere.

Such transformations of Muslim women and their roles post-genocide were confirmed in a three-year study undertaken after the Gujarat genocide. The study collected life-history narratives of female Muslim survivors of the communal violence in Gujarat, and also Mumbai and Hyderabad, cities in other states in India.[45] The researchers found that their preconceived categories—victim, agent, Muslim, woman, class, location—were simply not appropriate for the fluidity with which these women negotiated their changed lives. The most useful analytic concepts and tools were those being used by the women themselves in their own narratives of their current situations, and included such terms as *going out of the house* and *negotiating/managing*. The women also used concepts such as dignity/honour, belonging, identity, and justice. In the wake of the violence, women found themselves economically and socially "orphaned" by the death or disability of male family members. They described themselves as women who had to abandon the four walls of the home for the world outside, and as being without shelter or support.[46] Their changed circumstances were "not necessarily a negative way of looking at themselves," but more a matter-of-fact description of the "social norm/category they must now inhabit" out of necessity. In fact, many of the women in the study took great pride in what they had been able to achieve. There was, say the authors of the study,

> a shift or change in the consciousness of women. Many spoke of a changing sense of self that came about as a result of going out of the house and dealing with varied public institutions and spaces. They point to increasing confidence, awareness and understanding of the changing dynamics of their immediate surroundings.[47]

While many women have found themselves able to move into these new roles as their situation changed dramatically post-genocide, a common theme for these women has been frustration in trying to achieve justice for the violent and deadly events of 2002. For many women, accessing justice has been a harrowing journey, if they ever do find any sort of justice in the end. From filing a First Information Report at a police station with unsympathetic or hostile police, to prosecutors who identify with Hindutva, to the emotional struggle of going public about an attack, the legal system has made the pursuit of justice extremely difficult for the Muslim women of Gujarat. Regardless of the obstacles put in front of them, however, women such as Zahira Sheikh, Bilqis Bano, and Zakia Jafri fought tenaciously through the police and court system in search of a measure of justice for their losses. Not all outcomes were the same, and Zakia Jafri's case is still not resolved, more than 12 years after the genocide.

During the genocide, Zahira Sheikh watched as her family-owned business was set afire, and family members as well as employees were brutally murdered and burned. In what has become known as the Best Bakery Case, Zahira, with assistance from human rights activists, has pursued the perpetrators. They were successful in convincing the Supreme Court of India to have the case removed from Gujarat when it became apparent that it would be impossible to get a fair trial there. She won the admiration of many for her courage. The case is still being pursued, though Zahira eventually turned hostile witness, claiming under oath in court that she had been coerced. Post-genocide witness intimidation has been all too common, but for it to happen in this high-profile case stunned many. While some Muslims were bitterly disappointed and disillusioned by Zahira Sheikh's subsequent lack of cooperation in prosecuting the perpetrators, her case stands as testimony to the difficult and intimidating situation in which survivors have to live among the perpetrators, in constant fear of their lives, even today.[48]

Bilqis Bano, discussed earlier in this chapter, was also a woman determined not only to survive, but to find justice for the suffering and murder of her family. The young pregnant mother was left for dead, but after regaining consciousness climbed out from under the pile of corpses of family and neighbours that had shielded her. Once out of the pile of bodies, and finding that her family members, including her infant daughter, were all dead, she made her way to the police station. The police deliberately wrote an inaccurate account of what Bilqis told them. Not being literate, Bilqis did not know what was written in the report, and signed her approval with her thumb impression. Bilqis, however, refused to give up in her pursuit of legal recourse against the perpetrators. Assisted, like Zahira Sheikh, by human rights activists, she eventually saw justice when convictions were handed down to the key perpetrators of the violence against her family. But in order to assure a fair trial, she, again like Zahira Sheikh, had to plead to the court to have her case taken out of Gujarat. Post-genocide, Bilqis gave birth to the baby she had been pregnant with when she was attacked. She named her new daughter after the daughter who had been murdered during that fateful day in Gujarat in 2002. Bilqis is an example of Gujarati Muslim women taking back the agency that had been so violently stripped from them during and even after the genocide.[49]

Zakia Jafri is the widow of former MP, Ehsan Jafri. It was to the Jafris' home that many Gujarati Muslims ran for shelter when the violence first broke out. With their house full of terrified Muslims, and when it seemed that, despite assurances, relief was not forthcoming from the local police, Ehsan Jafri walked out of his house in an effort to plead with and calm the angry mob. Unfazed by his pleadings, the perpetrators stripped him and forced him to parade through the streets, naked. He was then slowly and sadistically murdered. Zakia Jafri has been pursuing justice for her husband's murder, refusing to give up despite the many obstacles, but the legal case plods on.[50]

While Bilqis succeeded in bringing the murderers of her family to justice, Zahira turned hostile witness, and Zakia still awaits a semblance of justice for her family, what they have done and are still doing speaks to the fact that women—when the circumstances demand—step out of the private sphere in the service of protection of family and community, as well as the pursuit of personal justice. These women have, either willingly or unwilling, put themselves into the spotlight in the hope of establishing justice for themselves and their loved ones. But there are many women who have remained silent for fear of ostracism, since the stigma of rape is so powerful that they fear being further victimized within their own community.[51]

Despite the strength that many Muslim women have demonstrated after the genocide, for many others, the genocide has taken a heavy toll, and moved them to keep their trauma—their words—bottled inside them. They find themselves unable to speak of their own trauma, their fears, or their anger, since they feel the responsibility of holding everything together for their families and their communities. In the words of a woman named Afroza, "I have never talked about myself like this before ... I've always been told not to get emotional, to keep my control.... I'm opening up to you for the first time today because I can't bear it any more. I'm so scared for my son."[52]

However, even as there seems to be a freeing from some patriarchal constraints as a result of post-genocide realities, the turning inward that the Muslim community has been experiencing has also led to normative reinforcement of the belief that women belong in the private sphere, rather than the public. There are more constraints on girls, which results in their being taken out of school and married off. As some semblance of normalcy returned to the Muslim population after the genocide, schools reopened; but, fearing for the safety of their daughters, many families prevented their daughters from continuing their education, and in other cases, the girls themselves were too afraid to venture out to attend school. An adult woman's identity being predicated on marriage means that remaining unmarried is unthinkable. Thus, the fear that a daughter might be raped before she could marry, thereby making her unmarriageable (because nobody would wish to marry a woman who had been raped), made families in refugee camps eager to get pubescent daughters married off, regardless of age. The patriarchal view was that if violence erupted again and resulted in the rape of a daughter, she would already be married, and so would not be made to suffer the ignominy of remaining unmarried as a consequence of rape.

Within the refugee camps, female volunteers reported how emotionally traumatized the girls often were. "They jump at the drop of the slightest object. They are very disturbed ... they go through long spells of silence ... they don't talk ... and at night they see those same scenes again." Mumtaz Bano, a volunteer at a refugee camp, who was also left traumatized by what she had seen and experienced during the genocide put this emotional toll into words: "I too have fallen sick.... I stopped eating, I had to be put on the drip for two days.... I can't bear it."[53] The loss of honour was palpable.

In recent years, there has been a rise in the activities of Muslim missionary organizations, such as the Tablighi Jamaat. The organization is building the first girls' school in Juhapura, in response to families' fears of having daughters travel to or through non-Muslim majority areas to reach their schools. A genocide survivor, Latifa, bitterly regrets the consequences of the genocide for her older daughter Sultana, who, prior to the 2002 violence, was interested in a career in education. Sultana had an appointment scheduled to take her final exams for a Bachelor of Science degree. Yet the young girl became too terrified after the genocidal actions to do so. Latifa explains, "Now her spirit is broken. She says she will never be able to take her exams again ... and my dream for her has turned to ashes."[54]

Just as the genocide resulted in some women coming out of the home and taking leadership in rehabilitiation and justice work, still other women have seemingly retreated inward. This, however, could be understood as women taking action to ameliorate the conditions in which they found themselves: socially, economically, and politically marginalized, but finding affirmation and strength within a smaller, cohesive group.[55] It could also be argued that as the material conditions deteriorated, some women found strength and solace in spiritual and religious practices within their home.

Immediate relief for the victims of the Gujarat genocide was organized not by government agencies, but by groups such as the Islamic Relief

Committee, the relief wing of the Muslim organization Jamaat-e-Islami. For women who may have begun to cleanse their lives in accordance with their religious beliefs, even prior to 2002, the violence of that year accelerated their religiosity and their desire to help other Muslim women through *isthemas* (religious congregations) organized in their living rooms. The Jamiaat-e-Ulema-e-Hind and the Tablighi Jamaat also had an impact on Muslims affected by the violence of 2002, in terms of worship, dress, and everyday behaviour.

Each year since 2002, anniversary reports on the lives of the survivors and the communal situation in Gujarat show that, after the intensity of the massacres of 2002, the survivors are being made to continue to suffer and die a slow death. The economic boycott of Muslims continues and takes many forms: harassment; being fired without cause; being unable to refinance businesses; small vendors being bullied; receiving no compensation; the banning of buffalo slaughter;[56] being chased away from their lands, their villages, their homes, their businesses, and areas of living and working (or simply feeling afraid and insecure enough not to return). All this has reduced a once-affluent and stable (relative to other parts of India) Muslim community to poverty and destitution. Perhaps the most destitute of all are the widows. In such women-headed households, children are pulled out of school because there is no money. People are reduced to eating one meal a day or less, because they cannot afford more food. Those who had regular work are now daily wage labourers—when they are lucky enough to find work.

Compounding the victimhood of these widowed heads of household is the effort it requires to negotiate the patriarchal parameters of their embattled community. In the face of great odds, female Muslim survivors of the Gujarat genocide have been rebuilding their lives and seeking justice for what they and their families have suffered. Muslim women and their communities want justice and to be able to regain their economic independence and autonomy. While there has been progress on some fronts, overall, much more needs to be done before survivors feel that justice has been served, and before the community can be economically and socially stable again. Further exacerbating the issue is the reality that the current prime minister of India, Narendra Modi, is the same man who was Chief

Minister of Gujarat at the time of the genocide, and his record since taking office, with respect to minorities, *Dalits* ("untouchables" in the caste system), and the indigenous population is very problematic. There have been many communal incidents in different parts of India.[57]

When we situate the Gujarat genocide within Ofer and Weitzman's framework, derived from Holocaust studies, we find a somewhat atypical case. Muslims in Gujarat experienced genocide swiftly and without warning. Also, unlike some of the other genocides written about in this volume, the Gujarat genocide did not happen in stages. The violence was immediate, frenzied, and devastating. Additionally, men and boys were not separated from girls and women. Whole families and communities came under attack suddenly, furiously, and simultaneously. Muslim men, women, and children faced violence, torture, and death without discrimination. However, the sexual violence perpetrated by Hindutva youths and men on Muslim women and girls speaks to hegemonic patriarchal thinking with respect to dishonouring a community with sexual violence against the community's female population. The savagery of the sexualized attacks on Muslim women needs to also be understood in the context of Hindutva—the Hindu nation that perceives Muslims as a demographic threat. If Muslims cannot reproduce, this perceived threat to the Hindu nation is then diminished. However, confirming Ofer and Weitzman's observations and conclusions, private sphere activities and gendered roles are very visible in Gujarat, especially in the aftermath. In the wake of the genocide, women rallied to try to provide some semblance of normality for their families; women who were left widowed had to take up the responsibility of assuming the normally male role of head of household; and Muslim women crossed gender boundaries into the public sphere in their tenacious quest for justice.

Questions

1. Why has there been a reluctance from many, even those who acknowledge the terrible violence that occurred, to call what happened in Gujarat a "genocide"? Is there still a sense that somehow the death toll needs to be higher to make an event important

enough to be labelled a genocide? Do you think this is what the people who drafted the 1948 Convention on the Prevention and Punishment of the Crime of Genocide were envisioning?

2. By focusing primarily on the outcomes for Muslim women and girls during and after the Gujarat genocide, is one drawing focus away from the Muslim community as a whole, which was clearly the targeted community of this genocide?

3. Does exploring the cases of some of the women who fought for, or are continuing to struggle through the legal process to achieve, justice translate to a useful understanding of the agency or lack thereof for women with respect to the genocide? Or does this individualizing approach take away from what women as a whole suffered and continue to experience in the wake of the genocide?

4. Consider what may be the fate of Muslims and other vulnerable minorities, when the prime minister of India has been linked to genocide. How can an oppressed and violated people receive justice in such a situation?

Notes

1. I would like to acknowledge that I am writing this in Montreal, Quebec, Canada, on Mohawk territory. Indigenous people in Canada have been subjected to genocide within the definition of the UN Convention on the Prevention and Punishment of the Crime of Genocide.

2. Dalia Ofer and Lenore J. Weitzman, eds., *Women in the Holocaust* (New Haven: Yale University Press, 1999).

3. Achyut Yagnik, "The Pathology of Gujarat," *Seminar* (2002): 513, www.india-seminar.com/2002/513/513%20achyut%20yagnik.htm.

4. In the context of South Asia, *communal* usually describes religion-based identities, often with respect to violent occurrences, usually between Hindus and Muslims.

5. In 1947 Britain withdrew and India was partitioned into India and Pakistan, ostensibly along religious lines—Hindu/Sikh and Muslim. There were massacres and violence in the run-up to Partition, as well as after. In 1984 there was a pogrom against Sikhs, when Prime Minister Indira Gandhi was assassinated by her Sikh bodyguards in retaliation for her ordering the

Indian army to attack the holiest Sikh shrine, the Golden Temple, because Sikh separatist militants had established themselves. Nearly 3,000 Sikhs perished.

6. Joseph Macwan, "This 'Unique' Land," *Seminar* 513 (May 2002), www.india-seminar.com/2002/513/513%20joseph%20macwan.htm.

7. Sanjiv Bhatt, Deputy Commissioner of the State Intelligence Bureau, Gujarat, at the time, in an affidavit to the Supreme Court of India, stated that he attended a meeting on February 27, 2002, after the Godhra train burning, at which Chief Minister Modi ordered police not to respond to calls for help from those being attacked. Mr. Modi "further impressed upon the gathering that for too long the Gujarat police had been following the principle of balancing the actions against Hindus and Muslims while dealing with communal riots in Gujarat." This time the situation warranted that "the Muslims be taught a lesson to ensure that such incidents do not recur ever again." The Chief Minister expressed the view that emotions were running very high among Hindus and it was imperative that they be allowed to "vent out their anger." Rohit Bhan, "Senior Gujarat Police Officer Implicates Modi in Riots," NDTV, April 22, 2011, www.ndtv.com/article/india/senior-gujarat-police-officer-implicates-modi-in-riots-100760.

8. At the time, 45 rupees = US $1.

9. Among these Hindu nationalist organizations are the following: Vishwa Hindu Parishad (World Hindu Organization), Rashtriya Swayamsevak Sangh (National Volunteer Corps), and Bajrang Dal (youth militia)—all part of the Sangh Parivar, a family of organizations that includes women's groups, trade unions, and the political party BJP (Bharatiya Janata Party), which was in power in Gujarat state as well as at the centre in Delhi (in the federal political system of India). The Sangh Parivar and its affiliates are Hindu nationalist organizations, committed to making India Hindutva—a Hindu nation.

10. India's National Human Rights Commission (an arm's length government organization), Amnesty International, Human Rights Watch, and PUCL (People's Union for Civil Liberties, an independent Indian citizens' group), to name a few.

11. Maya Kodnani, Minister for Women and Child Development, was found guilty and sentenced to 18 years in prison. Babu Bajrangi, a notorious Hindu nationalist, was sentenced to life in prison for atrocities committed.

12. Dolores Chew, "Women's Security in a Globalized World: Lessons from Gujarat, India," in *The Search for Lasting Peace*, ed. Rosalind Boyd

(Farnham: Ashgate, 2014), 7–87; see also Dolores Chew, "Living Genocide: Gujarat Today," (paper presented at Canadian Sociology and Anthropology Association Annual Meeting at the Congress of the Humanities and Social Science, York University, Toronto, May 30–June 2, 2006); Dolores Chew, "Not a 'Natural Disaster': Gujarat, Genocide and Gender," *Global Cinema*, 2004, www.jgcinema.com/single.php?sl=gujarat-genocide; Martha Nussbaum, "Genocide in Gujarat: The International Community Looks Away," *Dissent* 50, no. 3 (Summer 2003): 15–23; or Robert Petit, Stuart Ford, and Neha Jain, "Exploring Critical Issues in Religious Genocide: Case Studies of Violence in Tibet, Iraq and Gujarat," *Case Western Reserve Journal of International Law* 40, nos. 1/2 (2008): 163–214. Article 2 of the Convention on the Prevention and Punishment of the Crime of Genocide defines genocide as "any of the following acts committed with intent to destroy, in whole or in part, a national, ethnical, racial or religious group, as such: (a) Killing members of the group; (b) Causing serious bodily or mental harm to members of the group; (c) Deliberately inflicting on the group conditions of life calculated to bring about its physical destruction in whole or in part; (d) Imposing measures intended to prevent births within the group; (e) Forcibly transferring children of the group to another group."

13. Many women abducted to India or Pakistan in 1947 were repatriated, but often their own families rejected them. In the subcontinent there were also occurrences of Bengali women being raped by the Pakistani Army and kept as sex slaves in army camps during the 1971 War of Liberation. Later, these women received official recognition from the Bangladesh government as national heroines, and were known as *birangonas*, but their families and society frequently rejected them. Almost all who were pregnant sought abortions. If this was not possible, the woman generally gave her baby up for adoption. Suicide was a common occurrence among these *birangonas*.

14. SEWA Relief Team, "Re-building Our Lives," *Seminar* 513 (May 2002), www.india-seminar.com/2002/513/513%20sewa%20relief%20team.htm.

15. The Ghanchi community, which follows the Tablighi Jamaat, does not send its girls to school. See Sheela Bhatt, "How Can I Forgive Them?" *Rediff*, February 2004, www.rediff.com/news/2004/feb/26guj.htm.

16. Anumeha Yadav, "Only the Pawns Have Been Jailed Say Victims," *The Hindu*, September 1, 2012, www.thehindu.com/news/national/only-the-pawns-have-been-jailed-say-victims/article3845273.ece.

17. *Tempos* are small lorries or trucks.

18. Bhatt, "How Can I Forgive Them."

19. *Adivasi* means, literally, "original inhabitant"—this refers to an indigenous person.

20. Bhatt, "How Can I Forgive Them."

21. Mansi Choksi, "Narendra Modi's Shame: Muslim Survivors of the Gujarat Riots Are Still Suffering," *Vice News*, May 6, 2014, news.vice.com/article/ narendra-modis-shame-muslim-survivors-of-the-gujarat-riots-are-still-suffering.

22. *Encounter killings* is the term for custodial (police) murder/assassination, ostensibly in the process of apprehending "terrorists" or arrested individuals trying to escape. One of the best-known cases of encounter killings in Gujarat post-2002 is that of a young Muslim woman, Ishrat Jahan (aged 19), and three Muslim men, Javed Sheikh, Amjad Rana, and Zeeshan Johar, by officers of Ahmedabad Police Crime Branch in June 2004.

23. "Gujarat Carnage 2002: A Report to the Nation: How Has the Gujarat Massacre Affected Minority Women? The Survivors Speak," *Citizen's Initiative*, Ahmedabad, April 16, 2002, 13, cac.ektaonline.org/resources/ reports/womensreport.htm.

24. "Gujarat Carnage 2002," 4.

25. "Threatened Existence: A Feminist Analysis of the Genocide in Gujarat," *International Initiative for Justice in Gujarat*, December 2003, 43, www. coalitionagainstgenocide.org/reports/2003/iij.dec2003.report.pdf.

26. In India, assault, insult, humiliation, abuse, and gang-rape of lower-caste women by upper-caste men is used to intimidate, demoralize, punish, and exercise control over lower-caste groups, especially when they organize or offer resistance to caste oppression and atrocities perpetrated against them by upper castes.

27. While Gujarat does not uniquely bear this distinction, what is striking is that in a state of relative prosperity in India these practices exist among families that are socio-economically well off. Gujarat shares this abysmal distinction with Punjab and Haryana, the most prosperous states in India. See Rashmi Sharma and S. Mukherjee, "Comparative Study of Selected Parameters of Gender Discrimination in Rural versus Urban Population of Ahmedabad, Gujarat" *National Journal of Community Medicine* 2, no. 1 (January–June 2011): 111–115; see also Fred Arnold, Sunita Kishor, and T. K. Roy, "Sex-Selective Abortions in India," *Population and Development Review* 28, no. 4 (December 2002): 759–785.

28. Statistics from the 2001 census of India. This rate had improved by the 2011 census to 919 females for every 1,000 males.

29. Yagnik, "The Pathology of Gujarat."

30. *Evil Stalks the Land*, directed by Gauhar Raza (New Delhi, 2002), VHS.

31. "2001 Census of India," accessed July 18, 2014, censusindia.gov.in.

32. Purshottam Agarwal, "Surat, Savarkar and Draupadi: Legitimising Rape as a Political Weapon," in *Women and the Hindu Right—a Collection of Essays*, ed. Tanika Sarkar and Urvashi Butalia (New Delhi: Kali for Women, 1995), 50.

33. Naseem, interview by author, July 2003, Godhra, Gurjarat.

34. This is not easy, since some of the most popular actors are, in fact, Muslim.

35. Shabnam Hashmi, quoted in Soutik Biswas, "The Brave Muslim Women of Gujarat," *BBC News*, March 27, 2012, www.bbc.com/news/world-asia-india-17508814.

36. Noorjehan Abdul Hamid Dewan, quoted in Biswas, "The Brave Muslim Women of Gujarat."

37. Niaz Apa, quoted in Biswas, "The Brave Muslim Women of Gujarat."

38. It has been dubbed "Little Pakistan," a testament to the conflation of religious and national identities among many Hindu Gujaratis.

39. Darshan Desai, "The Hindu Across the Road," *The Hindu*, October 28, 2013, www.thehindu.com; see also Christophe Jaffrelot, "The Juhapura Model," *Indian Express*, April 25, 2014, indianexpress.com/article/opinion/columns/the-juhapura-model/99.

40. Biswas, "The Brave Muslim Women of Gujarat"; see also Desai, "The Hindu Across the Road."

41. Ibid.

42. Ibid. Attempting to cheat Muslims has become fairly common since 2002. There is an assumption that Muslims are so downtrodden that they will not protest and therefore can be exploited with impunity.

43. Biswas, "The Brave Muslim Women of Gujarat."

44. Rubina Jasani, "Violence, Reconstruction and Islamic Reform: Stories from the Muslim 'Ghetto,'" *Modern Asian Studies* 42, nos. 2/3 (March–May 2008): 432–433.

45. Diia Rajan, Deepa Dhanraj, and K. Lalita. "Bahar Nikalna: Muslim Women Negotiate Post-Conflict Life," *Inter-Asia Cultural Studies* 12, no. 2 (2011): 213–224.

46. Ibid.

47. Ibid.

48. Dionne Bunsha, "Two Steps Backward," *Frontline*, January 2–16, 2004, www.frontline.in/static/html/fl2101/stories/20040116004102200.htm.

49. Ram Puniyani, "Saluting Bilqis Bano: Reflecting on Gujarat," *Countercurrents*, January 26, 2008, www.countercurrents.org/puniyani260108.htm;

Ayesha Khan, "Three Stories of Resilience from Gujarat," March 2, 2012, kafila.org/2012/03/02/three-stories-of-resilience-from-gujarat-ayesha-khan; Malayala Manorama, trans., "Bilqis Bano Speaks," February 10, 2008, creative.sulekha.com/bilkis-bano-speaks_329413_blog; Dionne Bunsha, "Fight Goes On," *Frontline*, February 2–15, 2008, www.frontline.in/static/html/fl2503/stories/20080215250303100.htm.

50. Dionne Bunsha, "Can Zakia Jafri Take on India's Powerful Narendra Modi and Win?" *The Guardian*, November 22, 2011, www.theguardian.com/commentisfree/2011/nov/22/zakia-jafri-india-narendra-modi; Ram Puniyani, "India: Painful Path to Justice—Travails of Zakia Jafri," *Communalism Watch*, December 28, 2013, communalism.blogspot.ca/2013/12/travails-of-zakia-jafri.html; Press Trust of India, "2002 Riots Case: Zakia Jafri Moves HC against SIT Clean Chit to Narendra Modi," *Indian Express*, March 18, 2014, indianexpress.com/article/india/india-others/2002-riots-case-zakia-jafri-moves-hc-against-sit-clean-chit-to-narendra-modi; Press Trust of India, "2002 Gujarat Riots: High Court Adjourns Hearing on Zakia Jafri's Plea," *Economic Times*, July 15, 2014, articles.economictimes.indiatimes.com/2014-07-15/news/51542495_1_zakia-jafri-modi-and-others-closure-report.

51. Kavita Panjabi, Krishna Bandopadhyay, and Bolan Gangopadhyay, "The Next Generation: In the Wake of the Genocide—A Report on the Impact of the Gujarat Pogrom on Children and the Young," July 2002, 19, www.onlinevolunteers.org/gujarat/reports/children/pdf/full_report.pdf.

52. Ibid., 28.

53. Ibid., 19.

54. Ibid., 33.

55. Jasani, "Violence, Reconstruction and Islamic Reform."

56. In deference to Hindu majoritarian sentiments.

57. "Modi and Religious Minorities, Dalits and Adivasis," Narendra Modi—the 100 Day Report, accessed September 22, 2014, www.ghadaralliance.org.

JoAnn DiGeorgio-Lutz and Donna Gosbee

We began this study by asking if women's experiences in different genocidal contexts were comparable, and if so, in what ways. Women's voices give us a more complete representation of genocide that needs to be heard if we, as scholars and activists, hold any hope of raising global awareness of genocide's inhumanity that does not wholly discriminate on the basis of gender. We proceeded from the recognition that, regardless of the genocide under study, women's experiences were profoundly different from those of men, who were also victims and survivors. Additionally, we firmly believe that the women highlighted in these chapters each had an important story to tell apart from that of the larger genocidal context. Our aim was not to compare genocides per se; rather, we sought to compare women's accounts as victims and survivors across several distinct cases of genocide. To that end, our search for a framework of analysis took us to the scholarship on gender and the Holocaust that would allow us to utilize narratives, memoirs, testimonies, and literature to investigate the ways in which women's experiences in these genocidal events were comparable, and yet profoundly different.

Subsequently, we invited the contributors to this volume to consider Ofer and Weitzman's scholarship on women and the Holocaust, and to assess the applicability of their four structural sources relative to women's experiences within the respective genocide under investigation.[1] While each genocide in this work is defined by its own temporal and spatial characteristics, our aim was to search for both commonalities and differences among women's experiences. Our contributors examined the culturally defined roles of women, their anticipatory reactions in terms of what they believed would happen to them, the differences in the nature and degree of their treatment, and the different reactions of women to what was happening to them.

The contributors to this volume confirmed many of our initial assumptions about women and genocide. Women did experience genocide differently than men. They were classified as "others" in some identifiable context, and they all experienced some measure of dehumanization. In the aftermath of genocide, the women share the persistence of emotional suffering and all share in some form of loss. Although we knew that sexual violence defined particular cases in this book, such as in Kosova, and that it was widespread in others, such as Armenia, Rwanda, and Bangladesh, we did not realize the extent of sexual violence against women across all the cases we examined. Even though rape was prohibited by the Nazis under their policy of blood purity, Carol Mann's recounting of the rape and murder of French resistance fighter Marianne Cohn, and Michelle Kelso's chapter on Romani women who faced sexual violence in Transnistria inform us that sexual prohibitions did not shield women from this type of violence. In Cambodia, de Langis explains, even though the Khmer Rouge's Code #6 banned rape and other immoral offences, the growing body of research demonstrates that women experienced horrific sexual violence under Pol Pot's genocidal regime. Sexual violence toward women is a common thread within all the chapters. As such, we believe this subject should be explored in more depth across cases of genocide.

Another commonality has been women's culturally defined roles within society before the genocidal event. Each contributor identified roles that were fairly consistent. Depending on their socio-economic standing, women typically took charge of the home and child-rearing. In some cases, it might be common for the woman to also work outside the home, or have a skill that would allow her to earn money while remaining in the house, such as textile work, in order to help bring in money to make ends meet. The genocides covered in the various chapters relate to states or ethnic groups that were primarily patriarchal in nature. In each of the cases, women lacked a significant amount of autonomy or agency within society or the law. This lack of agency impacted women's ability to effect a measure of justice after the genocide ended. Yet we see, after almost all of the genocidal events covered in this book, that there were women who used the genocide as a springboard to becoming empowered after suffering emotional or even physical loss and violence. For examples, one only has to look at the advocacy groups created among survivors of the Rwandan genocide, the Bangladesh genocide of 1971, the Gujarat genocide of 2002, and more recently Cambodia and Guatemala. Many of the female survivors of these and other genocides became agents not only for themselves, but for other women who had suffered and survived genocidal experiences. In many of these cases, women found a voice within them that they had not even known existed. Yet, in other cases, such as we see with the Roma after the Holocaust, as well as many of the Kosovar women who had been sexually violated, the culture simply did not allow many women to find their voices, and the violence they experienced remains hidden away and unexplored.

Another generalization across our cases in this book is the relationship of genocide and war, and consequently its effects on women. While not every war is defined by genocide, every genocide we examined in this book occurred within the context of some manner of war, from the global reach of World Wars I and II to localized intrastate conflicts, civil wars, and wars of national liberation. Because war disrupts infrastructure, women are generally the ones who must navigate an uncertain terrain in search of food, shelter, and safety for themselves and their children. The dangers to women in the context of war and genocide exacerbate the inherent threat to women, particularly if they are members of a targeted group. Clearly, this is another area that should be explored in more detail across multiple cases of genocide.

How do women's experiences differ? One of the main differences we identified pertains to the temporal and spatial aspects of the genocide itself. Spatially, for example, in the cases of Armenia, the Holocaust, and Cambodia, we see a deliberate dislocation of women and children— a movement from one place to another. In contrast, in Guatemala, Rwanda, Gujarat, Bangladesh, and Kosova, the killing took place *in situ.* Additionally, the temporal aspects pertaining to each genocide in terms of duration are incomparable. Whereas the cases of Armenia, the Holocaust, Cambodia, and Guatemala encompass years, the remaining genocides in this study range from weeks to months in duration. The temporal and spatial natures of genocide and their impact on women should be examined in more detail as they may provide more insight into women's ability to survive once genocide commences.

Directions for Future Research

We asked each contributor to address what additional research is needed in reference to the particular genocide they study. Sona Haroutyunian has seen an evolution in Armenian genocide scholarship, so that it not only encompasses the historical, but also the cultural, artistic, visual, and literary aspects of the events. This evolution has shown us the importance of memoirs, literature, and oral histories in giving us an opportunity to gain a broader understanding of the genocide. However, a century after the genocide, Haroutyunian advises that we still do not possess an encyclopedic global compendium of the memoirs from victims or witnesses of the Armenian genocide. While she recently published a review of Italian literature pertaining to the Armenian genocide, it is Haroutyunian's goal to expand the range of study to map the Armenian genocide literature within different countries.[2]

Michelle Kelso asserts that almost all avenues to learning more about the genocide of Roma remain open for research. While she would like to point future research toward collecting oral testimonies of Romani survivors, given that their voices have been marginalized, the possibility of doing so dwindles with each passing year. Kelso contends that through local archival collections, there remains unexplored data that can be extracted about the lives of Roma prior to and immediately after the Holocaust. Local archives, due to the time commitment necessary to view them, have largely been passed over in attempts to sketch a broader picture of the genocide, especially in Romania. Additionally, she suggests reaching out to second- and third-generation Roma whose parents and grandparents experienced the genocide. Family photographs and stories handed down, as well as documents such as military records, yield tremendous and important knowledge as to how Roma culturally chronicle, remember, and commemorate the Holocaust, typically in the privacy of their homes. Social memory is a field that is underexplored concerning the Roma.

Carol Mann notes that the fate of women during the Holocaust has only attracted relatively recent and limited scholarship. She contends that practically nothing has been undertaken to explore the survival techniques women used in order to help their loved ones survive day to day and imagine a future after the war. Mann also brings our attention to Jewish women as part of the "homefront." While British women have become memorialized to an almost folkloric extent concerning their efforts to protect family during the infamous Blitz during World War II, the quiet heroism of Jewish women in trying to protect family and maintain a semblance of normalcy is overlooked. As Mann observes, Jewish women themselves have underestimated the heroic specificity of their own experience, which makes research challenging.

In her chapter on the 1971 Liberation War, Farah Ishtiyaque has provided readers with the various strategies the Bangladeshi state and other actors have used to effectively stifle the voices of the women belonging to the Bihari Muslim community. There has been little research on this marginalized group. Ishtiyaque indicates that other critical areas for further research would be examining the role of men within the Bihari Muslim community, looking at how they reacted to the war, and their role both as victims and perpetrators. Another overlooked group within the Bihari Muslim population of Bangladesh are the "war babies," the third-generation Biharis who continue to live in Camp Geneva, and who are still treated as "outsiders."

According to Theresa de Langis, oral history plays a unique role in post-genocidal contexts, where history is potentially decimated through the loss of human life to carry forward and record memory. In relation to the Khmer Rouge atrocity, and sexual violence in particular, much more research is needed; yet, as the conflict occurred 40 years ago, time is limited for the survivors to share their stories. Areas in need of further study and inquiry to fully understand the Cambodian case include the impacts on gender identity and family dynamics due to the consequences of forced marriage and collectivist policies; the unique effects on men, male roles, and masculinity as a result of being forced to marry and then consummate marriages under penalty of punishment and death; the variances of sexual violence as committed against men and women as part of the atrocity; intergenerational trauma suffered due to the gendered effects of the atrocity; and appropriate reparations and redress for these crimes.

On the Guatemalan genocide, Martha C. Galvan-Mandujano believes that more fieldwork needs to be undertaken to interview women about post-genocidal justice. Especially important is an examination of post-genocidal processes and measuring their success among the survivors, particularly the current living conditions of those whose villages were destroyed during the civil war. Moreover, further investigation is needed on the communities where the Maya became displaced as a consequence of the genocide. Research is also needed to understand how survivors themselves are working to create an awareness of the period of *La Violencia* in younger generations of Maya. Are Mayan survivors teaching their native languages to the next generation, and is that generation inheriting their traditions? Lastly, research is needed on Mayan survivors and their sense of security, and whether they still experience fears of being targeted because of their ethnicity.

Sara E. Brown suggests that to ensure a comprehensive rendering of the genocide in Rwanda, more research is needed on female rescuers. Female rescuers should be identified, their testimonies verified, and their efforts studied, publicized, and celebrated. This would benefit not only the academic community but Rwanda as well. Elucidating the complicated story of female rescuers during the Rwandan genocide would not only assist efforts to accurately document the genocide, it would also enable us to learn from and prevent mass violence. Equally important, these stories would serve Rwanda's future generations, who may then emulate the women who rejected the pervasive genocidal ideology and instead risked their lives to rescue.

Shirley Cloyes DioGuardi states that genocidal rape in Kosova has been known since the end of the Kosova war in 1999; however, it has only recently become a part of the arena of reflection and debate at a national level. Research needs to be conducted to identify the Serbian paramilitary and military troops who raped Kosovar women, in preparation for bringing the rapists to trial for war crimes and compensating the victims of rape. The extensive documentation of the survivors of genocidal rape by two Kosovar women's organizations that offer counselling and support for victims (Medica Kosova and the Kosova Rehabilitation Centre for Torture Victims) from 1998 onward needs to be examined by researchers who can be trusted by the survivors. Because of the stigmatization of rape victims in a society in which the patriarchal concept of rape as a crime against dignity and honour is still prevalent, access to the archives of these organizations has been limited and very few female survivors have been willing to come forward publicly. For this reason, too few women have claimed the compensation they deserve from the Kosovar government, which in 2014 passed a resolution giving rape victims annual financial and rehabilitation support on par with other civilian victims of war and veterans. Cloyes DioGuardi indicates that research also needs to be conducted about the degree to which the incursion of radical Islam (which is antithetical to Albanian secularism) into Albanian lands, first in Macedonia and then in Kosova, is creating a post-war patriarchal backlash, especially in rural areas, at the same time that there is a growing feminist movement, especially in urban areas, seeking to restore public dignity to rape victims and to make gender equality a reality at all levels of society. Finally, Cloyes DioGuardi argues that it is critical that oral history interviews be conducted with Kosova's rape victims, especially those who are willing to recount their experiences.

Rounding out the responses from our contributors is Dolores Chew, who examines the Gujarat genocide, which took place in the spring of 2002. She states that since then, the situation for Muslims in Gujarat has continued to be precarious—economically, socially, and even in regard to their physical safety. With the election of Narendra Modi (who was Chief Minister of Gujarat state at the time of the genocide) to prime minister of India, Hindu nationalists have felt further empowered. Those who link Prime Minister Modi to the genocide and raise questions about how his election impacts Muslims and other minorities are branded naysayers. In this environment, the voices of human rights activists get drowned out. Thus, there is great need for research that concretely demonstrates the ongoing nature of the impact of the genocide and the continuing threats to the lives of Gujarat's and India's Muslims and minorities. While there has been some work on the impact on the lives of women and girls post-genocide, more long-term research needs to be done on the effects of continuing restrictions being placed on them. Besides their precarious economic conditions, the Muslim women of Gujarat have also seen a lowering of the legal marriage age, greater religiosity, and ghettoization in order to ensure safety in the face of potential future attacks.

Ethics and Challenges of Conducting Genocide Research from a Gendered Lens

We also posed a more personal question to our contributors by asking them to situate themselves in their research and to reflect on the ethics and challenges of conducting genocide research from a gendered lens. For some, it will be an influential text or scholarly work that drives their research, while for others it is time spent among survivors. Their observations are deeply personal and sometimes painful; however, their commitment to document the experiences of women and genocide demonstrates their ethical and unshakable commitment to making sure these narratives are told. What follows are the reflections of our contributors, mostly in their own words. For purposes of consistency, we took editorial licence with their words to recount their reflections in the third-person voice. Their original voices are provided in quotes.

Sona Haroutyunian's approach to the field of Armenian genocide studies has been through translation, trauma, and memory studies. In 2007, she was commissioned to translate Italian-Armenian novelist Antonia Arslan's bestseller *La masseria delle allodole* (*Skylark Farm*).[3] That was her first direct immersion into trauma literature. She then translated the novel *La strada di Smirne* (*The Road to Smyrna*).[4] Working on these translations, and also working as a faculty member at the Nida School of Translation Studies, Haroutyunian came across Bella Brodzki's concept of "translation and memory."[5] She began thinking of trauma as a "translation of memory." Haroutyunian was subsequently invited to teach a course at California

State University, Fresno, on Armenian genocide through literature and translation. She began studying the role of memoirs on the birth of artistic literature, and recently published her book *The Theme of the Armenian Genocide in Italian Literature.*[6] Haroutyunian states, "It was not so much a decision to enter into the field of the Armenian genocide, but rather it was a direct consequence of more interconnected events" that led her to study that particular genocide.

Michelle Kelso's focus on the Roma began in 1993 when she volunteered for a humanitarian organization assisting at a Romanian state-run institution for abandoned children, where most of the residents were Romani children. She observed anti-Roma prejudice on the part of the locals when discussing her work with them. Having been reared in the United States, Kelso could not help but see similarities between the treatment by the Romanians of their Romani population and the discriminatory attitudes many American whites held and still hold against non-whites. The prejudice toward Roma, Europe's largest transnational ethnic minority, made her want to know more about Roma and their history, which she noted had been marginalized.

A year later, Kelso was able to return to Romania on a Fulbright fellowship and, while there, began researching Romani experiences during the Holocaust. She finds that one of the biggest challenges in her work has been overcoming outright denial of the genocide and gaining acceptance for the topic. As a Westerner researching the Holocaust, her operating paradigm is that the Holocaust not only happened in Romania, but also that it was perpetrated by the Romanian regime. Kelso believes it is imperative that the narratives of both the Roma and the Jews during the Holocaust be taught and discussed, especially given contemporary anti-Romani and anti-Jewish sentiments. For many Romanians, the Holocaust was a Nazi-perpetrated crime that, for the most part, did not happen in Romania. Kelso cites as an example of this disavowal the experience of being denied access to archives because those in power tried to keep hidden the atrocities committed by the Antonescu regime. During her research she has found that these different paradigms of knowledge have often led to tensions and a lack of acceptance for her work, although, Kelso states, "One positive aspect of my research has been working with Romani survivors.

They taught me about resilience and generosity of spirit. In retrospect, it has been a wonderful journey."

Carol Mann grew up in a family of Holocaust survivors. She observes that, as in so many such survivor homes, the Holocaust was something nobody ever spoke about. She writes that the silence was so poisonous that "I myself refused even to read or watch anything about the Holocaust for many years." When she initially became involved in research on gender and armed conflict by going to war zones to do both research and aid work, her first experience was in Sarajevo during the siege (1992–1996). Mann spent time there during the war and realized that what women (herself included, for a short while) were living through as women in the midst of a siege was not usually documented. The unspoken fear, the courage, the will to survive was something she understood that she had inherited unconsciously from her parents' and grandmother's experiences. When she went to Afghanistan and Pakistan shortly afterward, she intuitively understood what it meant to be a refugee. The experiences were eerily familiar. Mann indicates it was then that she was at last ready to envisage the study of the Holocaust from a women's standpoint.

For Farah Ishtiyaque, the need to investigate the 1971 War of Liberation was personal. Growing up in a small town in Jharkhand, erstwhile Bihar, she was constantly made aware of her identity. Her father was Muslim and her mother Christian, and Ishtiyaque recognized that being a Muslim constituted her "self." During her early years, Ishtiyaque bore the brunt of bullying by classmates who called her "cocktail," "mocktail," and "mixed breed"—which made her acutely aware that she was different. When she moved to Delhi, this "difference" became even more obvious as she had trouble, as a Muslim, finding accommodations. Ishtiyaque recalls that as a Master's program student, she chanced upon Urvashi Butalia's book *The Other Side of Silence: Voices From the Partition of India* and her life was forever changed.[7] It was then that she realized her questionable and quasi-threatening identity in being part Muslim. Nobody gave emphasis to the qualifier *part*—to others, she was viewed only as a Muslim. Growing up in India, Ishtiyaque was not aware of the 1971 War of Liberation and the making of Bangladesh. Reading more about the 1971 war, she came to learn about the plight of Bihari Muslims who became the victims of divergent streams of nationalism. Their muffled voices were not recorded in the official history of India, Pakistan, or Bangladesh. A particularly compelling force driving Ishtiyaque's focus on the plight of Bihari Muslim women was Yasmin Saikia's book *Women, War, and the Making of Bangladesh: Remembering 1971*.[8] Saikia's work spoke to Ishtiyaque at a personal level and pushed her to delve into the lives and liminal status of these women who were triply disempowered on the basis of their gender, ethnicity, and nationality.

Theresa de Langis informs us that in the academic and practitioner communities, the Cambodian genocide is often cited as an example in which sexual violence was not used as a constituent part of the armed conflict. However outdated, the thesis that the Khmer Rouge were exceptional in this regard has proved tenacious and has served as a means to illustrate that, with enforced policy and military discipline, sexual violence can be prevented in periods of war, genocide, and atrocity. De Langis indicates that, in fact, as more sexual violence survivors and witnesses come forward to share their personal stories, we are learning that the Khmer Rouge regime, as is typical of so many vicious dictatorships, used sexual violation as a means to exert power and control over the population. Rather than exceptional, the regime is illustrative in this regard.

According to de Langis, the information needed for a correction to the established thesis is available to us only through the courage of survivors and witnesses who come forward to share their stories. Researchers and oral historians dealing with sexual violations in particular have an ethical obligation to mitigate the risks entailed in truth-telling that counters those established "master" narratives. De Langis has been deeply involved with the Cambodian Women's Oral History Project (cambodianwomensoralhistory.com), an organization that has adopted a victim-centred, life-story, shared-authority approach: narrators understood that their information would be made public (with the option of anonymity) and, at their request, these narratives have been used to raise awareness locally and globally on the issue of violence against women in times of atrocity.

Martha C. Galvan-Mandujano became interested in the Guatemalan genocide as a result of her visits to Guatemala during her undergraduate global seminars in Central America. When she met the widowed women from CONAVIGUA, members of Guatemalan NGOs for displaced persons such as CONDEG, the mothers who worked tirelessly on behalf of the disappeared through FAMDEGUA, and female members of the communities in popular resistance (CPRs), she was haunted by their testimonies. Galvan-Mandujano recalls repeatedly asking herself how people could commit such atrocities against their fellow human beings. She kept a journal of all she heard and saw on her visits to Guatemala, and she quickly became interested in meeting and interviewing people who lived in the zones of conflict during the Guatemalan civil war. She was part of a project that interviewed Mayan survivors in the highlands of Nebaj, and she travelled to Guatemala on several occasions to record these testimonies. Galvan-Mandujano vividly recalls hearing the women speak about similar stories of torture, killings, and abuses and how great the pain still remains for many of the female Mayan survivors as they recounted the horrors of murdered relatives, and the rapes, abuses, and struggles they endured in the conflict areas.

Galvan-Mandujano recalls that the women spoke with her about the genocide in the hopes that their stories would be told. They wanted people to know what had happened to them during *La Violencia*, and entrusted her with their stories so that she could become a voice for them to the outside world. Her main goal afterward was to bring those stories that had been entrusted to her to the academic community. She has relayed the survivors' narratives at Rhetoric Symposiums and has written poetry based on their experiences. In this way, then, she is able to give voice to some of the Guatemalan orphans, widows, and men who were victims of *La Violencia*.

Sara E. Brown researches the role of women before, during, and after mass violence and human rights atrocities because without that narrative, "we will continue to perpetuate gendered misunderstandings about the myriad of women's roles during mass violence and produce incomplete and possibly ineffectual prevention strategies." She has worked and conducted research in Rwanda since 2004 but it wasn't until 2011 that she asked herself, "where are the women?" Brown states that Cynthia Enloe had been asking that question for years, and one day, standing outside the Kigali Genocide Memorial, she herself realized that the narratives of the 1994 genocide in Rwanda—narratives she had learned, accepted, and regularly utilized for her research—were incomplete. There existed at the time a number of studies on genocide perpetration but most of the perpetrators profiled were men. The few female perpetrators included were often represented as monstrous, hyper-sexualized, or deviant anomalies, while their male counterparts were normalized, with charts and graphs emphasizing their middle-of-the-road averageness. And female rescuers were all but omitted from the limited discourse on rescue. Brown asked herself, "Where were the women?" Once she had asked this first key question, a subset followed: "Did women participate in the genocide?" "If yes, why did they participate?" "How many participated?" "Why aren't we talking about them?" and finally, "Why do we assume that women would not participate? Isn't genocide comparable to other mass movements?" Brown continues to ask, "What subjective lens are we applying to the study of genocide that blinds us to the participation of women?" These questions led her to her current research.

Brown notes that renowned Holocaust historian Yehuda Bauer reminds us to be cognizant of our biases, and she readily admits that she is decidedly (and unapologetically) biased in her decision to research the role of women during genocide. She indicates that this bias is rooted in a desire to compare, contrast, learn from, and prevent instances of mass violence and human rights atrocities. She asserts that to develop effective prevention strategies, we need to know and understand what we are preventing. With respect to Rwanda and the genocide that took place there in 1994, Brown explains that there are existing gaps in our analyses, which then lead to ineffective strategies. Some of these gaps result from gendered research that erringly casts women solely as victims or bystanders. Women who exercise agency as rescuers or perpetrators are omitted, minimized, or "othered." This, according to Brown, leads to misunderstandings, incomplete prevention strategies, and misprescribed antidotes to mass violence. In Rwanda, due to the assumption that women did not exercise agency during the genocide, measures intended to prevent a recycling of the violence, rehabilitate the population, and rebuild the country focus overwhelmingly on men, with little regard for women who participated in the genocide. Brown reflects that it remains to be seen how this omission will impact Rwanda in the coming years.

Shirley Cloyes DioGuardi became involved in studying the Balkan conflict, and ultimately the Albanian dimension of it, because she was influenced as a child by the trial of Nazi war criminal Adolf Eichmann, and the failure of the West to save Jews during the Holocaust. Cloyes DioGuardi recounts that when the Bosnian war began, she was watching, along with other Americans, jarring images on television news programs of genocide in Bosnia, and later the concealment of the concentration camps at the hands of the Serbian military and paramilitary forces under then-dictator Slobodan Milosevic. She recalls being told that "this was not our war"; "this had nothing to do with us"; "it was a quagmire we must not get trapped into"; and "'these people' have been fighting for centuries, and interethnic hatred in the Balkans is almost genetic." She also recalls being appalled because, in her opinion, "there is nothing more morally corrosive than showing scenes of carnage to a largely privileged population in the United States, compared to the peoples of Southeast Europe, and then insisting that we have no responsibility."

Cloyes DioGuardi became a tireless advocate for Kosovar women who suffered brutal violence, rape, and abuse during the war. When the issue of the rape of Kosovar women came to the forefront, she recalls recognizing the need to direct her work to breaking the protracted silence about rape and bringing it to the attention of a wider audience. For Cloyes DioGuardi, a gendered lens is essential to a complete understanding of the occupation, the Kosova war, and post-conflict nation-building; hence, conducting genocide research from a gendered lens is an ethical act of historical restoration. As she asserts, conducting genocide research from a gendered lens is, on the one hand, key to the recognition and healing of female Kosovar survivors of genocidal rape. On the other hand, by integrating women's voices into the narratives of the war and the post-conflict peace process, a more authentic understanding of Kosova's past and present emerges and enhances the capacity for achieving gender equality and political and economic progress in a nation that still lacks full sovereignty.

Dolores Chew reflects as both an academic and an activist in the South Asian diaspora. She notes that her research on the Gujarat genocide began with a desire to participate in Indian and diasporic efforts to get justice for the victims of the Gujarat genocide. For Chew, the gendered lens became integral to understanding the genocide and working toward justice for the victims because of the particular targeting of women and girls in the genocidal violence and massacres. She writes that the highly sexualized nature of the violence directed toward them was very different from previous violence directed toward Muslim minorities in India and the South Asian subcontinent. Chew writes as a feminist historian, familiar with the histories of women in the Indian subcontinent, stating she was drawn to try to understand and explain this violence in order to gain justice for the victims. A challenge for Chew is that in this particular instance, Muslims as a community were also targeted; by focusing solely on women, the research might be drawing attention away from the religious nationalism that targeted an entire community. She observes that another difficult aspect of her research topic is that of narrating and describing the horrendous violence perpetrated against women and girls—almost a pornography of violence. Chew asked herself, "Should I stay away from vivid descriptions that may distract or in some way play into voyeuristic preoccupations with sexualized violence?" But then further asks, "By not graphically describing, am I doing a disservice to the pain and suffering of those who were attacked?"

*   *   *

One of the limitations of our study was the incomplete attendance of women's experiences within the individual genocides in this study and across the spectrum of genocides that we could have considered. The genocide in Darfur with its ongoing rapes and killings is unfortunately missing from this volume, as is the current genocide warning against the Rohingya in Myanmar. Moreover, also missing from this book is a chapter on the "First Nation Genocide" of Canada and the attempted cultural annihilation of First Nations, Metis, and Inuit through the appropriation of their children and the government policies that subjected the Plains Indians to starvation and eviction from their ancestral lands. There remain far too many current and past unheard memories and narratives to be recognized, and to that end, we prefer to think of our work as prologue rather than a conclusion.

While not by design, all the contributors to this book are women. Women's voices matter, and through our scholarship we can bear witness to these events and demonstrate that genocidal violence against women will not go unheard. As long as the crime of genocide persists, women's voices as victims and survivors will endure and so will our commitment to represent them.

Notes

1. Dalia Ofer and Lenore J. Weitzman, eds., *Women in the Holocaust* (New Haven: Yale University Press, 1998).
2. Sona Haroutyunian, *Hayots tseghaspanityan teman italakan grakanoutyan medj* [*The Theme of the Armenian Genocide in Italian Literature*] (Yerevan: Yerevan State University Press, 2015).
3. Antonia Arslan, *Artoytneri agarake* [*Skylark Farm*]. Translation from Italian into Armenian, preface and notes by Sona Haroutyunian, introduction by B. L. Zekiyan (Yerevan: Zangak-Sahak Partev, 2012).
4. Antonia Arslan, *Zmiwrniayi djanaparhe* [*The Road to Smyrna*]. Translation from Italian into Armenian, introduction and notes by Sona Haroutyunian (Yerevan: Zangak-Sahak Partev, 2012).
5. Bella Brodzki, *Can These Bones Live? Translation, Survival, and Cultural Memory* (Stanford: Stanford University Press, 2007).
6. Sona Haroutyunian, *Hayots tseghaspanityan teman italakan grakanoutyan medj* [*The Theme of the Armenian Genocide in Italian Literature*] (Yerevan: Yerevan State University Press, 2015).
7. Urvashi Butalia, *The Other Side of Silence: Voices from the Partition of India* (Durham: Duke University Press, 2000).
8. Yasmin Saikia, *Women, War, and the Making of Bangladesh: Remembering 1971* (New Delhi: Women Unlimited, 2011).

Sara E. Brown is the Stern Family fellow and the first comparative genocide doctoral candidate at the Strassler Center for Holocaust and Genocide Studies at Clark University. Her dissertation, "Gender and Agency: Women Rescuers and Perpetrators During the Rwandan Genocide," explores women who exercised agency during the 1994 Rwandan genocide. Brown has worked and conducted research in Rwanda since 2004. She regularly travels there to conduct first-hand interviews with survivors, perpetrators, rescuers, and witnesses of the Rwandan genocide. Brown was an adjunct lecturer at Worcester State University; researched globalization and conflict at the Interdisciplinary Center (IDC) in Herzliya, Israel; worked in refugee resettlement in the Dallas Metroplex; and served as a project coordinator in refugee camps in western Tanzania. She received her MA in Diplomacy and Conflict Studies from the IDC.

Dolores Chew, Ph.D., currently resides in Montreal, Canada, where she teaches humanities and history coursework on South Asian civilization and culture, women, gender, the 20th century, and Western civilization survey courses at Marianopolis College. She is also a research associate for the Simone de Beauvoir Institute at Concordia University. Chew is a founding member and current president of the South Asian Women's Community Centre in Montreal, a service, support, and advocacy organization for South Asian women and their families. Her research interests are gender, race, and colonialism. Reflecting her research interests and her concern with gender inequality and justice, she became interested in documenting and researching the Gujarat genocide, and continues working for justice for the victims. Chew's publications include "'Not a Natural Disaster': Gujarat, Genocide and Gender" (www.globalcinema.eu/single.php?sl=gujarat-genocide) and a chapter entitled "Women's

Security in a Globalized World: Lessons from Gujarat, India," in *The Search for Lasting Peace* (Ashgate, 2014).

Shirley Cloyes DioGuardi is Balkan Affairs Adviser to the Albanian American Civic League, a position she has held since 1995. She has lectured widely and written more than 75 articles about the Balkan conflict. She has made 40 trips to Southeast Europe, including 15 to Kosova since the end of the Kosova war in 1999. Together with her husband, Civic League President and former congressman Joseph DioGuardi, she has worked with members of the U.S. Congress to bring lasting peace and stability to the Balkans. Cloyes DioGuardi has assisted House and Senate members responsible for U.S. foreign policy in preparing legislation on the Balkans, and she has testified before the Committee on Foreign Affairs in the US House of Representatives on six occasions—in 1996 regarding contested elections in Albania, in 1998 in support of U.S. ground troop deployment to Kosova, in May 2003 on the future of Kosova, in October 2003 on the status of Albanians in Montenegro, in May 2005 on the current and future status of Kosova, and in April 2013 on the EU-sponsored agreement between Serbia and Kosova.

JoAnn DiGeorgio-Lutz is a professor of political science and department head of liberal studies at Texas A&M University at Galveston. She has taught courses on the Holocaust, Jewish ghettos, comparative genocide, foreign policy, and international relations. She has authored five book reviews (three invited), written three invited encyclopedic entries, contributed chapters to edited books, co-authored and edited a book on women in higher education, and presented her research at numerous international and national conferences. She is the recipient of two J. William Fulbright awards—one as a Fulbright Scholar to Jordan and the other as a Fulbright Specialist to Cambodia. She was also a fellow in the Jack and Anita Hess Faculty Seminar on the Holocaust and Other Genocides with the United States Holocaust Memorial Museum.

Martha C. Galvan-Mandujano is from San Luis Potosí, Mexico. She has her Ph.D. in Spanish from the University of Oklahoma and is analyzing the works of female writers such as Sor Juana Inés de la Cruz, the

Colombian Madre Castillo de Tunja, Gertrudis Gómez de Avellaneda, Cristina Peri-Rossi, and Mayra Montero. Galvan-Mandujano also holds a graduate certificate in women's and gender studies from the University of Oklahoma, and several of her investigations have incorporated gender and women's perspectives, such as in the works of Gloria Anzaldúa and Cherrie Moraga. Galvan-Mandujano has a political science background, and works actively on Latin-American women's issues. She is currently working on a project on contemporary Central American fiction from the Salvadoran writer Horacio Castellanos Moya, and is also co-author of "Mujeres de Acción: La figura femenina en *Adiós muchachos*," an essay that explores the role of women during Nicaragua's Somozan dictatorship. She has also collaborated in the *Encyclopedia of U.S. Military Interventions in Latin America* (ABC-CLIO, 2013), with an entry on the murder of Archbishop Óscar Romero in 1980.

Donna Gosbee completed her master's degree in political science at Texas A&M University-Commerce, where she also completed their Holocaust Studies certificate program. She is a Jack Kent Cooke Undergraduate Transfer Scholar as well as a Jack Kent Cooke Graduate Scholar. Her research and writing have primarily focused on the experiences of the Roma and Sinti during the Holocaust as well as looking at the Holocaust from a more gendered perspective. She has presented her research at several international and national conferences. Gosbee has taught Holocaust coursework at Texas A&M University-Commerce, and is currently pursuing her Ph.D. in the history of ideas through the Ackerman Center for Holocaust Studies at the University of Texas at Dallas.

Sona Haroutyunian is a professor of Armenian language and literature at the University of Venice, Italy. She received her first Ph.D. in philology from Yerevan State University, and her second Ph.D. in linguistics from the University of Venice. In 2013 she had the honour of being the 10th Henry S. Khanzadian Kazan Visiting Professor in Armenian Studies at California State University, Fresno, where she taught a course on the Armenian genocide in literature and translation. Author of many scholarly papers as well as translated books, Haroutyunian is now working on a new book on the literary expression of the historical event, concentrating on the presentation of the Armenian genocide within Italian literature.

Farah Ishtiyaque is pursuing her M.Phil./Ph.D. from the Centre for English Studies, School of Language Literature and Culture Studies, Jawaharlal Nehru University, New Delhi. She is interested in partition studies, and her research is on the Bihari Muslims/stranded Pakistanis who were left stateless after the 1971 War of Liberation. A budding academic, she has both presented papers at international conferences and published papers. Ishtiyaque's recent publications include a chapter in *Tabish Khair: Critical Perspectives* (Cambridge Scholars Publishing, 2014).

Michelle Kelso is an assistant professor of human services, sociology, and international affairs at George Washington University in Washington, DC. Her research interests include collective memory, the Holocaust, gender, education, and migration. She has been the recipient of several prestigious national awards, including two Fulbright fellowships to Romania and a Charles H. Revson fellowship at the U.S. Holocaust Memorial Museum. She has written and published books on the Holocaust and the Roma. Kelso also made a well-received documentary film in 2005, *Hidden Sorrows: The Persecution of Romanian Gypsies During WWII*, that has screened in several countries and numerous film festivals, and aired on national television channels. She also worked for several years in civil society before joining George Washington University faculty.

Theresa de Langis is an independent researcher and senior consultant on women's human rights in conflict, post-conflict, and transitioning settings, with a focus on the Asia Pacific region. Based in Cambodia since 2012, she has worked with such organizations as the Extraordinary Chambers in the Courts of Cambodia (the Khmer Rouge Tribunal) and UN Women, examining general women's human rights issues and gender-responsive approaches to transitional justice measures. She is currently undertaking independent research on sexual and gender-based violence as part of the general atrocities committed during the Khmer Rouge regime, and in 2013, she launched the Cambodian Women's Oral History Project to collect life-story testimonies of female survivors for the historical record. De

Langis holds a doctoral degree from the University of Illinois at Chicago. She is currently affiliate fellow at the Center for Khmer Studies and adjunct faculty at American University of Phnom Penh.

Carol Mann has her Ph.D. in sociology from the EHESS (École des hautes études en sciences sociales) in Paris. She is a Franco-British historian and sociologist specializing in gender and armed conflict. She is the founder and administrator of Women in War and she teaches gender and armed conflict at the Paris School of International Affairs at Sciences Po. Mann has numerous publications and presentations on women and armed conflict and war. Her most recent book is *La resistance des femmes de Sarajevo* (Editions Le Croquant, 2014).